TRENT FRAYNE'S
Allstars

AN ANTHOLOGY
OF CANADA'S
BEST
SPORTSWRITING

Recent books by Trent Frayne:

The Best of Times

The Madmen of Hockey

The Tales of an Athletic Supporter

TRENT FRAYNE'S
Allstars

Trent Frayne (ed.)

Doubleday Canada Limited

Canadian Cataloguing in Publication Data

Main entry under title:

Allstars: an anthology of Canada's best sportswriting

Includes bibliographical references
ISBN 0-385-25540-3

1. Sports – Canada. I. Frayne, Trent, 1918–

GV585.A55 1996   796'.0971   C95-932388-0

CONTENTS

INTRODUCTION

For years there was this private conviction that American sportswriters had an easier time than Canadians in finding inspiration for their work. That wasn't because we were inferior mentally or lazier or were paid less (one of which may be true) but mostly because of the nature of the two countries' national games.

Hockey, which is life's blood north of the border, is a bang bang game in a cold cold land (no time for commas here). There is an understandable lack of desire for an inquisitive scribe to stand in snow up to his navel or freeze to death at ice level indoors to invite the superstar left-winger to turn philosophical. Hockey is not a game that inspires leisurely conversation.

Conversely, American sportswriters capture the atmosphere of baseball, the national game south of here, in the warm sunshine of summer and, as the French-born historian Jacques Barzun has been quoted dozens of times, "Whoever wants to know the heart and mind of America had better learn baseball." Accordingly, memorable lines and verse are numerous in American baseball literature.

However, this notion of mine that the Canadian climate is too heavy a burden for our sports scribes is quickly dispelled by the people contributing to this collection. Maybe the atmosphere is gentler down south, but if this is an advantage it ends there. For illustration, read Brian Preston's hilarious account of a road trip with the Victoria Cougars of the Western Hockey League, "the second-worst team in the second-best hockey league in the world." Or try to find a more concise analysis of *any* trade other than

Ken Dryden's classic reflection on goaltending. Examine Earl McRae's insight into the bizarre character who became Harold Ballard and ran the Toronto Maple Leafs (almost into oblivion) for 18 years. Then turn to Red Fisher and absorb the Montreal sage's long look at the former Canadien genius, Sam Pollock.

One thing our hockey writers haven't managed to do — and this may have some bearing on climate — is seal memorable lines into the language. Hockey, the furious game, contrasts sharply with baseball, a game that can inspire introspection. Writers, even serious ones more often given to more serious matters (George F. Will, David Halberstam), can be caught jotting down batting-cage chatter or sitting on the dugout steps while the manager dangles his feet and muses on the endless turmoil of his massive decisions.

In such a tranquil setting the impish manager of the old New York Yankees, Casey Stengel, remarked about baseball, "Now there's three things you can do in a ballgame. You can win, or you can lose, or it can rain." Or with time to think about his success in winning the American League pennant ten times in his 12 years as Yankee manager, to suggest thoughtfully, "I couldn't have done it without the players." Expounding on the importance of a catcher, he pontificated, "Now you take the catcher; without a catcher the ball rolls right to the wall."

In this atmosphere a scribe such as Jim Murray, the sage of the *Los Angeles Times*, can observe of the hometown Dodgers, "This team has a chance to go all the way. So did the *Titanic*."

Contrast these quiet ruminations with the thunder of hockey. Think of the immortal line of Conn Smythe, wearing his game face. "If you can't beat 'em outside in the alley," trumpeted the guiding light for 35 years of the Toronto Maple Leafs, "you can't beat 'em inside on the ice."

Most hockey people think that way or every team wouldn't have a goon — beg pardon, a policeman — in the lineup. Hockey being a violent game, much of its literature reveals its fiery nature, once expressed best by the gentlemanly Montreal novelist, the late Hugh MacLennan, in the old *Holiday* magazine. "To spectator and player alike, hockey gives the release that strong liquor gives to a repressed man. It is the counterpoint of the Canadian self-restraint, it takes us back to the fiery blood of Gallic and Celtic ancestors who found themselves minorities in a cold, new environment and had to discipline themselves as all minorities must."

Of course, any anthology of sportswriting must contain considerably more than hockey to hold a fan's interest, and no exception is brooked here. The reader, even if he or she doesn't know a thoroughbred from a Percheron, is invited to examine the wondrous betting coups of Barry Callaghan in Hong Kong, and David Macfarlane's brilliant account of how thoroughbreds became international currency, led by the unmatched Northern Dancer.

Baseball? Assuredly, with the Expos owning the game's best record of 1994 until the strike came, and the Blue Jays the World Series twice in a row, baseball is high on space in magazines and newspapers. Here too. Such as Paul Quarrington's closeup view of Blue Jays manager Cito Gaston and Michael Posner's no-holds-barred look at the all-star second baseman Roberto Alomar.

Golf is here, from the country's best golf writer, Lorne Rubenstein, and even a dazzling piece on wrestling, of all weird games, by Gare Joyce. Whatever you do, don't miss *the* piece for any anthology anywhere, Harry Bruce's *The Alchemy of Sailing*.

The work of some people suggests they enjoy what they're doing, although my own feeling is that sportswriting is not the rewarding occupation it once was. If you read Jim Coleman here on his threat to purchase Maple Leaf Gardens or Ralph Allen reciting the golden opportunity available for a midget of ambition, you'll appreciate that sportswriting once inspired an inventiveness not easy to find nowadays. I think the change can be traced to the money television has put into the pockets of professional athletes. It used to be that players and scribes shared a mutual economic scale and a common social level. Today's athletes have climbed to such heights on the economic ladder that setting up an interview with one is like making an appointment with the prime minister (reminding me of the old story about Babe Ruth — inevitably an American story — being advised he made more money than the U.S. president, Calvin Coolidge. "Well, why not?" said the Babe, "I had a better year.")

Of course, there are also people who wonder why grown men and women bother writing about children's games, or indeed why they've chosen to be writers at all. For them, Mordecai Richler, the Montreal novelist and essayist whose piece in this collection relates to his favourite hockey team, *les Canadiens*, has a quite reasonable reply. "Strangers who accept without question a man who has put together a life dealing in pork belly futures or manufacturing zippers demand to know *why you did it*," he wrote in the *New York Times Book Review*. "Such a weighty query begs for an appropriate pretentious answer. Something about artistic compulsions. Muses. Inspiration. But the truth is, everybody I knew in my Montreal high school who wasn't going to be another Ted Williams or Barney Ross or Maurice (The Rocket) Richard was willing to settle for being a writer. As far as we could make out, Hemingway set his own hours. He seemed to go fishing whenever he felt like it. He was on first-name terms with Ingrid Bergman and Marlene Dietrich. It had to be a good life."

Whatever *their* reasons, more and more women are writing sports these days. Once, few publications carried a woman's byline over a sports subject. I can't recall any writing in magazines and the only ones I remember from early newspapers were a pair of former Olympic track stars, Myrtle Cook at the *Montreal Star* and Bobbie Rosenfeld at the Toronto *Globe and Mail*, and a stalwart of the Toronto *Star*, Alexandrine Gibb. But these writers were confined almost exclusively to women's sports.

These days women cover everything. Christie Blatchford leads off this collection with a sensitive reflection on Canada's Olympic hockey team as it prepared for the gold-medal game against the Russians in France in 1992. Here too is a tough, perceptive piece by Rosie DiManno on the hockey player Wendel Clark. At the time, gossipers circulated tales of the player's sexuality. Rosie, in typical style, got to the crux of the matter: she asked him point blank.

Speaking of sexuality, within these covers is an excerpt from Muriel Lennox's book on Northern Dancer, the definitive work on one of the great stallions in thorough-bred racing history. Moving right along, when *Sports Illustrated* magazine's editors wanted a piece in the World Series issue on the new American League champions, the 1992 Blue Jays, they turned to a Canadian woman sports-writer. This was Alison Gordon, an Ottawa native, who had been *The Toronto Star*'s beat writer on baseball before turning to novel writing and producing four books involving baseball and murder.

Jane O'Hara is here, too, once Canada's No. 1 ranked women's tennis player, recalling her return to the sacred grass of Wimbledon. When Jane quit competitive tennis she headed *Maclean's* magazine bureaus in New York and Vancouver, went to London for FP Publications and did three years' hard time as sports editor of the *Ottawa Sun*.

And so, between these covers there's something for everyone — women's stuff, funny stuff, newspaper stuff, men's stuff, some earnest stuff, nobody bogged down in permanent adolescence. Blood-and-thunder is scarce here and gee-whiz is outlawed. As the one-time columnist for the *New York Times*, Red Smith, once said of the games people write about, "It ain't Armageddon."

CONTRIBUTORS

Allen Abel is a freelance writer whose sports column ran for six years in the Toronto *Globe and Mail*. He was the *Globe*'s man in China for two years in the mid-1980s, then spent nine years with CBC television's *The Journal* and *Prime Time News*.

Ralph Allen is perhaps best remembered as editor of *Maclean's* magazine for the decade of the 1950s. Earlier, he wrote a sports column in the Winnipeg *Tribune* and then the Toronto *Globe and Mail*. Later, he wrote novels (*Home Made Banners*, *The Tall White Forest*) and was managing editor of the Toronto *Star*. He died in 1966 at age 53.

Jack Batten writes mystery novels about a lawyer-sleuth named Crang and also is the author of several sports books, the most recent of which is *The Leafs*. On "the side," he is the movie reviewer for CBC radio's morning show in Toronto.

Christie Blatchford writes a general-interest column for the *Toronto Sun*. She is a former *Globe and Mail* sports columnist.

Harry Bruce lives and writes in St. Andrews, New Brunswick. He wrote regularly for *Maclean's* and *Saturday Night* during more than a decade in Toronto. A *Toronto Star* series on neighbourhood walks became a book called *The Short Happy Walks of Max MacPherson*. Of his several books, his favourite is *Down Home: Notes of a Maritime Son*.

Stephen Brunt's forte is writing on boxing, though he writes commentary on all sports at *The Globe and Mail*.

Barry Callaghan is a novelist, poet, journalist, and professor of English at Toronto's York University. He has won national magazine awards in politics, sports, and travel.

Neil A. Campbell wrote on baseball and horse racing in *The Globe and Mail* until 1994 when the paper sent him to its Vancouver bureau to cover western sports.

James Christie specializes in amateur sports and the Olympic Games for *The Globe and Mail*.

Cam Cole, has written about sports for the *Edmonton Journal* since 1975, and for the past 10 years has been his paper's lead sports columnist, as well as a syndicated national columnist with the Southam News Service. He has covered sports in 22 countries and twice has been nominated for a National Newspaper Award for sportswriting.

When **Jim Coleman's** father, D.C. Coleman, was president of the CPR in the 1920s he'd sometimes take his young son to the Saratoga race course in his private railway car. Thus was born a lifelong racing fan who became a sports columnist for *The Globe and Mail* and later a syndicated columnist for the Southam newspaper chain. Jim is now retired in Vancouver.

Rosie DiManno, who writes a daily general-interest column for *The Toronto Star*, turns to sports when the Blue Jays or the Maple Leafs need attention.

Ken Dryden is the five-time Vezina Trophy winner for the Montreal Canadiens. His 1983 book, *The Game*, was short-listed for a Governor-General's prize in non-fiction. His most recent book is *In School, Our Kids, Our Teachers, Our Classrooms*.

Milt Dunnell retired in 1994 at age 88, following a long career as sports editor and columnist for *The Toronto Star*. A collection of his columns, *The Best of Milt Dunnell*, was published in 1993.

Michael Farber has won two National Newspaper Awards as sports columnist for the Montreal *Gazette*, after which he joined *Sports Illustrated* magazine in 1994. He lives in Montreal.

Red Fisher has covered the Canadiens for the old *Montreal Star* and the current Montreal *Gazette* through the most recent 17 of their 24 Stanley Cup victories. He won a National Newspaper Award in 1993.

Don Gillmor, a contributing editor of *Saturday Night* magazine, has won National Magazine Awards in such diverse fields as travel, business, and the environment. He is the author of three books for children, *The Trouble with Justin*, *When Vegetables Go Bad*, and *The Fabulous Song*.

Alison Gordon writes mystery novels with baseball backgrounds. Earlier, she was a baseball beat writer on the Blue Jays for *The Toronto Star*.

Gare Joyce, for 10 years a freelance writer and winner of three National Magazine Awards, joined *The Globe and Mail* as a hockey columnist in 1994.

Muriel Anne Lennox writes about horses for magazines about thoroughbreds. Her biography of Northern Dancer, Canada's greatest racehorse and the world's most productive sire, *Northern Dancer: The Legend and His Legacy*, was published in 1995.

David Macfarlane is a contributing editor of *Toronto Life* magazine. He has won National Magazine Awards for humour, travel, and sports, and published a non-fiction book, *The Danger Tree*, in 1992.

Roy MacGregor, a columnist for the *Ottawa Citizen*, turned to sports from political writing on the grounds that covering Parliament Hill for 11 years had made him ill. He collaborated with Ken Dryden on *Home Game* and last fall brought out *The Home Team*.

Allan Maki is a sports columnist for the *Calgary Herald* and frequent commentator on CBC television.

Earl McRae writes a sports column for the *Ottawa Sun*. Two collections of his magazine pieces have become books, *Requiem for Reggie* and *The Victors and the Vanquished*.

Jane O'Hara resigned as sports editor of the *Ottawa Sun* in 1994 to spend a year as the Max Bell Visiting Professor of Journalism at the University of Regina. She ghosted *Mark My Words*, the autobiography of the *Ottawa Citizen*'s political columnist, the late Marjorie Nichols.

Mary Ormsby is a sports writer for *The Toronto Star*. Her specialty is tennis.

Michael Posner wrote occasional sports pieces during 11 years on the staff of *Maclean's* magazine. He has written two books, one on the Canadian film industry, and currently is a freelance magazine writer.

Brian Preston of Vancouver is a freelance magazine writer, about a third of whose output is on sports.

Jim Proudfoot has been a *Toronto Star* sportswriter since 1954 as hockey writer, sports editor, and as columnist. He won a National Newspaper Award for a series on the mysterious death of jockey Don Beckon.

Paul Quarrington is a novelist, screenwriter, and playwright. He won the Governor-General's Award for his novel *Whale Music* and a Genie for his screenplay for the film *Perfectly Normal*. His latest book is *Fishing With My Old Guy*.

Mordecai Richler writes novels, screenplays, and book reviews. His fiction hero is Duddy Kravitz. Three collections of his essays have become books, of which the excerpt here is from *Home Sweet Home*. He lives and writes in his native Montreal in summer and England in winter.

Lorne Rubenstein writes almost exclusively about golf. He is a regular contributor to *The Globe and Mail* and numerous U.S. golf magazines, and has authored three books about the game, *The Natural Golf Swing* (with George Knudson), *Links, an Insider's Tour Through the World of Golf*, and *Touring Prose: Writings on Golf*.

Steve Simmons began his current column in the *Toronto Sun* in 1987, following eight years in Calgary divided between the *Herald* and the *Sun*. In Calgary he wrote a biography of hockey star Lanny McDonald.

Robin Short is the sports editor and columnist for the St. John's *Evening Telegram* in Newfoundland.

Jim Taylor is a Vancouver sports fixture whose columns ran in the *Sun*, then the *Province*, for three decades. In the autumn of 1995 he joined the weekly *Sports Only* as associate publisher. A collection of his columns is called *Forgive Me My Press Passes*.

Scott Taylor is a sports columnist for the *Winnipeg Free Press*, specializing in football and hockey.

Kenneth Whyte became editor of *Saturday Night* in 1994. He was executive editor of *Alberta Report* in Calgary and contributed to *Saturday Night* and *The Globe and Mail*.

Scott Young, author, columnist, left-handed golfer, has settled exclusively into writing mystery fiction at home in Peterborough, Ontario. He is a former *Globe and Mail* columnist and *Toronto Telegram* sports editor.

FOR YOU, FOR ME... FOR CANADA

Christie Blatchford

MERIBEL, FRANCE — This game was for you, and me, and all our small towns and the rinks that are their cold, clear centres, and all the players who have gone before and all of those yet to come.

This was for the public address announcer in Drumheller, Alta., who called for the mayor to walk out on the ice for the opening ceremonies, then handed over the microphone to the guy beside him, and walked onto the ice himself. *He* was the mayor. This was for the people of Barrhead, Alta., where the $25-a-seat section was separated from the $50-a-seat section by a line of red tape on the floor.

This was for Miss Kapuskasing, Ont., and Miss Maniwaki, Que., both of whom, at their respective arenas, were part of the official welcome for the team.

This was for the morning man at the only radio station in Powell River, B.C., who, when the PA system died on him while he was making the introductions, threw the mike on the ice and shouted out the players' names. This was for the fishing village of Shippagan, N.B., where they wanted a game so much they didn't care what it cost (the national team gets a guarantee before it comes to town), and upped their perfectly acceptable offer of $25,000 to $30,000 just to be sure.

This was for New Liskeard and Iroquois Falls, Elliot Lake and Chilliwack, B.C., Sydney, N.S. and Fort Frances, Granby and Rosetown and Williams Lake — 192 games in 95 Canadian cities and towns and dots on the map in the past seven years. This was for all the rinks, all the games on the road, all those lovely opening ceremonies where the Zamboni drivers wore tuxedos and ordinary working stiffs paid $100 a pop and the arena was in darkness until the spotlights lit the ice and a deep-voiced announcer said, "Ladies and gentlemen, *mesdames et monsieurs*, the members of Canada's national hockey team..."

Canada's National Hockey Team. How fine that phrase feels on the tongue.

"That's what it's all about," says Donnie Beauchamp, the team's communications manager. Beauchamp has been with Dave King and the boys for seven years.

He just turned down a big job with the new Ottawa Senators in the National Hockey League. "You don't buy these experiences," he says of his decision to stay with the national team. "This is what it's all about. Our players have been everywhere in this country, every small town we played in has a piece of us. We were their big show. They [the small towns] wanted a game and they couldn't care less about the price.

"They didn't want to make money, they wanted the game. We took the game back where it belongs, we kept it where it belonged, that's what it's all about."

What is it all about?

Well, while the federal government was fiddling away your tax dollars on unity commission after unity commission, the national team, in the deep dark nationalist heart of Quebec, was wowing them in Rimouski. The announcer didn't speak a word of English, and in the player introductions buggered up everyone's name, and nobody cared a damn. It was beautiful. They had the disco lights going and the big crowd and they were cheering for the Canadian hockey team.

About the time two Quebec backbenchers were standing up and saying Eric Lindros shouldn't be allowed to play for the national team because he wouldn't sign with the Quebec Nordiques, the folks in Maniwaki, Que., were working up a special dinner for the boys. Tourtière. Sugar pie. It was December 23 last year. "That was our Christmas," says Don Beauchamp. "Go ask the boys about this stuff. Watch their eyes glisten."

When Brett Hull and Adam Oates were renegotiating their only-just-negotiated million-dollar contracts, Brad Schlegel, the gentle, diligent Canadian captain from Kitchener, was signing autographs and posing for pictures for nothing. Schlegel has been with the team for four years. He has many memories — not just of the towns, "but the people we got to meet there" — but his favourite was in Shippagan, N.B., four years ago, for a game against the touring Russians. When he got to the rink for a practice, it was sold out, and the people were still lining up outside.

"It makes you realize," he says, "how much hockey is a common thread. We have different languages, different interests, but hockey is what we have in common."

While in Ottawa and at Queen's Park the deficit was growing by leaps and bounds, the Canadian national team was meeting its budget — about $3-million to $3.5-million a year, only five lousy per cent of it from the taxpayers. The rest the program raises itself — through gate receipts, through three valued corporate sponsors (Labatt's, Air Canada, and Esso) and with much help from the government of Alberta and the Calgary Flames.

While governments all across Canada fought to reduce the size of the bureaucracy, the national team slugged along with one senior V.P., Ron Robison (whose brainchild, with Beauchamp, it was to tour small-town Canada) and the 44-year-old King doing three jobs — V.P. of hockey operations, general manager, and head coach.

Every value worth valuing — thrift, perseverance, hard bloody work, loyalty, patriotism, co-operation, grit, and tenacity — is a part of this team and a part of this program.

This is what Dave King means when he talks about how he would like to see young Canadian kids dream of being Olympians. He knows how the experience broadens a young man, pushes him, teaches him about his country; it is no accident, I think, that every member of the Olympic hockey team felt it was worthwhile to come out for the official flag-raising ceremony two weeks ago.

He is a difficult man to know, Dave King, thoughtful and a little shy and self-contained, one kind of Canuck where Terry Crisp is the other kind, loud and profane and funny. These last days in France, King has all but burst at his seams. He has spent nine years of his life selling a dream. When Canada clinched a berth in the gold medal game, Linda King, Dave's wife, did what he may do later today. She stood in the hockey rink and cried.

Among the dozens and dozens of places this team has been in Canada was a northern Quebec mining town named Rouyn-Noranda. This was my home town, where I grew up. The boys played in the Forum, which is in Rouyn. My father ran the other hockey rink, the Rec Centre in Noranda. He loved hockey, and hockey rinks, and hockey players, and his country, so much that he used to say that when he died, he would like to be buried at centre ice.

He would have loved this team as much as I do. And this game, I like to think, was for him, too.

(That afternoon, Canada's team lost to the Russians 3-1 and thereby won a silver medal.)

(First appeared in the *Toronto Sun*)

IT'S BEISBOL OR LIFE IN THE CANE FIELDS

Allen Abel

BARRIO HATO MAYOR, CONSUELO, DOMINICAN REPUBLIC — The storm rolled off the sea and drenched the fields where the sugar cane grows taller than the men whose lives depend on it, the red stalks fanning into dark green leaves that wave in the steady breeze from the coast. It was good for the sugar cane, the summer storm, good for *el ingenio* — the mashing factory — good for the people of the village that surrounds it.

It was bad for the streets of the town, the summer storm, and now there is a muddy pit in front of the chicken killer's stand, muddy and bloody. He is a practised man, the chicken killer. A customer points to a white hen in a crowded crate. The vendor grabs it by the neck and, with a motion that is being studied intently by two naked boys beside his cart, snaps the fowl into the air like a jockey's whip and breaks its neck, and more blood flows into the muddy street and the two boys run away.

The burros do not mind the mud, but the car does. It bucks and groans slowly through a rocky ditch while the life of the republic passes by on foot and horseback and children stare out from the doorways of houses that have no doors. It is a busy day in the village, the main street filled with mules and Mazdas and the shouts of men in the market.

Around the corner from the stalls where red meat and green plantains stand for sale in the morning sun of Hispaniola, a woman sits in a stiff-backed wooden chair and clasps her hands to her breast.

"Oh God, I cried when he went away," the woman says. "Oh, God, I cried plenty. For three months, I didn't eat. And still, I pray for him. Three times a day, I pray for him. I get down on my knees and I pray for a base hit. Maybe I should ask for a homerun."

Her name is Mary Griffin and all her prayers will not make her son a power hitter. Summer is a lonely time for Mary Griffin, although she has sons who work at *el ingenio* and sons who live in the capital, Santo Domingo, 70 kilometres to the west. Her youngest and, she laughs, smallest son toils far from the rocky streets of his home town and she prays for him. He plays beisbol in a strange place called Canada and for seven months is only a postcard, a name on the radio and a line in *El Nacional*.

This is the Dominican Republic, an island state that lives off its sugar cane and for its ball-playing sons. Next door, across the *cordillera* and a border that can be crossed only with "written Presidential permission," the Haitians ignore Abner Doubleday's game and care only for soccer, sharing the Dominicans' island but not their passion. It is, it seems, not a matter of climate alone.

More than any other place where diamonds have been laid out on rocky lots or groomed expanses, this is the fount whence allstars gush. At last count 41 Dominicans graced major-league rosters, among them four men from this little town of 25,000 in the cane fields — Alfredo Griffin and Rico Carty of the Toronto Blue Jays, Pepe Frias of the Atlanta Braves and Nelson Norman of the Texas Rangers. If Consuelo's seems a paltry contribution to the big leagues, consider that, by the same ratio, Toronto would have 400 in the majors. (It boasts, at the moment, one.) Puerto Rico, a 40-minute flight across the blue water, can claim only about 20 current big-leaguers; Venezuela,

Panama, Nicaragua, Cuba, Mexico, and Canada have sent a handful, or fewer.

The ballplayers of Consuelo begin their careers by throwing rocks at wandering goats. Later, in the years before they are old enough to have to work in the fields or the mashing factory, there are endless pickup games on the stony streets, the players decked out in bare feet and bare chests and the caps of the Braves or the Blue Jays or the winter-league team that plays in the big sta-dium down at the harbour — las Estrellas of San Pedro de Macoris. There are two standard diamonds in the town, directly across a pitted road from the new, modern home built by Frias, a home that boasts one common item in Consuelo and one rarity — a major-leaguer's family, and a telephone.

"My boy called me once," Mary Griffin says. "They ran from the central office and told me. But then he wrote and said it was too expensive. Ninety-five dollars, he said it cost. So now he writes to me. He says he is very happy, very happy in Toronto." Behind her, on a wall of the green wooden-slatted house with the corrugated steel roof, are photographs of Alfredo in various baseball uniforms, post-cards from stops along the American League circuit, a painting of *The Last Supper* and a wall hanging of provin-cial coats-of-arms that says "Souvenir of Canada."

Their language is English; in the parlour of the green house, it bubbles from their mouths with a Caribbean lilt. The whole family is there — cousins, brothers, girl friends, uncles, countless townspeople who can claim, on some branch or other of the matrilineal family tree, kin-ship to the faraway big-leaguer. To greet a visitor from the city where Alfredo plays, the men are in wool suits and silk neckties. Alfredo's stepfather, Joseph Alexander, is there. "Raised him from a baby with my own hands," he says.

Their Spanish is acquired but fluent, the language of the conquerors of half an island the Griffins would not reach until the 1920s, when Mary's brother left the island of Nevis, in the Leewards, and came with her man to

Consuelo seeking work. At 85, Mary's mother is not fit for the walk through the rocky streets to meet the foreign visitor, so the car once more must wrench its way through the marketplace and the mud. Mary is in the front seat, her husband in the back.

"It is not right, Mary, it is not right," a woman shouts from a doorway as the car lurches by. "Man should sit in front, woman in back."

It is a land of strong traditions, some athletic, some foul. "I was at a dinner at the company office," says Moses, Alfredo's oldest brother. "I was the only black man there of 20 men. Before, they did not know I was Alfredo's brother. Every day, they would read in the newspaper how well he was doing and everybody would say, 'Look at this boy Griffin!' and one day I say, 'Yes, and that is my brother'.

"Well, from that day on, I am a hero at the sugar company. So we are at this dinner, and I am the only black man, but they say, 'Let him be served first, he is Griffin's brother'. I am thinking if Alfredo makes the allstar team some day, they will make me president of the company."

Moses laughs. A hard-working man, he has read books that tell of the history of the mashing factory that rules his life and that of the town. "It was owned by Canadians in 1889," he says. "Then it was taken away by the Americans. They named it Consuelo — consolation — for the poor man they took it from. Now the government owns all the factories, since 1956, but it was better when the Americans were here. We had more rights, more salary."

Mary has gone to fetch some letters from Alfredo. Girlfriends and cousins have gone to the kitchen for bottles of Quisqueya beer. Moses leans over and softens his voice to a conspiratorial whisper.

"I don't want Mary to hear it," he says, "but I'm still a Cardinals fan. Marty Marion, now *there* was a shortstop."

They know the game from the papers and the brand-new radio in the parlour of the green house. On the infrequent occasions when the U.S. Armed Forces Radio Network picks up the dulcet tones of Tom Cheek and Early Wynn for relay to fans in the Caribbean to the South China Sea, the house is jammed with family and friends who cheer for their hero and his hapless Azulejos. They are still waiting for the Blue Jays to be deemed worthy of one of Dominican television's weekly broadcasts; it may be a long wait.

"He always wanted to be a baseball player," Mary says, and she could be speaking of any boy in the town. "He never liked to get his hands dirty, never wanted to work in the factory. He is such a good boy. He sends me money every month. Maybe soon he will buy a bigger house so we can have more space to live.

"He was always such a quiet boy. Even when he comes home for the winter, all he wants to do is sit here with friends and listen to his music. The others drink, but he doesn't drink. He always had the stamp on his heart. He was going to be a baseball player."

Many hearts have been stamped in the Dominican. A Blue Jays scout stands on a street corner, watching a pickup game, and the players are watching him. "Look at this!" they shout. "Toronto, hey! Toronto!"

"Maybe I should just sign every boy in town the day he is born and take my chances," the scout laughs, shaking his head at the wonder of such a gold mine of talent. He is Epifanio (Epy) Guerrero, once a blue-chip outfield prospect who headed north to Waycross, Ga., at the age of 17, with a countryman named Rico Carty, later a coach of the Dominican national team at the Pan-American Games in Mexico, now the chief Caribbean scout for the last-place Jays. An ebullient Jonah, Guerrero last was encountered on a long bus trip with the Jays' lowliest farm team in Medicine Hat; the bus crashed. Driving from Santo Domingo to Consuelo, he barely averts a head-on meeting with a stray horse. "I haven't had an accident yet this week," he says.

(That was *last* week. A few days ago, Epy was involved in a smackup on a busy Santo Domingo street. "The car was hurt but Epy wasn't," reported his brother, Mario, who labours as shortstop for the Oakland A's. "He was only in the hospital long enough for somebody to steal his watch.")

Epy Guerrero scours bumpy diamonds from Monterey to Maracaibo for talent and directs an underground network of spies that would be the envy of the KGB. At the ballpark in San Pedro de Macoris, he is standing idly in the outfield, admiring an advertising sign featuring a nearly bald Carty and a pack of filtertips, when a local teenager comes sprinting up, breathlessly.

"I've seen him! I've seen him!" the youth pants in Spanish.

"Can he hit?" Guerrero asks.

"Oh, *si*."

"Can he throw?"

"Oh, *si*."

"Can he run?"

"Oh, *si*."

"Tell him I'll be back Monday to see him," Guerrero says, and the lad runs off. They have not mentioned the prospect's name. Later, the scene is repeated in a San Pedro eatery and the Santo Domingo airport bar. Guerrero says the waiter looks like a second baseman.

"What position?" Guerrero asks.

"Second base," says the waiter. "I'll need a week of practice before you look at me."

"Friday," says Guerrero. "See you Friday."

From these tryouts come a few signings each year by each of the 26 major-league organizations. The players, their hearts stamped by a common dream, head off to Waycross and Medicine Hat, but many are home by midsummer, disenfranchised by loneliness or the language barrier or beaten out by a hotshot Yanqui from the amateur draft. The free-agent lottery does not apply beyond the U.S. border, so Guerrero and the other Latin American scouts are the last soldiers in what used to be a continental war, racing each other to green-slatted shacks to sign 16-year-old boys.

"It is the only way," Guerrero says. "We take them when they are so young because here they would never improve. Here, they would play in a real game only every Sunday on bad fields like these, they go to ballparks in the States and it's no sweat. No bad hops; that is why they are such good fielders, the Dominicans."

Guerrero's new home in Santo Domingo stands two blocks from the prison where Cesar Cedeno, whom Epy signed for the Houston Astros a decade ago, spent a month before it was determined that he was not criminally liable for the shooting death of a young woman with whom he was arguing at the time the gun went off. Cedeno, and the sadly slumping Carty, are the two big names in Dominican baseball since the retirement of the flashy pitcher Juan Marichal, the dynamic, popular dandy.

Had the ruling gone against Cedeno, his punishment would have been severe indeed: a lifetime of hard labour, without pay, for the Government of Presidente Antonio Guzman. Guzman's forces took over from ex-president Juan Balaguer, a sports-minded autocrat who built a magnificent complex of diamonds, swimming pools, and basketball courts in the heart of Santo Domingo.

It is a city of palm beaches and tin shacks, of grandiose squares and monuments, Columbus' tomb and banners proclaiming the inspirational messages of El Presidente: THE GOVERNMENT WORKS, THE PEOPLE PROSPER. TO LOVE A CHILD IS TO LISTEN TO HIM. IMPROVE YOUR FAMILY'S DIET — EAT MORE POTATOES.

In the offices of Licey Tigers, the capital's representative in the winter league, a bulletin board lists the prospective roster for the season that opens in November. Included, on a team that can claim at least as much talent as the big league Blue Jays, are such familiar names as Carty, Pedro Borbon, Manny Mota, Jesus Alou, and the roly-poly ex-Jay, Victor Cruz. (A team official says that Cruz, who claimed to be 21 when he was acquired by the Jays last year, actually was 28. The relief pitcher has since been traded to Cleveland.)

The winter league satisfies the island's passions; there

is no fooling these fans. A recent experiment, the Class AAA Inter-American League, died quickly here because customers were not about to spend money to watch professional baseball in the summertime, when they know that all worthy Dominican talent is off toiling on the mainland.

The president of the Licey team is a hearty fellow named Monchin Pichardo, and he has heard the question many times before. Asked why there are so many Dominicans in the major leagues, he does not pause.

"It is not that there are so many," Pichardo says sagely. "If there were not so much prejudice against Latin ballplayers, there would be many more. Now, we have *mucho*. If not for the prejudice, we would have *muchisimo*."

Indeed, the well of talent appears bottomless. On one of the city diamonds on a steaming Sunday, the Epy Guerrero Youth League is in action. At the instant the league's patron pulls up to watch an inning or two, the batter hits a bouncer back to the pitcher, who fires to second base, where the tag is slapped on a sliding baserunner, who comes up punching. In a moment, the benches have emptied and fists are flying and Guerrero is in the middle of it.

"Hey, I tell you," he says, brushing himself off. "Down here, we play *hard*."

Back in Consuelo, the car rolls along a side street and pulls up at the Church of the Apostolic Faith, where an old man spends his time away from the sugar factory. The children said he could be found here, the thin man in the grey wool cap. Jacobo Carty, whose mother came from St. Maarten and whose son went off to play baseball, steps out into the blinding sunshine and speaks of his son as a stranger.

"Self-praise is no praise," the elder Carty says when asked if he is proud of the batting champion he raised with his earnings from odd jobs, from carpentry and truck driving and labour in the factory. "If I do something grand, I do not need to stand on a street corner and shout about it."

English is his language but the Bible is his tongue. Quoting chapter and verse, Carty tells of a break with the sins of his youth, sins that included, he says, watching baseball. He tells of rejecting his past habits and of years of hard work, but then a visitor remembers Rico's talking about his father's love for boxing and the wall comes down.

"I learned boxing by correspondence," he says, flashing a smile and shaking his head to dislodge the memory. "There was a trainer in New York. We wrote to him, asked about how to throw certain punches.

"It was a great time for boxing then. I watched them all in the films. Dempsey, Tunney, Kid Chocolate. It was all we had then in this place, the boxing and the guitars. Now, we still have the guitars, but not the boxing. It was what we all wanted to be in those days. Some went professional, but they made little money.

"Myself," Jacobo Carty says, standing outside the church, "I never made no speed at it, but I loved it plenty well."

LORDS OF THE RINK

Jim Coleman

I am afraid that the premature publication of the news that a group of local real estate promoters has failed to purchase Maple Leaf Gardens has spoiled one of my own dazzling financial coups. My bank manager, pointing a shaky finger at my overdraft, was reminding me, just the other day, that it's high time I engineer another of those *putschs* which, in the past, won me the nickname, "The Wolf of Bay Street." (My memory is hazy and I'm not quite sure whether I won that nickname on the Toronto Stock Exchange or in a bar of the Savarin Hotel.) In any event, they haven't showered me with ticker-tape since that autumn afternoon in 1944 when I bet $50 on Broom Time and he paid $56.10 for every $2 in winning The Breeders' Stakes at Woodbine.

No longer is there any point in concealing the fact that up until Thursday a group of my friends and I were "interested" in purchasing Maple Leaf Gardens. We were in firm agreement, however, that the sale was contingent on the National Hockey League granting us permission to change the name of the Toronto Maple Leaf hockey team to Coleman's Comets.

We realize now we were hopelessly old-fashioned and naive in our campaign to gain control of Maple Leaf Gardens. The rival group of real estate promoters had acquired the services of an intermediary and, in order to conduct their negotiations as secretively as possible, they had employed an advertising agency which shyly arranged a press conference, complete with television cameras, klieg lights, food, and drink.

My associates in our offer to purchase Maple Leaf Gardens have given me permission to identify them publicly. We do this merely to clear up any public misconception that we might have been "fronting" for the Chase National Bank or J. Paul Getty. My associates were: Phil "Canvasback" Lisner, Meat-Wagon Joe Brown, and a taxi-driver named Tex.

We were sitting in Tex's cab outside the King Edward Hotel late one night — waiting for Tex to pick up a fare — when we decided to buy Maple Leaf Gardens.

"Aw — that sounds nuts," said Lisner. "How do you go about making an offer to buy Maple Leaf Gardens?"

"You just phone Stafford Smythe, stupid," I said. "Has anyone got a dime? I'll make the phone call."

Well, no one had a dime so we didn't phone that night. Of course, if we had been out-of-town, we could have conned the long-distance operator into phoning Stafford Smythe, collect.

It was decided that we should persuade an intermediary to make our offer to Stafford Smythe. I have a friend named Rose, who is a hat-check girl in a local hotel. Rose doesn't know Stafford Smythe personally, but Rose has a cousin who worked for the Conn Smythes at their summer cottage a few years ago.

It was a pretty flimsy connection, I'm prepared to admit now, but it was arranged for Rose's cousin to transmit our offer to Stafford Smythe. Then, I was to meet Stafford Smythe at the end of the second period of last Wednesday's game between the Maple Leafs and the Canadiens. He would give me "the sign" if he was agreeable to the deal.

All this may sound very confusing to you innocents who haven't attempted to engineer a financial coup. Just stick to your television sets and leave the Big Deals to those of us who are destined to be Captains of Industry.

It was a crushing blow which fell when, the next afternoon, Conn Smythe announced from Florida that he doesn't propose to sell Maple Leaf Gardens at this time.

This is merely a temporary setback in our financial campaign. My associates and I have embarked upon another more adventurous, more imaginative project.

Within 48 hours, we propose to make an offer to purchase Mount Pleasant Cemetery — provided, of course, that we can hire the right advertising agency to handle our publicity campaign with becoming dignity.

(First appeared in *The Globe and Mail*)

PEACE IN A DIM-LIT POOL

Michael Farber

Sylvie Frechette dove into the pool as dark, haunting music boomed from a hidden speaker, a dive as much an act of ablution as it was of training.

In these 3½ minutes Frechette was rinsing away the tragedy of a 24-year-old lifetime, embellishing the drama of the music with thrusts and spins and taking synchronized swimming places it never has dreamed of going.

There was a spirituality to her routine, a quality that existed before last weekend but that never was more appropriate than now.

Even in the dimly-lit practice pool, there was no mistaking a gold-medal swim. But the fantastic part of the routine isn't the glory it will bring Frechette or the push it will give her down the road to wherever it is she wants to go. The best part is when she swims to Vangelis' *Mask*, she does not have to smile.

"I held my funeral when I went to see him in the morgue in Montreal," Frechette said. "For me tomorrow is not the funeral, but the opening ceremonies of the Olympic Games."

The crying stops. The Games begin.

Sylvain Lake, Frechette's companion, will be buried

today and a little bit of her will go with him. He took his life a week ago. Four days later she boarded a plane for Barcelona and began putting her life back together in the pool, one element at a time.

"The water is my home," Frechette said. This is where she lives now, where she is most herself. She can't go back to her home in Laval, not after finding his body.

Lake took his own life. That was his decision.

Frechette will swim in the Olympics. This is hers.

"I knew deep down inside this is what Sylvain wants," Frechette said. "It was his dream to come to the Olympics, first as an athlete and then as a journalist. I'd been with him a couple of years. He knew what the Olympics meant to me.

"At first I thought only of myself, but that was a little egotistical. I had worked hard for me but also for him, for my coach [Julie Sauve], for all those people who supported me. Julie has been my coach for 18 years. This is for us, not for me."

The training session went surprisingly well, her thoughts falling into step with the music after two sessions in Montreal where the anarchy of grief had jumbled her mind. She was composed yesterday, all grace and sense of purpose. There was red in her eyes and her skin looked pale against a purple Canada swimsuit, but it only heightened her beauty in this shadowy place. She glowed.

"On the plane something washed over her like travelling often does to people," said Sauve, who has seen her grow up but never have to be this grown up before. "At home the crying didn't stop. You know, I was getting a little ticked off by it. You tell her you know she feels like crying so cry, cry, cry, and get it all out, and you take her in your arms. But you hoped her family would say, 'OK, Sylvie, let's go,' but it was always cry, cry."

Frechette is having a difficult time.

"But," she said, "I don't want to be reminded about it."

"When I reached the Athletes' Village, the first person I came across was [Canadian backstroker] Mark Tewksbury, who I only know a little," Frechette said. "He gave me a big hug and said, 'Ah, Sylvie.' That's all he said. From that hug, I felt I was getting energy from him. It was great for me.

"I don't talk about it yet. But there are little gestures, little signs I've been getting from the athletes. A pat on the shoulder. A thumb's up. It's all a little superficial, but it's what I need right now."

The condolences are piling up in mailsacks, at home, and in the Village. There is a bag of sympathy in her room that will wait because what do you say when there is nothing to say? Frechette has chosen to check her mind at the Olympic Village gate, to escape into a Stephen King novel. Go ahead, Mr. King. Take your best shot. There is nothing in that bizarre imagination that can be more horror-filled than what Frechette and Lake's family went through last Saturday.

Are you angry with him?

"I'm not angry," Frechette said, and her eyes grew wide. "It never crossed my mind to be angry with him.

"No one in the world can judge what he did. No one should make comments on that. If they do, they are only hurting me.

"I've heard the theories, and they are like a blow to my heart. I also have a lot of unanswered questions. But no one — *no one* — in the world can judge him."

Her coach, her friends, and her family are a human safety net now, prepared to catch her when the mourning dawns. Frechette calls them "my smile." Originally she and Sauve considered inviting her sports psychologist, Luc Pelletier of Ottawa, to Barcelona but changed their minds because it was not one of the old ways.

"If he's here, he'd be asking me how do I feel and I'd be wondering whether I should be talking to him and then I'd be asking myself whether I was fine or what?" Frechette said. "I have his phone number. I can reach him 24 hours a day. He'll be my crutch if I have a crying fit. But Julie is here, and I tell her everything. I've also been writing in my diary."

"She's stronger than I thought," Sauve said. "She's

stronger than she thought."

Frechette met the future in a pool tucked away on a downtown side street, a striking silhouette in a world with shadow and lights. The routine wasn't perfect — Sauve stopped the modern musical *Walpurgis Nacht* to correct a leg movement — but it was at least good enough to repair one loss. Frechette had her confidence back.

After Vangelis' *Mask*, she did smile.

(First appeared in the Montreal *Gazette*)

NASTY

Brian Preston

At six o'clock on a drizzly morning in the parking lot behind the Memorial arena in Victoria, 22 weary hockey players board an idling Volvo touring bus. Over the next five days it will carry them eastward through mountain snowstorms and across the bleakest winter prairie, to a place where all water turns to ice and hockey enters the blood and dreams of every boy. They are on a 4,600-kilometre highway pilgrimage to Manitoba and back for the sake of three hockey games and three wildly variant sporting experiences: an old-time brawl fought on pride and rubbery legs in Regina, a long, painful night of penitence in Moose Jaw, and a sudden finale of near-redemption in Brandon, Manitoba.

These are the Victoria Cougars of the Western Hockey League, the second-worst team in the second-best hockey league in the world. They're still mostly kids — the youngest is 17, the oldest 20. As a team they are heirs to a long tradition of hockey in Victoria, dating back beyond 1925, when the pro Cougars of the Western Hockey League won the Stanley Cup. It was in 1912 that Lester Patrick, who later founded the New York Rangers, opened the Willow Arena, Canada's first artificial rink, and started the Cougars' predecessors, the Senators, in what was then a very keen hockey town.

The Cougars are also heirs to a junior tradition in the WHL that since 1971 has seen the team send more than

40 players to the NHL, among them Mel Bridgman, Grant Fuhr, and the Courtnall brothers. But lately that tradition has been eclipsed by another. In 1989–90, the team dropped dramatically from second place to last with a 5-65-2 season, entering the record book as the worst team in the history of Canadian Major Junior hockey.

This year's model, although already doomed to miss the playoffs, boasts an almost entirely new lineup, including a fracas-fond goalie who will manage two fighting majors in the same game, an amiable hayseed who transmogrifies into an on-ice animal, a captain they call the Toothless Wonder, a 20-year-old named the Colossal Fossil, a Finnish import who imagines "Who are you fuck?" is an acceptable English greeting, and a host of teenaged bruisers from tiny towns like Duck Lake, Saskatchewan, where they still call aftershave "hooer lure." They're mostly castoffs from other teams, thrown together by Rick Hopper, 36, a hungry coach possessed of a profound sense of humour, a two-year guaranteed contract, and long-term vision that expects no more of this year's motley crew than keeping the score respectable and, most especially, "answering the bell" when the rough stuff starts.

Two hours out of Vancouver, every player is asleep. The Cougars, marginally improved over last year, played at home last night, falling 7-5 to the Medicine Hat Tigers, their 27th loss this season against six wins. Most players slept only an hour or two between the game and the early-morning rendezvous at the bus. Outside, through the frosted windows, mountain streams tumble from the peaks of the Columbia Range, shrouded in snowstorms. But the boys are not interested in scenery. When they awaken hours later, they raise a post-adolescent plea to the bus driver: "Billy, slap in a video!" The bus is equipped with a VCR and two television screens; they want Arnold Schwarzenegger in *The Terminator*, Eddie Murphy in *48 Hours*, then the hockey movie *Slap Shot*. They know by heart every word uttered by the Hanson brothers, the movie's heroic, bespectacled goons; their laughter competes with the sound of big wheels splattering slush against the underbelly of the bus.

It's early in the trip, and the bus's heater is still working; players lounge in long johns, some shirtless, more comfortable here than with their own families. They are close enough, emotionally and physically, that when one player squeezes the pimples on another's back, it's an act of charity that passes unremarked upon.

Near the back of the bus, defenceman Dwayne Newman, at 19 a four-year veteran, built tall and lean like a cowboy, keeps one eye out for the coaches, and offers a dip of chewing tobacco. Two days from now the empty Coke bottle he employs as a spittoon will hold two fingers of frozen spit in a brown lump in the bottom. Dwayne, a Winnipegger, is the team captain, a result of on-ice tenacity and off-ice likeability. He lost his two front teeth early in 1990 to a high stick, so his nickname is "the Toothless Wonder." "They shattered," he says. "Two hours in the dentist's chair getting the fragments pulled out of my gums."

Newman hasn't scored a goal in 107 games, a streak he attributes to bad hands and bad luck. "I play a defensive style, but not by choice," he smiles. A season without a goal is called a doughnut, and Newman has bitten into his second. "If I go the double doughnut, that'll be brutal." Still, he'll probably be back next year on the off chance he'll improve and be discovered by the NHL, but mostly because he loves playing hockey, and the other guys love having him.

From a few seats back Colin Gregor, a.k.a. the Colossal Fossil, the Cougar's leading scorer with 17 goals in 33 games, launches into his best Bob Cole "Hockey Night in Canada" parody: "... in his 107th game of futility, Dwayne Newman, it's back to the point, *he shoots, he scores!* The whole Victoria bench empties, they've won the Stanley Cup! *Dwayne Newman* has scored his first goal, and they're carrying him around the rink!"

Gregor is one of the three "over-age" 20-year-olds league rules permit the team to carry, and a year's maturity sets him apart from his teammates: his glasses give him a cerebral look, and he speaks with the deliberate caution of an adult. The younger players tease him about being in his last year of major-league hockey, but it's too close to the truth to be funny.

The WHL, affectionately known to its players as "the Dub," is one of three loosely affiliated Major Junior hockey leagues in Canada (the other two are the Ontario and Quebec leagues). The Cougars compete with 13 other teams in non-NHL towns on both sides of the border, including the bottom-of-the-league Portland Winter Hawks and the league-leading Kamloops Blazers. The WHL game is played at a level of skill and emotion most hockey people consider to be second to the NHL. But no kid grows up dreaming about being second-best. A young player comes to the Dub because it's the closest to the pro style game — and to the pro scouts. About a quarter of last year's NHLers came from the WHL. But players are eligible for the pro draft only until age 19. Last season was Colin Gregor's last draft year. He went undrafted. There's still a chance he could be invited to an NHL tryout as a free agent. "I never dreamed about playing in the Dub," he says. "I dreamed about playing pro, period. I'm still dreaming about it, but not all the time like other years."

A few seats away, three younger players, for whom junior hockey's version of the mid-life crisis is a year or two away, are preparing themselves for a homecoming. All are from small-town Saskatchewan: Johnny Badduke, 18, from Watson; Shane Stangby, 17, from Duck Lake; and Dave McMillen, 18, from Carievale. Whether any of them has a future in the pros is, at this point, questionable. But all three are promising scrappers: Badduke, 6'2" with huge fists, admits with a false modesty he broke Stangby's nose in a bout in training camp, and McMillen, "Macker" to his teammates, with a choirboy face and a good-natured farm-boy grin, demonstrates how he transforms himself into an on-ice horror. He sucks the breath out of his cheeks and bulges out his eyes to psychokiller proportions. He describes his style: "I don't beat up the guy. I hold my own. I never really out-and-out win a fight, but I haven't lost one either." He rubs a nasty scar above his left eyebrow. "Well, one."

Late Sunday afternoon, an hour and 20 minutes before game time, the big Volvo pulls up to the Agridome, home of the Regina Pats (14-17-1), and the players stumble off, suffering from bus legs and bus brain. Gregor the Fossil watches as the rookies unload the ice-cold equipment in their west coast clothes: jackets, street shoes, and glove-less hands in the bone-chilling -20°C wind. "You learn from your mistakes as a rookie. One time I set down a big box like that one with the skate sharpener in it, and left all my skin on the metal handle."

In the dressingroom, defenceman Chris Catellier sits in a corner scowling. Coach Hopper has just told him he'll have to sit out tonight's game, even though his folks are driving all the way from Winnipeg to see him play. Steve Passmore, the fervent little goalie, blows into the boot of his ice-cold skate and watches his breath emerge as a frosty vapour. Hopper surveys his team and worries, "Sometimes they get off a bus like this and have *nothing*." The comment is prophetic. By the end of the first period, the team is down 3-0 and looks lifeless. Two thousand three hundred and ten paying customers fill less than half the seats, and the Agridome, known for its quiet crowds, is tomblike: when Stangby rallies his mates at the bench with a phrase made up mostly of the f-word, a woman 15 rows up yells, "Hey, quit swearing, there's kids in the audience."

At the start of the second period, Macker, true to form, gets in a fight before the puck is even dropped. In the third, he's in another, this time with a kid named Weenks; they claw at each other's helmets and throw a few sloppy rights before they go down in a heap: Weenks' skull and the ice combine to produce a crack heard in every corner of the arena.

The game degenerates into a series of fights and

ejections, culminating with a brawl among all the players on the ice in the dying moments. Passmore, the goalie, takes on two different Pats to earn a double major and a game misconduct. When the game is over, the Cougars, outscored 7-0 and outshot 44-18, come off the ice hooting and hollering with delight. They've won the fights. In the dressingroom — after the boys have buoyantly compared their individual shares of the game's 338 penalty minutes, and pantomimed slow-motion replays of some of the more brutal collisions of fists with faces — Coach Hopper offers a tempered chastisement: "It's not what we wanna get a reputation for, but I'm glad you guys had the nuts to stand up for yourselves."

The next day in his room at the Regina Travelodge, Rick Hopper can be found studying a depth chart of the Cougars' "list", containing the names — 50 in all — of the team's current players, along with the minor-league players aged 15 and up whose options, should they ever be inclined or enticed to play Major Junior hockey, are pledged to Victoria alone. In the margin of the chart, surrounded by doodled sunbeams, are the words "tough idiots" and "skills". "I was thinking about our guys," he explains. "They're tough and they're idiots, but we need skills."

Hopper is 36, but the boyish cut of his fair red hair makes him look younger. Last year Hopper, who once played college hockey in Ontario, coached the quite respectable Powell River Paper Kings of the B.C. Junior League, a Tier II "A" league one level below the WHL. Last spring, for a raise in pay ($40,000 this year, $45,000 the next) and what he terms "a bigger challenge", Hopper was hired by Cougars owner Bob Vranckaert as coach and director of hockey operations.

Vranckaert, 50, a Burnaby-raised construction company owner now living in Anchorage, took possession of the team in April 1989. He bought it, he says, from "a Scotsman who measured success by having the lowest budget in the league". Since then, Vranckaert has increased the part-time scouting staff to nine and doubled their wages. He also hired Hopper before this season began, attracted to the coach's two-fisted attitude to the game. The team is losing money — $200,000 last season — and is unable to get more than 1,700 paying customers to the home games when 2,400 are needed to break even. Vranckaert is bitter about the lack of support. When a Victoria sportswriter reported the owner was thinking of moving the Cougars elsewhere, there was not a single call or letter of complaint. "We're spending enormous amounts and working our tails off," says the owner, "and the people in Victoria don't give a shit. In most cities, if you threatened to move a franchise, people would be burning your house down."

In this blase climate, Hopper must try to build a winner. When he took over last spring, he found the remnants of a demoralized team that had gone through 49 players and four coaches the previous year, and a scouting network unsure of the team's direction (there having been no one coach there long enough to provide one). To add to Hopper's troubles, none of the younger "skill" players on the list was willing to come and play for a team that won five games the year before. Who could blame them? The lure of a comprehensive hockey scholarship from a major U.S. college keeps many kids playing Tier II "A", where they maintain the amateur status required by the colleges. For many others, even staying with a winning Tier II "A" team is preferable to joining a losing Major Junior. Thus it was that the manpower-strapped Hopper spent the summer putting close to 32,000 kilometres on his car looking for hockey players.

"What I look for is decent young guys who are hard workers. How many teenaged kids do you know who could do what those kids did last night? Step off that bus and skate out on the ice — and sure it's fighting and all that, it looks stupid" — he lowers his voice for emphasis — "but it's scary out there. Real scary. A kid like Dave McMillen, he's been beat up so many times this year it isn't funny, and he doesn't even feel it."

How Hopper discovered McMillen reveals a lot about

his coaching style. Last summer he was going through stats from the Saskatchewan Junior League: "I'm running my finger down the penalty minutes first to find the tough guys — 365 minutes, hmm, I like that. I got right on the phone."

"I said, 'Look, I don't know anything about you, but if you can get 365 minutes in penalties as a 17-year-old, you can play for me.' I figured he might not be able to skate, but shit, I didn't mind what I saw in training camp. And then he went through four days of camp really shy, I mean he hit a few guys, mucked it up and down the wall, but never fought. So I sat him down after the fourth day and said, 'Look, Davey, you're either gonna show me what you got or you're goin' home'. " The coach breaks into a grin for the punchline: "And he went out and just *tooned* on this guy! That kid can be a pro. He's gonna fill out, his old man's a giant, he's right off the prairies.

"That's the kind of kid I like to have, a good farm boy from out here. When it's nutcuttin' time on the ice, those guys will show. I've given lots of kids chances like him, that nobody else would even give shit for. With the other coaches in this league, it's all 'skill level, skill level' — well, sure, go find a kid with skill, put him in the line-up, he just naturally gets better and away you go. But I've had to use a bit of guile and find guys who in a year or two might be players for me, because they're not being given to me.

"Of course, you'll never win a championship being brutes. Never. We're just trying to win some respect for now, until we can build our skill level up. We've got some good young players coming up, but you have to get the kids to come and play. So how do you judge success for us? For me, it'll be the ability to recruit young skill players." In the meantime, the Cougars can at least gain some respect for being tough.

The team has a night off in Regina. The players have been given seven bucks meal money and an 11 p.m.

curfew. For the coach, there's more work to be done — he'll take a look at some local minor-league talent. Three blocks from the hotel at the Murray Balfour Arena, a suburban rink so bare-bones the coffee comes from a coin machine. Hopper, his face close to one of the small plex-iglass windows more suited to an aquarium, peers out at the swirling randomness of a Bantam "AA" game. He's checking out a "76", a player born in 1976 and therefore eligible this year to join a WHL team's list. "Wish he'd quit holding his stick funny," he mutters. "He's got a few bad habits, but he's a good player. Some of the qualities that'll make them a decent hockey player you'll never see at this level anyway."

After the game, it's back to the hotel to talk hockey with the scouts, one of whom is Frank Harding, the team's Manitoba man, a Winnipeg janitor who for a $2,000 hon-orarium from the team watches more than 300 Bantam, Pee Wee, Junior "A" or Midget-level hockey games each winter. He reports the Cougars are developing a reputa-tion whether they want one or not: other scouts are calling them "Hop's Hooligans". Hopper just smiles. He men-tions a time last spring when he ended up at the same beer-parlour table with two legendary fire-breathing old WHL coaches, Paddy Ginnell and Ernie "Punch" McLean. Ginnell got to reminiscing about a bench-clearing brawl when he coached the Cougars back in the '70s. The hor-rified mayor of Victoria, the story goes, came out of the stands to order technicians to shut off the lights; the fighting continued, so His Worship headed down to the bench to plead with the coach. Ginnell felt the mayor's hand on his shoulder, but, thinking it must be an irate enemy fan, he wheeled and started punching.

The days are gone when any coach can afford a repu-tation like that. The Regina game has earned Hopper a grim phone call from the Calgary-based league's president, Ed Chynoweth. "He feels, and maybe rightly so, that we're starting fights that wouldn't normally start, simply because we're losing. He said I'll be suspended or fined if it continues." The coach accepts the judgement without rancour. "He doesn't think it's good for the image of the league." So the next night at the Moose Jaw Civic Centre, an architectural marvel referred to locally as "the crushed beer can" (its roof rests on slung cables and sags in the middle), Hopper quiets the troops in the dressingroom and lays down the law: "Keep the mitts on." There'll be no fighting tonight.

Sketching a rink in chalk on the dressingroom floor, he outlines a no-frills game plan for his no-frills team, who watch glassy-eyed: dump it in, bang 'em along the boards, "two on two down low and whoever's in the middle lane is the high guy." The building's odd acoustics amplify the roar of the 1,795 fans and make on-ice communication impossible. The boys stick to the plan for about 10 minutes. They score the first goal. But the thrill of a lead is seductive and destroys all concentration; the Cougars' game descends to the random spontaneity of wide-open shinny. The Moose Jaw Warriors (17-16-3) play a fast, high-skilled skating game, and run away with it 9-2. So much for keeping the mitts on. The bus ride back to the hotel in Regina is mighty quiet.

Next morning, during the five-hour ride to Brandon for the last game of the road trip, the players recover their high spirits. Newman, who broke two ribs when landed upon in one of the preliminary bouts in the Regina game, yet continues to play without complaint, sits up and announces, "We must be getting close, I can smell the shit at the Keystone." The Brandon Keystone Centre arena is part of a complex that includes facilities for livestock shows, and the melange of smells is part of the league's folklore.

Today there's not a trace of an odour. The big Volvo has delivered the team early for once, and 22 hockey players suddenly find themselves with an hour to kill amid the gentility of the annual children's Christmas party of the Brandon Figure Skating Club. Mikko Outinin, 19, the melancholy Finn from Kuusankoski, whom the other players insist on calling "Sven from Sveden" ("Just to bug him," says John Badduke), loiters by the snacks and goodies table that the local ladies have set up for their tiny skaters. For his indifferent play, Mikko has been dropped from tonight's lineup in favour of Chris Catellier, but it doesn't seem to bother him. When the assistant coach asks him if he thinks he can play better, he shrugs, and says, "No." In Canadian hockey, that's the wrong answer.

Several hours later, the Brandon Wheat Kings, 13-22-2 and missing their all-star goalie, have spent most of the evening around the Victoria net and outshot their visitors 50-21 in regulation time, but somehow the Cougars manage to finish 60 minutes of hockey tied 2-2. Less than a minute into sudden-death overtime, Colossal Fossil Gregor picks up a loose puck along the boards near centre ice, freezes the lone defenceman with a fake to the outside, and flips the puck to the centre of the rink. A few swift strides and he's caught up with it for a break-away from the blueline in. He gives the goalie a big-league fake and shifts to his backhand. The puck trickles over the goaltender's pad — and *Colin Gregor scores! The Victoria Cougars win the Stanley Cup!*

Well, not quite, but as they pour off the bench to embrace their hero, to celebrate his 18th goal, and to celebrate each other, they're as intoxicated by this victory as any champions. In the delirium of the dressingroom — between the gleeful torching of Billy the bus driver's ugly red and blue tie, and chants of "Shitfaced, shitfaced" from teenaged boys enthralled with the promise of a few days off at Christmas away from curfews and strictly enforced prohibition — Gregor's linemate Gerry St. Cyr, a tough guy who is the team's second-highest scorer, takes a reporter's tape recorder and interviews the giggling goal-scorer:

"Colin, are you planning higher goals after Christmas, or what?"

"I'm just trying to roll with the punches, keep my head above water, keep playing with Gerry St. Cyr number 22 from Nanaimo, 19 years of age, eligible for the draft this year — draft this kid! He's a gamer, he's a player — I would be nowhere without him, goodnight."

Before he leaves the rink, Gregor phones his parents in New Sarepta, Alberta. They're as pleased and as happy as he is that he scored on a breakaway in overtime in the last hockey game he'll ever play in the Brandon Keystone Centre. Will he miss playing in Brandon? He answers with a swift, "No." Then, more thoughtfully, he weighs a long, uncertain future against what is suddenly the past, and corrects himself. "Maybe someday, yeah."

The coach has a parting message, as he strokes the scraggle of hair sprouting from Macker's chin: "Next time I see you all, there's a $20 fine for any bullshit on the face!" Then it's back on the bus, boys, passing around Vaseline to rub on the lips "so they'll be soft for the girl-friend", wrapping up in sleeping bags (the heater's conked out for good) for what is supposed to be a marathon 28-hour nonstop ride back to Victoria, but turns into 48 hours because of weather and bus trouble.

Gregor will probably be a university student by next fall. Badduke, McMillen, Passmore, and Stangby most likely will be back on the bus for another year. The first game back after Christmas — his 111th match — Newman will score a goal. And Mikko Outinin, the forlorn Finn, will be released by the Cougars in mid-January. But for now, as the bus pulls away from the Keystone Arena, Mikko's thinking is short term. He holds up an open palm, spreads his fingers. "Five hours," he says with a smile, anticipating the holidays in Regina. "Five hours, then I will be drunk."

(First appeared in *Vancouver*)

WOMEN'S TENNIS TOUR PREFERS DENIAL TO DISCREET

Mary Ormsby

What a group of Grand Slam wimps. Scared of a little tampon. The Women's Tennis Association Tour last week rejected a $10-million proposal from the maker of Tampax because the product might make other sponsors squeamish and, therefore, cost players prize money.

This decision brought to you by those who felt Monica Seles needed only a week off after being stabbed.

Strange, women's tennis wasn't afraid to maintain a long, lucrative, and controversial relationship with Virginia Slims. The game blissfully ignored growing medical evidence that cigarettes destroy healthy people. A walk through a cancer ward will jolt even the most dedicated addict to butt out.

Not surprisingly, the women on the tour don't smoke. They know better. And the rare exceptions do so in private because a public puff is bad for the image of athletic excellence.

But all female tennis pros menstruate — at least, the ones allowed to finish grade school do. It's something healthy young women do and unless one was raised by wolves, this natural process is common knowledge. So is the understanding that women — including those bashing away on the baseline — use sanitary protection during their monthly cycle.

It's no big deal.

Feminine hygiene products have been flogged on TV for years. Sure, the ads are discreet — fields of flowers, sunrises/sunsets, aerobics classes, etc. — to soft-sell the items. But clearly, viewer discomfort is no longer a concern.

Yet, women's tennis doesn't even want discreet. The tour wants denial.

Good girls don't do the sorts of things that require tampons. And in that misguided thinking, the tennis tour has sold out to society's unrealistic beauty standard of women.

Sports Illustrated, under the guise of sports journalism, panders the magazine's ideal woman in its annual swimsuit edition. The supermodels on display have no physical flaws, their only body hair is on their head (check out some of the bikini bottoms) and posing half-naked in steamy jungles/foaming surf appears to be how they spend their days. Not exactly the girls next door.

Consciously or not, women have been fighting to destroy this sort of media-perpetuated beauty myth through sport. Female athletes are muscled, powerful, smart, aggressive, competitive and their natural beauty shines through. They are real women, not fantasies.

But the WTA is running scared that women may somehow displease men and therefore, cost the athletes money. Martina Navratilova, who bravely fought prejudice over her lesbian lifestyle, buckled at the knees over tampons.

"We couldn't risk losing the local tournament sponsors, which is where our $35-million in prize money comes from, because they didn't want to be associated with a WTA tour presented by Tampax," said Navratilova, president of the WTA Tour Players Association.

"It shouldn't be a stigma," she continued, "but apparently it still is."

The tour claims differently, but it's really the women

in tennis who see this as a stigma. This stand grossly underestimates people's tolerance today and, shockingly, their own power as women. Can you imagine what would happen if a tournament was cancelled because the thought of tampons made a promoter queasy? The twerp would be run out of town.

Harlan Stone, a vice-president of the firm that recruited the rejected sponsor, said it best.

"Women's tennis had the chance to do something cutting edge, to lead instead of follow, and instead they've opted for the path of least resistance," Stone said.

Game, set, match, Mr. Stone.

(Reprinted with permission from *The Toronto Star* Syndicate)

CITO'S SECRET

Paul Quarrington

"**P**aul! Paul!"

For the dozenth time, I spin around and stare at the people leaning across the top of the dugout. I search there for a familiar face, but find none. The autograph hunters wave programs, scraps of paper, baseball mitts and gloves. One small boy, a Blue Jays cap obscuring his vision, clutches a large piece of wood. "Paul! Paul!" It occurs to me that I'm standing beside Paul Molitor, who stares placidly at the field and awaits his time in the batting cage. I take a moment to feel stupid, but at least my spinning around has caused me to spy my quarry. Clarence Edwin Gaston is returning to the clubhouse. I bolt after him, fumbling in my briefcase for my notepad and the futuristic recording device I've purchased, a small machine that resembles a phaser from the first *Star Trek* series. I catch up with Gaston in the passageway that has been hacked through the Toronto Skydome's inner rib work.

"Cito!" I call out. I resist the urge to call him "Mr. Gaston" only because I don't believe people like it anymore when I assume they're elders (although Gaston is, at 50 years of age.) Perhaps this is a tactical error — I don't know. All I know is, when he turns around, there is a decided cast to his eyes, guarded and wary.

Gaston is larger than I'd expected, taller — at six feet four inches — and muscular. He is a handsome man, as many have pointed out, with high cheekbones, large eyes, and a thick but orderly moustache. I gesticulate with my appurtenances, explain that I'm writing a story about him. This news doesn't seem to mean much to him one way or another. We shake hands. "So whenever you get a chance," I go on, "I'd really like to talk to you." I whip out my little recording device; Gaston, I fear, mistakes it for a phaser, because he almost startles at the sight of it.

"All right, Paul," he says, friendly enough, but then he turns and takes a few stairs to the clubhouse door with huge determined strides. He disappears.

Okay. I've always admired those writers who wax rhapsodic about the glories of such things as batting practice. They gaze at the stadia and discern mathematical and geometric interconnections. I didn't know it was because people wouldn't talk to them at the ballpark. I walk back toward the field through the Skydome's skeleton. In the shadows, huge and oddly-shaped girders rest on what looks like airplane landing gear, everything set in place to roll away and open up the heavenly vault; although, despite the fineness of the day, whoever decides such things has decided against it. I take the few steps and lift myself up on to the pitch. I enter the dugout and wander down to the manager's end. There is a piece of tape attached to the dark blue vinyl back and seat, as if to sequester Gaston in some small way, to mark off his territory. I sit down and stare out at the domain.

There is always something unlikely about the Skydome's aspect, no matter what the vantage point, be it driving along the expressway and seeing it squatting there like a giant white spacetoad, or sitting in the stands looking out at the roiling sea of humanity. But this view is perhaps the weirdest. The field seems dreamlike, a huge expanse of green, a gaudy and colourized reproduction of the Elysian Fields in Hoboken, New Jersey, where the New York Nine and the Knickerbockers first contested a game. I see my chance to make one of those insightful mathematical connections; it's 60 feet (6 inches) from the mound to home plate, 90 feet between the bases, and it looks to be a very tidy 120 feet from the pitcher's mound to where Cito Gaston sits. The insightfulness of this observation is not immediately evident, but it's worth remembering.

I take my place in the small scrum of beat reporters that badgers Cito Gaston on a daily basis.

He deals with the press in a prescribed manner; two-and-a-half hours before game time, he emerges out into the dugout, usually working a hot beverage with a plastic stir-stick. He wanders down toward his spot; the press follows. Despite the white tape that sequesters the manager's actual seat, he is not proprietorial about it; in fact, radio commentator Jerry Howarth is usually sitting there, a look of unmitigated pleasure on his face, as if being in the ballpark is the best thing in the world. (The tape, I discover, is leftover from the Obus Forme support that Gaston needed three years back, when his back caused him so much pain that he missed 33 games.) He sits down beside Howarth, concentrates on working the stir-stick. "What's up, guys?"

Although Gaston seems to bristle in one-on-one interview sessions, his eyes narrowing whenever a phaser is stuck in his face, he quite often loosens up in this situation. He seems to enjoy remembering his own playing days. Gaston had a ten-year career, spent mostly in San Diego's outfield. He likes to recall the parks, the players, and he likes it very much when someone else returns a story, Jerry, Buck Martinez, or one of the reporters. Then he will listen, staring ahead, always watching what's going on in the field. Gaston is not afraid in those situations to be candid, personal; the death of a player's sister causes him to speak, very quietly, of losing two of his sisters in the past five years. But he will end these sessions abruptly. "You got everything you need?" he'll ask, and reporters flip their notebooks shut and turn off their tape recorders.

"If you can't communicate with Cito, you're the one with the problem," says Dave Winfield. He doesn't mean *me* specifically, he means the average Toronto Blue Jay. Winfield, now with the Minnesota Twins, was one of the most popular Blue Jays ever and, of course, the man who drove in the run that won Toronto its first World Series. Winfield first met Gaston some 20 years ago, when they both played for the Padres. "He was before me," Winfield points out, "but we played together a little, roomed together."

"And back then," I ask, "did he exhibit any qualities that led you to think, *this man would be a good manager*?"

"Well, you couldn't say that," responds Winfield. "He was black. They didn't allow black managers then."

Don't think it hasn't occurred to me that the reason Cito Gaston is reluctant to talk to me is that I tend to ask somewhat bone-headed questions like that one — although, in my own defence, Gaston had once roomed in spring training with one of his childhood heroes, Hank Aaron, when he played for Atlanta, and Aaron evidently saw some sign of a guiding hand; it was he who would convince Gaston, fresh from his last year of Mexican winterball, to become a hitting instructor. "He called three times and asked me to come back and work with him," remembers Gaston. "He never said work *for* me, always work *with* me, and I finally said yes." That was in 1981; he came to Toronto the following year.

"Do you think Cito gets the recognition he deserves?"

"No," Winfield replies, picking up a bat. "The biggest reason is, I think, that Canada is not the United States. Cito doesn't get the credit, even the Blue Jays don't get the credit." Winfield stands back and begins swinging his bat idly. "I hope people understand how good a manager he is."

I think he's referring to the American public, and I begin to address a thought such as, "Well, the more they see the Blue Jays on television..." but Winfield shakes his head.

"No, I mean... " He gesticulates with his bat toward the seats over the right field wall, which are beginning to fill with Toronto Blue Jay fans. "They still get on his case, don't they?"

"Hello, Stormin'?"

This is how I address Norm Rumack — by assuming a familiar first name (he broadcasts under the sobriquet of Stormin' Norman.) For one thing, Rumack is clearly not my elder. He is a dark-haired man with an evident intelligence. For another, all of Rumack's callers call him Stormin'. Come to think of it, most fans call Gaston "Cito", using the childhood nickname that was borrowed from a villainous Mexican wrestler. So people will call up Rumack and say, "Stormin'? I want to talk about Cito."

I have turned to Rumack because Winfield's comment has got me thinking about Cito's relationship with the city of Toronto. His admirers are legion — there's no denying that — and he's fulsome in his praise, calling Toronto "one of the great cities of North America." But despite a record that is by any standards astounding — four divisional titles, two league championships, two World Series victories — the Blue Jays' manager still has detractors. Rumack is in a position to know; he has a call-in show on the Fan, 1430, and quite often the lines crackle with anti-Cito sentiment.

"Any time there's a losing streak, people are going to start calling in and saying they should fire Cito," says Stormin' Norman. "Some people who play Rotisserie League think they know more about baseball than Cito."

There is, of course, a long and time-honoured tradition of second-guessing baseball managers. "No matter what you do," writes Leo Durocher in his book *Nice Guys Finish Last*, "you're going to be second-guessed. The manager is the only person in the ballpark who has to call it right *now*. Everyone else can call it after it's over."

Second-guessing may be intrinsic to the game of baseball, in that the fans are often left sprawling in the stadium seating or on their sofas with nothing better to do. It's fun to try to anticipate the manager's next move, although with Cito Gaston, that can be tricky. Even professionals have some difficulty; during last year's World

Series, it seemed like whenever broadcaster Tim McCarver offered an opinion — *he'll leave the pitcher in, he'll pinch-hit now* — Gaston would do the opposite.

Cito himself downplays all this. "That's just a few people who call in," he says. "A minority. It doesn't bother me." Certainly, it's true that few of the 50,000 boosters in the Skydome are looking to jump all over his butt, but in other haunts of fandom — barrooms leap to mind as an example — the treatment is not so kind.

"I just don't understand some of the things he does," says one such denizen of a local watering hole, who refused to be named (or rather, I lost the matchbook cover I'd scribbled his name down on.) "Why does he bat Olerud and Delgado together? Two left-handers, I mean. That way, the other manager can bring in just one leftie to get them both."

Cito Gaston simply doesn't "manage" in a commonly accepted way. In one game, April 7th, which went into extra innings, John Olerud drew a walk off former teammate Tom Henke. Most managers would have replaced him with a pinch-runner. Gaston did not. Gaston merely sat on the bench rather serenely and allowed history to unfold according to its own will.

Olerud came around to score.

Should this have backfired, of course, the lights would have lit up on Stormin' Norman's console. It is Gaston's propensity for doing *nothing* that most rankles some people. Before the Blue Jays won two World Series he was criticized roundly for this passivity. Now the attitude has changed somewhat. People seem to feel that the passivity is somewhat justified. They don't like it any more, but they understand it. The Blue Jays are a stacked team, they are rife with talent, and all Gaston has to do is fill out the lineup card, hand it to the umpire, and he gets to sit down and relax and watch a good game of baseball.

I sometimes wonder if part of Cito Gaston's problem with Toronto has to do with his ascension to manager status, a messy affair that conveyed the impression that no one, neither the Blue Jay management nor Cito himself, felt he was the right man for the job. In the early days of 1989, the Blue Jays were the losingest team in baseball, and the blame fell, as the blame usually does in such situations, on skipper Jimy Williams. There was a feeling that Williams was, in effect, too nice, that he had failed to command the players' respect. So on May 15th, batting instructor Cito Gaston was named interim manager. It was made clear by Pat Gillick that the search for a new manager was on-going. The Blue Jays needed someone tougher, a real butt-kicker from outside the organization.

It didn't seem to matter that the Blue Jay players seemed very enthusiastic about the choice of Gaston. They won their first game under the interim manager, beating the Cleveland Indians 5-3, and over the next two weeks amassed a winning record. The Blue Jay executives, however, continued their search for a butt-kicker. They were reluctant to promote from inside the organization, a mistake they felt they'd made with Jimy Williams, third-base coach under Bobby Cox. And Cito, for these same reasons, seemed reluctant to assume the position. "I'm too friendly with the players," he said at the time. He was very happy as the Blue Jays' hitting instructor. "I'm still proud of the work I did with some of the guys, no matter where they've gone to," he says. "Guys like [Cecil] Fielder, [Fred] McGriff. A lot of guys." Cito was also happy in his Mississauga home with his wife Denise, and he had no great desire to willingly embrace a governance of turmoil.

The situation became even more snarled when Harry Edwards, special assistant to major league commissioner A. Bartlett Giamatti, announced that he was keeping a close eye on the situation. "It can be interpreted to have racial overtones," he explained. I suspect that the Blue Jay management was as surprised as anyone by this view. But a situation had existed ever since Al Campanis, then vice-president in charge of player personnel for the Los Angeles Dodgers, had flapped his gums on Ted Koppel's *Nightline*, declaring that black people "may not have some of the necessities to be, let's say, a field manager or perhaps a general manager." He had this to offer by way of explanation: "Why are black men or black people not good swimmers? Because they don't have the buoyancy." As embarrassing as this may have been, Campanis was only voicing what a lot of baseball people felt. There had only been a handful of black managers — Frank Robinson, Larry Doby, Maury Wills — and none had achieved much success.

Other than pointing out that he can swim, Gaston doesn't have much to say about these racial matters. "I don't see colours. I wasn't raised that way." He was raised in Corpus Christi, Texas, a lone boy among five sisters. Although Gaston can remember sitting in the black section in the movie theatres and riding in the back of a bus, he doesn't allow those memories to cloud his vision of humanity. "I haven't got a prejudiced bone in my body, I hope, because my Mom never taught me to hate anybody, no matter what colour they are." Despite being Baptist (his grandfather was a preacher) Cito spent some time in Catholic schools. "One of my teachers, Sister Cobrini, was very concerned about other people all the time, and she taught us that, to care about other people." This moral education certainly helped at the start of his career, when Gaston toured around South Carolina. "We'd roll into some towns and I couldn't get off the bus to eat."

Gaston has, framed in his office, an old broadside promoting the Negro Leagues. His wife, Denise, is white. On one of the occasions that I manage to get the phaser aimed, I ask how he feels when referred to as "the first black manager to win the World Series."

"You're not going to get around that," he answers. "I *am* black."

Okay, fair enough. Torontonians don't care about that, at least, I'd like to think we don't. I'll return to my theory that what got Cito and the city off on the wrong foot was that confusing two weeks, where it was easy to misinterpret his reservations for a lack of confidence. But when Paul Beeston and Pat Gillick did offer him the full-time job, Gaston accepted. "They said, we want you to take it if you want to take it," he said upon becoming full-time manager May 31, 1989. "After two weeks of doing it, it's not as bad as I thought. Not yet, anyway."

I've had occasion to think about the process of decision making, particularly decision making that is not based on hard data. The kind of decision that requires wisdom and insight, in short, the sort of decision that Cito Gaston is called upon to make day after day. You see, this fine magazine had suggested a story about Gaston, an opportunity at which I'd leapt. However, at our first editorial meeting, I was told they'd had a re-think: now, they were considering a story about Joe Carter.

Now, I love Joe Carter as much as the next fan. No one will forget those images of him galloping, bucking, and leaping uncontained after the World Series-winning homerun. But Cito seemed the much more intriguing study. With Joe, I suggested, what you saw was more-or-less what you got.

That was my decision, which I have reason to rue.

Forget the fact that Carter, despite playing with a thumb that had been broken in spring training, sets a new major league record for runs batted in during the month of April. What really rankles is that I can't go anywhere without encountering Joe Carter being charming, eloquent, and funny.

The nadir of all this occurs as I sit on the bench, staring out at batting practice (which has lost much of its poetic sheen) trying to think of a whiz-bang question to fire at Gaston. Five feet away, the comedian John Lovitz has given a video camera to a companion, asked that the lens be turned on Joe Carter and him. "So, Joe," asks Lovitz, "where did you hit that homerun?"

Carter waves toward the wall in left field. "Over that wall."

"The wall?"

Carter nods briefly. "Absolutely. Some guys, like Carlos Delgado, they can hit that second deck, that restaurant, those hotel rooms, but then, if it's an important ball, you have to pay to get it back from a fan. I've heard of players spending five hundred dollars getting a ball back. That's after you find the guy. So I just knock them over that wall. That way, the groundskeeper brings them to me at the end of the game."

Lovitz nods uncertainly and reminds himself that he's the one who used to be on *Saturday Night Live*. Carter returns an expression of angelic guilelessness. Lovitz pulls the bat near and points at the inscribed signature near the top. "That bat has your name on it," he points out.

"Sure. Because sometimes I'll be sitting in the dugout and I'll look at my bat and realize that it's me."

The next time I get close to Cito Gaston I ask about Preston Gomez. The novelist Alison Gordon suggested this course of action. As the former baseball beat writer for the *Toronto Daily Star*, she has great acquaintance with Gaston. "I think he's an extraordinary manager, and an extraordinary man," she tells me. "A very emotional, warm human being. He weeps."

"He *what*?"

"The guy is Mr. Ducts. That's something very sweet about him, that he weeps."

I *have* noticed that Gaston's face is not always a veil of impassivity. Quite often emotions cross it. Once, as I fumbled near the back of the beat-scrum with my phaser, anxious to do something that resembled *bona fide* journalism, I'm fairly certain he smiled at me in a friendly manner. And he will laugh, as he sits on the bench and chews the fat, staring straight ahead, always watching, his arms driven downwards for support, his hands gripping the side of the vinyl bench cover. His eyes are the most telling gauge of his mood, flashing with anger, wariness, and mirth.

"Ask about Preston Gomez," Alison suggests, and I do this, although it's not the best sort of question to ask while the other fellows are wondering about the baseball game that just finished. Preston Gomez managed the San Diego Padres when Gaston first started out, and Cito based much of his managing style on him. "Preston was a very stern man, but a fair man," Gaston answers. "Very smart as far as what's going on in the game. I'll give you an example of how intelligent Preston was. He used to be third-base coach for the Los Angeles Dodgers and he had 15 players and all 15 of them had different signs. He'd memorized 15 sets of signs. That is almost impossible.

"He was easily two or three innings ahead of everyone else as far as knowing what he was going to do before it happened. He could see very deeply into a game."

"See into a game?"

"Sure. You try to see ahead into the game, see what's going to happen. That way, when it does, you don't panic. You've already decided what to do. That's one thing I learned from Preston. And he was kind of a father figure to me, being away from home and all."

I refer to my notes. "What's interesting is that Gomez didn't have a very good record ..." I think I'm being tactful here; his record stands at 346 wins and 529 losses, for a winning percentage of .395. Gaston turns defensive on behalf of his mentor. "He didn't have good ball clubs. Our team in San Diego in '71 was second in the league in homeruns, but we didn't have any pitching. Then he managed in Houston; he didn't have a real good team down there either. He wasn't fortunate enough to have a team like I've had over the years."

One thing is certainly clear; no one is more conscious of how blessed the Blue Jays are, talent-wise, than Cito Gaston. It was suggested to me by Stompin' Norman that often a so-called "stacked" team is harder to manage than a mediocre one. That would certainly be true, I think, if the Blue Jay players came equipped with egos commensurate with their abilities, but they don't appear to. "I don't have any guys here who'd be upset if they went 0 for 4 but the team still won," says Cito, "though I've played with guys like that." Like Joe Carter, the players tend to exhibit a certain graciousness. Here's a maddening but telling bit of conversation I overheard from one media type to his crew: "Okay, guys, this is the plan. Paul Molitor has invited us up to his house to do the feature."

And as for the Blue Jays being stacked with talent, I believe Stormin' Norman put it best: "Where are these championship teams with all the bad players?"

I believe I'm on to something here, what with the disparate influences of Sister Cobrini and Preston Gomez — that is, a nun and a man with a losing record. There is something in all this having to do with *character*, something along the lines of Grantland Rice's poem — you know it, the one about the One Great Scorer marking, not that you won or lost, but how you played the game. So at the next opportunity I press ahead. "Are there aspects to managing even more important than winning and losing?

"No."

I have abandoned the phaser altogether, as its presence seems to clam Cito up. This works much better. I write *no*.

"Not in the major leagues," he continues. "Not if you want to keep your job."

"But..."

"It's not my job to raise anyone," he pronounces with finality. I scribble away. "Maybe *help* a little bit."

I have found a moment that helps to explain both what Gaston does and who he is.

Let me set up the situation for you: the Jays are leading, 7 to 6, against Minnesota. Mike Timlin is pitching late in the game, a young man who, according to one of the local scribes, "cannot turn talent into on-field success." There are two on base, nobody out. Timlin rears back and hurls, hitting the batter, Knoblauch. Now the bases are loaded and Alex Cole, Kirby Puckett, and Dave Winfield are licking their lips.

Gaston sits in the dugout without expression. He does nothing, makes no move. His decision to leave Timlin in isn't based on statistical information or any of those other managerial strategies. His decision to leave Timlin in is based on a very simple thing: the look on the young man's face. Cito Gaston, sitting on his bench 120 feet away (I *told* you that would be significant) looks at his pitcher and can see no panic.

Timlin strikes out Cole and Puckett, Winfield hits a long ball that doesn't escape the ballpark. And what if it hadn't worked out?

"The thing to remember," he says, "is there's a lot of things more important than baseball. It's just a game."

Calmness is the heart of Gaston's managerial style. "It's something I found as a hitting instructor, that if I was down, if I was upset, the hitters sometimes didn't do as well. Maybe I wasn't vocalizing something, I don't know."

Cito believes that a calm player will outperform an agitated one, a sensible piece of thinking that still manages to fly in the face of traditional managerial thinking. It is for this reason, for example, that he prefers a set lineup, so that his players will know their role and function. It is for this reason that he will sit, staring straight ahead and ruminating in the most literal sense, at points in the game that have the rest of us barely containing our beer and footlongs. Such is his tranquillity that some fans actually read it for indifference. But Cito Gaston is actually the centre of the calm — it emanates from him. And when one remembers key match-ups — a placid Joe Carter versus a visibly frazzled Mitch Williams, for example — Cito's managerial style seems brimming with good sense.

One morning, I am sitting on the bench in the dugout, looking out upon the realm. Cito emerges from the dugout and sits down beside me. He grips the edges of the vinyl seat cushion and stares forward. I ask my questions and he responds, his answers forthright but circumspect.

I have the questions written on my steno pad, and I dutifully run them down and tick them off. After the last, something changes and Cito and I are actually having a conversation. It has to do with journalism, in a general way, but Cito still relates it to the rule that informs his existence; treat others as you would be treated. "I wonder what writers would write," he asks, turning suddenly to look at me, "if they had to write about themselves."

"I know what I'd write, that I'm pretty stupid. I was standing out there during batting practice, and I kept turning around when people yelled out *Paul*."

Cito Gaston laughs gently and returns his gaze to the baseball field.

(First appeared in *Saturday Night*)

THE GOALTENDER'S GAME

Ken Dryden

I have always been a goalie. I became one long enough ago, before others' memories and reasons intruded on my own, that I can no longer remember why I did, but if I had to guess, it was because of Dave. Almost six years older, he started playing goal before I was old enough to play any position, so by the time I was six and ready to play, there was a set of used and discarded equipment that awaited me — that and an older brother I always tried to emulate.

I have mostly vague recollections of being a goalie at that time. I remember the spectacular feeling of splitting and sprawling on pavement or ice, and feeling there was something somehow noble and sympathetic about having bruises and occasional cuts, especially if they came, as they did, from only a tennis ball. But if I have one clear image that remains, it is that of a goalie, his right knee on the ice, his left leg extended in half splits, his left arm stretching for the top corner, and, resting indifferently in his catching glove, a round black puck.

It was the posed position of NHL goalies for promotional photos and hockey cards at the time and it was a position we tried to re-enact as often as we could in backyard games. There was something that looked and felt distinctly major league about a shot "raised" that high, and about a clean, precise movement into space to intercept it. Coming as it did without rebound, it allowed us to freeze the position as if in a photo, extending the moment, letting our feelings catch up to the play, giving us time to step outside ourselves and see what we had done. In school, or at home, with pencil and paper, sometimes thinking of what I was doing, more often just mindlessly doodling, I would draw pictures of goalies, not much more than stick figures really, but fleshed out with parallel lines, and always in that same catching position. Each year when my father arranged for a photographer to take pictures for our family's Christmas card, as Dave and I readied ourselves in our nets, the shooter was told to shoot high to the glove side, that we had rehearsed the rest.

To catch a puck or a ball — it was the great joy of being a goalie. Like a young ballplayer, too young to hit for much enjoyment but old enough to catch and throw, it was something I could do before I was big enough to do the rest. But mostly it was the feeling it gave me. Even now, watching TV or reading a newspaper, I like to have a ball in my hands, fingering its laces, its seams, its nubby surface, until my fingertips are so alive and alert that the ball and I seem drawn to each other. I like to spin it, bounce it, flip it from hand to hand, throw it against a wall or a ceiling, and catch it over and over again. There is something quite magical about a hand that can follow a ball and find it so crisply and tidily every time, something solid and wonderfully reassuring about its muscular certainty and control. So, if it was because of Dave that I became a goalie, it was the feeling of catching a puck or a ball that kept me one. The irony, of course, would be that later, when I finally became a real goalie instead of a kid with a good glove hand, when I learned to use the other parts of the goaltender's equipment — skates, pads, blocker, stick — it could only be at the expense of what had been until then my greatest joy as a goalie.

I was 19 at the time. It surely had been happening before then, just as it must before any watershed moment, but the time I remember was the warm-up for the 1967 NCAA final against Boston University. For the first few minutes, I remember only feeling good: a shot, a save, a shot, a save; loose, easy, the burn of nerves turning slowly to a burn of exhilaration. For a shot to my right, my right arm went up and I stopped it with my blocker; another, low to the corner, I kicked away with my pad; along the ice to the other side, my skate; high to the left, my catching glove. Again and again: a pad, a catching glove, a skate, a stick, a blocker, whatever was closest moved, and the puck stopped. For someone who had scooped up ice-skimming shots like a shortstop, who had twisted his body to make backhanded catches on shots for the top right corner, it was a moment of great personal triumph. I had come of age. As the warm-up was ending, I could feel myself becoming a goalie.

Goaltending is often described as the most dangerous position in sports. It is not. Race drivers die from racing cars, jockeys die, so do football players. Goalies do not die from being goalies. Nor do they suffer the frequent facial cuts, the knee and shoulder injuries, that forwards and defencemen often suffer. They stand as obstacles to a hard rubber disc, frequently shot at a lethal speed, sometimes unseen, sometimes deflected; the danger to them is obvious, but it is exaggerated — even the unthinkable: a goalie diving anxiously out of the way of a 100 m.p.h. slapshot, the shooter panicking at his own recklessness, the fans "ah"-ing at the near miss. Except for that one, feared time, the time it doesn't happen that way, when the puck moves too fast and the goalie too slow, and, hit in the head, he falls frighteningly to the ice. Moments later, up again, he shakes his head, smiling as others slowly do the same, again reminded that he wears a mask which at other times he sees through and forgets. The danger of playing goal is *potential* danger, but equipment technology, like a net below a trapeze act, has made serious injury extremely unlikely.

From the time I was six years old, until as a freshman at Cornell I was required to wear a mask, I received 15 stitches. Since then I have had only four — from a Dennis Hull slapshot that rebounded off my chest, hitting under my chin, in my first playoff year. I have pulled groins and hamstrings, stretched, twisted, and bruised uncounted times various other things, sent my back into spasm twice, broken a toe, and torn the cartilage in one knee. In almost eight years, after more than 400 games and 1,000 practices, that's not much.

Yet, I am often afraid. For while I am well protected, and know that I'm unlikely to suffer more than a bruise from any shot that is taken, the puck hurts, constantly and cumulatively: through the pillow-thick leg pads I wear, where straps pulled tight around the shins squeeze much of the padding away; through armour-shelled skate boots; through a catching glove compromised too far for its flexibility; with a dull, aching nausea from stomach to throat when my jock slams against my testes; and most often, on my arms, on wrists, and forearms especially, where padding is light and often out of place, where a shot hits and spreads its ache, up an arm and through a body, until both go limp and feel lifeless. Through a season, a puck hurts like a long, slow battering from a skillful boxer, almost unnoticed in the beginning, but gradually wearing me down, until two or three times a year, I wake up in the morning sore, aching, laughing/moaning with each move I make, and feel a hundred years old. It is on those days and others that when practice comes, I shy away.

The puck on his stick, a player skates for the net. Deep in my crouch, intent, ready, to anyone watching I look the same as I always do. But, like a batter who has been knocked down too many times before, when I see a player draw back his stick to shoot, at the critical moment when concentration must turn to commitment, my body stiffens, my eyes widen and go sightless, my head lifts in the air, turning imperceptibly to the right, as if away from the puck — I bail out, leaving only an empty body behind to cover the net. I yell at myself as others might ("you chicken"). I tell myself reasonably, rationally, that lifting my head, blanking my eyes, can only put me in greater danger; but I don't listen. In a game, each shot controlled by a harassing defence, with something else to think about I can usually put away fear and just play. But in practice, without the distraction of a game, seeing Tremblay or Lambert, Risebrough, Chartraw, or Lupien, dangerous, uncontrolled shooters as likely to hit my arms as a corner of the net, I cannot. In time the fear gradually shrinks back, manageable again, but it never quite goes away.

I have thought more about fear, I have been afraid more often, the last few years. For the first time this year, I have realized that I've only rarely been hurt in my career. I have noticed that unlike many, so far as I know, I carry with me no permanent injury. And now that I know I will retire at the end of the season, more and more I find myself thinking — *I've lasted this long: please let me get out in one piece.* For while I know I am well protected, while I know it's unlikely I will suffer any serious injury, like every other goalie I carry with me the fear of the *one big hurt* that never comes. Recently, I read of the retirement of a race-car driver. Explaining his decision to quit, he said that after his many years of racing, after the deaths of close friends, he simply "knew too much." I feel a little differently. I feel I have known all along what I know now. It's just that I can't forget it as easily as I once did.

Playing goal is not fun. Behind a mask, there are no smiling faces, no timely sweaty grins of satisfaction. It's a grim, humourless position, largely uncreative, requiring little physical movement, giving little physical pleasure in return. A goalie is simply there, tied to a net and to a game; the game acts, a goalie reacts. How he reacts, how often, a hundred shots or no shots, is not up to him. Unable to initiate a game's action, unable to focus its direction, he can only do what he's given to do, what the game demands of him, and that he must do. It is his job, a job that cannot be done one minute in every three, one that will not await rare moments of genius, one that ends when the game ends, and only then. For while a goal goes up in lights, a permanent record for the goal-scorer and the game, a save is ephemeral, important at the time, occasionally when a game is over, but able to be wiped away, undone, with the next shot. It is only when a game ends and the mask comes off, when the immense challenge of the job turns abruptly to immense satisfaction or despair, that the unsmiling grimness lifts and goes away.

If you were to spend some time with a team, without ever watching them on the ice, it wouldn't take long before you discovered who its goalies were. Goalies are different. Whether it's because the position attracts certain personality types, or only permits certain ones to succeed; whether the experience is so intense and fundamental that it transforms its practitioners to type — I don't know the answer. But whatever it is, the differences between "players" and "goalies" are manifest and real, transcending as they do even culture and sport.

A few years ago, at a reception at the Canadian Embassy in Prague, the wife of Jiri Holecek, former star goalie for Czechoslovakia, was introduced to my wife Lynda, and immediately exclaimed, "The players think my Jiri's crazy. Do they [my teammates] think your husband's crazy too?" (No more of this conversation was related to me.) For his book on soccer goalies, English journalist Brian Glanville chose as his title *Goalkeepers are Different*. It is all part of the mythology of the position, anticipated, expected, accepted, and believed; and in many ways real.

Predictably, a goalie is more introverted than his teammates, more serious (for team pictures, when a photographer tells me to smile, unsmilingly I tell him, "Goalies don't smile"), more sensitive and moody ("ghoulies"), more insecure (often unusually "careful" with money; you might remember Johnny Bower and I *shared* a cab). While a goalie might sometimes be gregarious and outgoing, it usually manifests itself in binges — when a game is over, or on the day of a game when he isn't playing — when he feels himself released from the game. Earlier this season, minutes before a game with the Rangers in the Forum, Robinson looked across the dressingroom at me and asked, "Who's playing?" Before I could answer, Shutt yelled back, "I'll give ya a hint, Bird," he said. "Bunny's in the shitter puking; Kenny hasn't shut up since he got here." While teams insist on togetherness, and on qualities in their teammates that encourage it both on and off the ice, a goalie is the one player a team allows to be different. Indeed, as perplexed as anyone at his willingness to dress in cumbrous, oversized equipment and get hit by a puck, a team allows a goalie to sit by himself on planes or buses, to disappear on road trips, to reappear and say nothing for long periods of time, to have a single room when everyone else has roommates. After all, *shrug*, he's a goalie. What can you expect? Flaky, crazy, everything he does accepted and explained away, it offers a goalie wonderful licence. It was what allowed Gilles Gratton to "streak" a practice, and Gary Smith to take showers between periods. In many ways, it is also why my teammates accepted me going to law school.

Good goalies come in many shapes, sizes, and styles. So do bad goalies. A goalie is often plump (Savard, a defenceman, always insists "I like my goalies fat"), sometimes unathletic, and with reflex reactions surprisingly similar to those of the average person (recently at a science museum, with a flashing light and a buzzer I tested my eye-hand reactions against Lynda's; she was slightly faster). While most might agree on what the ideal physical and technical goalie-specimen might look like, it almost certainly would be a composite — the physical size of Tretiak, the elegance of Parent, the agility of Giacomin or Cheevers, the bouncy charisma of Vachon or Resch — with no guarantee that *supergoalie* would be any good. For while there are certain minimum standards of size, style, and agility any goalie must have, goaltending is a remarkable aphysical activity.

If you were to ask a coach or a player what he would most like to see in a goalie, he would, after some rambling out-loud thoughts, probably settle on something like: consistency, dependability, and the ability to make the big save. Only in the latter, and then only in part, is the physical element present. Instead, what these qualities suggest is a certain character of mind, a mind that need not be nimble or dextrous, for the demands of the job are not complex, but a mind emotionally disciplined, one able to be focused and directed, a mind under control.

Because the demands on a goalie are mostly mental, it means that for a goalie the biggest enemy is himself. Not a puck, not an opponent, not a quirk of size or style. Him. The stress and anxiety he feels when he plays, the fear of failing, the fear of being embarrassed, the fear of being physically hurt, all are symptoms of his position, in constant ebb and flow, but never disappearing. The successful goalie understands these neuroses, accepts them, and puts them under control. The unsuccessful goalie is distracted by them, his mind in knots, his body quickly following.

It is why Vachon was superb in Los Angeles and as a high-priced free-agent Messiah, poor in Detroit. It is why Dan Bouchard, Tretiak-sized, athletic, technically flawless, lurches annoyingly in and out of mediocrity. It is why there are good "good team" goalies and good "bad team" goalies — Gary Smith, Doug Flavell, Denis Herron. The latter are spectacular, capable of making near-impossible saves that few others can make. They are essential for bad teams, winning them games they shouldn't win, but they are goalies who need a second chance, who need the cushion of an occasional bad goal, knowing that they can seem to earn it back later with several inspired saves. On a good team, a goalie has few near-impossible saves to make, but the rest he must make, and playing in close and critical games as he does, he gets no second chance.

A good "bad team" goalie, numbed by the volume of goals he cannot prevent, can focus on brilliant saves and brilliant games, the only things that make a difference to a poor team. A good "good team" goalie cannot. Allowing few enough goals that he feels every one, he is driven instead by something else — the penetrating hatred of letting in a goal.

The greatest satisfaction of playing goal comes from the challenge it presents. Simply stated, it is to give the team what it needs, when it needs it, not when I feel well-rested, injury-free, warmed-up, psyched-up, healthy, happy, and able to give it, but when *the team* needs it. On a team as good as the Canadiens, often it will need nothing; other times, one good save, perhaps two or three; maybe five good minutes, a period, sometimes, though not often, a whole game. Against better teams, you can almost predict what and when it might be; against the rest, you cannot. You simply have to be ready.

During my first two years with the team, for reasons none of us could figure out, we would start games slowly, outplayed for most of the first period, occasionally for a little longer. It happened so regularly that it became a pattern we anticipated and prepared for, each of us with a special role to play. Mine was to keep the score sufficiently close in the first period, usually to within one goal, so as not to discourage any comeback — their role — that otherwise we would almost certainly make. We were a good combination. I could feel heroically beleaguered for the first period, all the time knowing that it would end, that we would soon get our stride, and when we did that I would become a virtual spectator to the game.

That has changed. It began to change the next season, and for the last four years, the change has been complete. A much better team than earlier in the decade, it needs less from me now, just pockets of moments that for me and others sometimes seem lost in a game. But more than that, what it needs now is not to be distracted — by bad goals, by looseness or uncertainty in my play. It needs only to feel secure, confident that the defensive zone is taken care of; the rest it can do by itself.

It makes my job different from that of every other goalie in the NHL. I get fewer shots, and fewer *hard* shots; I must allow fewer goals, the teams I play on must win Stanley Cups. Most envy me my job, some are not so sure. Once Vachon, my predecessor in Montreal, in the midst of one of his excellent seasons in Los Angeles, told me he wasn't sure he would ever want to play for the Canadiens again, even if he had the chance. He said he had come to enjoy a feeling he knew he would rarely have in Montreal — the feeling of winning the game for his team — and he wasn't sure how well he could play without it. In a speech a few years ago, my brother talked about the heroic self-image each goalie needs and has, and is allowed to have because of the nature and perception of his position. "A solitary figure," "a thankless job," "facing an onslaught," "a barrage," "like Horatio at the bridge" — it's the stuff of backyard dreams. It is how others often see him; it is how he sometimes sees himself. I know the feeling Vachon described because I felt it early in my career, when the team wasn't as good as it is now. It is a feeling I have learned to live without.

But something else has changed, something that is more difficult to live without. Each year, I find it harder and harder to make a connection between a Canadiens win and me — nothing so much as my winning a game for the team, just a timely save, or a series of saves that made a difference, that arguably made a difference, that *might* have made a difference, that, as with a baseball pitcher, can make a win feel mine and ours. But as the team's superiority has become entrenched, and as the gap between our opponents and us, mostly unchanged, has come to seem wider and more permanent, every save I make seems without urgency, as if it is done completely at my own discretion, a minor bonus if made, a minor inconvenience, quickly overcome, if not.

A few months ago, we played the Colorado Rockies at the Forum. Early in the game, I missed an easy shot from the blueline, and a little unnerved, for the next 50 minutes I juggled long shots, and allowed big rebounds and three additional goals. After each Rockies goal, the team would put on a brief spurt and score quickly, and so with only minutes remaining, the game was tied. Then the Rockies scored again, this time a long sharp-angled shot that squirted through my legs. The game had seemed finally lost. But in the last three minutes, Lapointe scored, then Lafleur, and we won 6-5. Alone in the dressingroom afterwards, I tried to feel angry at my own performance, and to feel relieved at being let off the uncomfortable hook I had put myself on, to laugh at what a winner could now find funny; but I couldn't. Instead, feeling weak and empty, I just sat there, unable to understand why I felt the way I did. Only slowly did it come to me: I had been irrelevant; I couldn't even lose the game.

I catch few shots now, perhaps only two or three a game. I should catch more, but years of concussions have left the bones in my hand and wrist often tender and sore, and learning to substitute a leg or a stick to save my hand, my catching glove, reprogrammed and out of practice, often remains at my side. Moreover, the game has changed. Bigger players now clutter the front of the net, obstructing and deflecting shots, or, threatening to do both, they distract a goalie, causing rebounds, making clean, precise movements into space — commitments to a single option unmindful of possible deflection or rebound — an indulgence for which a price is too often paid. What I enjoy most about goaltending now is the game itself: feeling myself slowly immerse in it, finding its rhythm, anticipating it, getting there before it does, challenging it, controlling a play that should control me, making it go where I want it to go, moving easily, crushingly within myself, delivering a clear, confident message to the game. And at the same time, to feel my body slowly act out that feeling, pushing up taller and straighter, thrusting itself forward, clenched, flexed, at game's end released like an untied balloon, its feeling spewing in all directions until the next game.

I enjoy the role I play — now rarely to win a game, but not to lose it; a game fully in my hands, fully in the hands of my teammates, and between us an unstated trust, a quiet confidence, and the results we want. Our roles have changed, but we remain a good combination, and I find that immensely satisfying.

(From *Home Game* by Ken Dryden. Used by permission of the Canadian Publishers, McClelland & Stewart, Toronto)

IF YOU CAN'T BEAT 'EM IN THE ALLEY

Conn Smythe with Scott Young

I couldn't see why the Toronto Maple Leafs shouldn't keep on winning Stanley Cups year after year, now that we'd won the first one in our first season. And in Maple Leaf Gardens that next year, 1931–32, we would have won at least one more Cup if it hadn't been for circumstances that I don't think would be allowed to happen today.

We had pretty well the team that had won the Stanley Cup back in the spring, except that Ottawa, after suspending operations for a year, decided to come back in. That meant that Ottawa players spread around the league had to be returned. We lost Frank Finnigan, but brought up Ken Doraty and Bill Thoms from the farm system I'd been building. Both of them came through well, Doraty especially. He only got five goals during the season, but scored another five in the playoffs, including one that has been a highlight of many a hockey history since.

You could see the effects of the Depression in arenas that fall: only 2,000 for the opener in Detroit; 4,000 for our first game in Chicago. We didn't have that kind of trouble at home because we were winning and we were exciting, an unbeatable combination. Over the 48-game season we led the league's Canadian section (Toronto, Maroons, Canadiens, New York Americans, and Ottawa, finishing in that order) while Boston took the American section (Boston, Detroit, Rangers, and Chicago). That meant the Leafs would play Boston a best-of-five series while the second and third place teams fought it out to decide who would play the survivor in the final.

As it turned out, the Rangers won their elimination rounds easily while the Leafs and Boston fought through a very tough series. We split the first four games, three of them in overtime. When we came up to the deciding game in Toronto on Monday, April 3, the winner was supposed to play the Rangers in the first game of the final in New York the very next night, April 4.

With only 14 players each, counting Lorne Chabot in our goal, and Tiny Thompson in theirs, it was not exactly a game of blazing speed by the time we got into sudden-death.

The clock wound on past midnight. We played period after period. King Clancy scored in the fourth overtime period, but the whistle had just gone. In the intermission players lay on the benches, on the floor, anywhere flat, then went out, and played the fifth overtime. By that time there had been 160 minutes of hockey, one period short of three full games. It was 1:30 a.m. Many people had gone home, but others, listening to Foster at home on their radios, came down. I said, "Let 'em in free." In a little room down a corridor NHL president Frank Calder called Art Ross and me together about what we should do. There were stories later that Ross and I went to Calder to suggest that we call this game a draw and play again the following night. Or that we decide the winner by the flip of a coin. Neither was true, although both alternatives were discussed. Calder kept saying that something had to happen. If we were going on, the winner had to play in New York less than 17 hours later and it took almost that long to get there, by train. If we were going to call the game, though, both teams had to agree.

I knew that if I could get an extra five or ten minutes

rest for the Leafs, they'd be all right. So I kept the discussion going. I took my time. I did a lot of saying, "On one hand ..." and "On the other hand." When I thought the rest had been long enough, I said I would like to consult my players while Ross consulted his. It turned out that Boston players were in favour of calling the game. I wasn't, but I didn't want to go in and announce it. I wanted the decision to come from my players.

So I went in. Baldy Cotton was lying on the floor. To look at him, you'd want to take his pulse and see if he was dead. He could put on a death act better than anyone living; he was dead, dying, pinned to the floor, no life or breath in him, until I said, "Listen, there's talk about calling this game ..."

Cotton was on his feet in one wild leap, yelling, "No son of a bitch is going to call this game!"

That's what I wanted to hear. The others started to yell too. They were suddenly goddam mad, in fact. I just about got run down with them going out of there to get on the ice. I went and told Calder and Ross, "My team wants to play."

In the fifth minute of that sixth overtime period, Eddie Shore, tired as he was, tried to clear the puck from a corner in the Boston end. Andy Blair was fresher than most; he hadn't played as much as some, earlier. He jumped in to intercept the puck, passed to Ken Doraty in front of the net, and zip — it was in, the only goal of the game, at 1:50 a.m., 4.46 of the sixth overtime.

Then all we had to do was get to New York to play that night.

We went from the Gardens to Union Station and after 3 a.m. boarded our special car to be hitched onto the New York train. Dick Irvin and I fell into our bunks in the compartment we shared and for once the playboys on the team beat us to sleep, if anything. I might say that with Irvin, myself, and Hap Day, the captain, all being non-smokers and non-drinkers, it was rather hard for anybody to live it up on one of our train rides. For the rest of the night and the next day we rattled across northern New

York until we pulled into Grand Central at 4:10 p.m., about four hours before game time. The rottenest thing was that when I tried to have the game postponed, the Madison Square people said it had to go on because the circus coming in later in the week needed the time to set up. That was a lie, because now they suggested to me that we play the second game of the series there too, meaning that there really had been time to get the first one postponed. I told them, "You guys told me that because of the circus coming in there'd be no ice, we couldn't even postpone the first game ..."

They said, "Well, we've changed our minds."

I said, "Well, you can change your minds again! I wouldn't play the second game here now if it was the last place in the world!"

When it was announced during the game that the second game would be played in Toronto because of the circus, the crowd of 17,000 raised such an uproar that the announcer couldn't go on to ballyhoo the circus. It made us angry, too, but we couldn't do anything about it, we were so tired. We lost 5-1. The game ended at 10:45 p.m. We went straight to the station to board a train that left for Toronto at 11:25 p.m. We'd only been off the train for seven hours.

(From *If You Can't Beat 'Em in the Alley*)

THE GREATEST FIGHTER WHO EVER LIVED

Trent Frayne

Upstairs in a venerable boarding-house in an ancient section of Boston a blind old black man sits all day rocking in a creaking wooden chair. His sightless eyes are masked by a pair of cheap plastic-rimmed spectacles, long since scratched and smudged by age. His greying bullet head is covered by a faded maroon baseball cap and his lean age-ing body swaddled in a nondescript bathrobe. He is a man with many ailments, few hopes and only one amusement: On Wednesday nights, when the fights come on the little mantel radio, as they do on radios all over the continent, his head cocks and his face lights up as he lives once again in a golden past.

For this is Sam Langford, a living legend from Weymouth, Nova Scotia, and perhaps the greatest fighter of his size who ever lived.

Hype Igoe, the most renowned of all boxing writers, made no bones about it in the old *New York Journal*. "Langford is the greatest fighter, pound for pound, who ever lived," he wrote. Just this year, Joe Williams, the respected sports columnist of the *New York World-Telegram*, echoed Igoe's words. "Langford was probably the best the ring ever saw," he wrote in his current TV box-ing book. The great Grantland Rice described Langford as "about the best fighting man I've ever watched."

Langford's old manager, Joe Woodman, put it a little more colourfully last month. "At 'seventy-two,'" he said, meaning 172 pounds, "he'd have eaten Joe Louis."

Langford was a small man — five feet six inches — who took on opponents as much as ten inches taller and 60 pounds heavier than himself because he couldn't get enough fights with men his own size to keep him busy. He was so good that he could actually name the moment he'd knock out an opponent. One night in 1910 he was fighting a pug named Dewey, who weighed 205 and stood at six foot two. The bout was in Cheyenne, Wyoming, a section where the trains came and went irregularly. His manager was anxious to get back quickly to Los Angeles. When he consulted timetables he discovered that the only train that day left half an hour after the fight was to start.

"Why, I'm surprised you're worrying," Langford said. "That gives us lots of time." Whereupon he knocked out Dewey in a minute and 42 seconds of the first round.

He was so good that he once knocked an opponent into the lap of an unfriendly writer. In San Francisco in 1908, when he weighed about 155 pounds, he fought a 210-pound bruiser named Fireman Jim Flynn who was six feet one. In the first round Langford jostled Flynn towards the ropes above the ringside seat of a west-coast sportswriter named H.M. Walker. Walker had written that Flynn ought to stop mixing with "clowns like Langford" if he wanted to prove he was a genuine threat for Jack Johnson's heavyweight crown.

"Mr. Walker," grinned Sam, "here comes your champion." And he knocked Flynn into the writer's lap.

Langford fought in an era when black fighters were in a highly anomalous position. Jack Johnson, the champi-on, was black, and largely because of this there was a national wave of sentiment against him. Managers strove to find a "white hope" who could beat him.

The "white hope" industry was launched in 1908 right

after Johnson followed Tommy Burns to Australia and beat him to a pulp in 14 rounds in Sydney to win the world's championship. Johnson thus became the first man to cross the colour line established by John L. Sullivan, the first American heavyweight champion of the world, who had refused to meet Peter Jackson, an outstanding Australian black fighter. For years the colour line was invoked by each succeeding champion. But Johnson refused to keep what most whites regarded as "his place." As champion he was once compelled to flee to Paris after being charged with violation of the Mann Act — he was accused of transporting a white woman, Lucille Cameron, whom he later married, across a state line for immoral purposes. In Paris he bet lavish sums on racehorses, wore a beret and sipped champagne through a straw, habits that swelled the sentiments against him.

In this turbulent atmosphere, not all white hopes were worthy challengers; rather, many were products of skilful manipulation by their managers and the worked-up fervour of prejudiced fans. White hopes were usually too wary, or their handlers too discreet, to risk their reputations against black fighters of Langford's talent. Langford's manager, Joe Woodman, told me that Sam "almost always" had to "do business" to get a fight with a white man. In other words, white fighters exacted promises that Langford would carry them so far.

To get fights and to keep eating, Langford had a long series of bouts with Harry Wills, Sam McVey, and Joe Jeannette, who, with the champion Johnson, were the best prize fighters in the world. During the time Johnson was champion, from 1908 until 1915, the other four tried constantly to track him down, but Johnson avoided them. "On a good night Sam is just liable to beat me or make it close," the champion said when a match with Langford was proposed in Paris in 1914, "and what's the sense of that for the kind of money we'd draw?"

They did meet once — but that was before Johnson was champion. When Langford weighed 151 pounds in 1906 he fought 15 brutal rounds with Johnson in Boston.

Although Johnson, who weighed 186, won the fight, he resolutely refused to meet Langford again. Two years after he became champion he was cornered by Langford and Joe Woodman in the sports department of the Boston *Globe*, and offered $10,000 if he would agree to a return bout. He did, but when the two fighters were to meet at ten o'clock the next morning to sign papers for the fight, Johnson didn't show up. The bout naturally died.

In his fights Langford invariably got the worst of physical odds. He fought 15 times with the brawling Harry Wills, who outweighed him by almost 50 pounds and was seven inches taller — unbelievably violent clashes. Wills, who chased the heavyweight champion Jack Dempsey for a fight in the early Twenties and was bypassed in favour of Gene Tunney, who won the championship in 1926, once knocked Langford down nine times in the first four rounds of a bout in New Orleans in 1916, and then was knocked out by Langford in the 19th round.

Langford fought McVey and Jeannette 14 times apiece and lost only two bouts to each. Sam broke even in two fights with Fred Fulton, who weighed 210 and who, at six feet four, was a full ten inches taller. When Langford was crowding 40 in 1920 he twice knocked out a black fighter named George Godfrey, who stood six foot three and weighed 240 pounds.

The phrase, pound for pound, fits naturally into any comparisons with Langford because he was so much smaller than such heavyweight champions as Johnson, Jess Willard, Dempsey, and Joe Louis. He had exceptionally long arms, heavy shoulders, and a deep, thick torso. He started fighting as a youngster in the lightweight division at 132 pounds and when he added weight almost all of it was in his upper body. He outgrew the lightweight, welterweight (147) and middleweight (160) divisions. Most experts agree his best fighting weight was 172.

Under his barrel build and with his long strong arms, Langford's short legs gave him a curiously gnomelike appearance. Then, as now, he had a broad, flat nose, a cauliflower left ear, thick, heavy lips, and crisp, short, curly

hair that fitted the broad contours of his head so tightly
it looked almost like a skullcap.

He would come loping out of his corner, his face
impassive. He fought in a crouch that made him a difficult target for taller opponents and he usually offset their
superior height by working inside their defence, pound-
ing solidly to the body and then hooking to the jaw. His
judgement of distance was uncanny. One old-time boxing writer in Boston, William A. Hamilton, described it
this way:

"He would glide out in a crouch and when his opponents led he'd move just a fraction and let the blow graze
his head. He could hit like a terror with both hands."

Langford was never able to get a fight for a world's
championship in any division. Johnson refused to meet
him and so did Georges Carpentier when he was the light-
heavyweight champion. When Stanley Ketchell was middleweight champion his manager, the astute Willis Britt,
refused repeated offers to meet Langford in California,
but finally consented to a no-decision, six-round bout in
Philadelphia on April 27, 1910.

Langford had instructions from Woodman to go easy,
the theory being that Ketchell might then consent to a
championship bout. Newspaper reports relate that "they
gave a pretty boxing exhibition, with Langford having
something of a shade on points in the first three rounds.
After that Langford contented himself with blocking
Ketchell's punches, without making any attempt to fight
back." Woodman's plan for a return match faded forever
six months later when Ketchell was shot and killed.

Langford got $300 for fighting Ketchell. Throughout
his 21 years in the ring his purses were small. Although
one of the greatest ringmen of his time, he never drew
more than $10,000 for a fight and reached that level only
once — in London in 1909 when he knocked out Ian
Hague, the English heavyweight champion, in four rounds.

"I once fought Joe Jeannette on a percentage of the
house and the gate was only a few hundred dollars,"
Langford recalled. "One time I boxed for a Negro pro-

moter in New Orleans. The bout drew 75 dollars and I got a fourth of that. Most of the time I got a couple of hundred dollars."

But prices were low too. In 1914 eggs were 23¢ a dozen and a man could buy a Ford runabout for $440. Tailored suits were $22 and newspapers were 1¢ apiece. Boxing was in low repute socially and few women attended fights, which were often held in smoky billiards rooms in men's clubs. In many states, boxing was illegal, although police often looked the other way.

Finally in 1920 New York State adopted the Walker Law, which set up a state boxing commission. Other states followed suit and the National Boxing Association was formed, legalizing boxing in the United States.

Langford fought most of his early bouts in and around Boston, frequently at the Armoury Athletic Association where billiard tables were removed to make room for ringside chairs and long heavy boards that served as bleacher seats. Club members and their friends attended. Membership was $15 a year and a friend could become a "temporary member" for $1 on the day of the fight. Later, after World War I and just before Prohibition, a few emancipated women began to appear at fights, although reformers shouted that boxing was "brutal bear-baiting."

If he wasn't highly paid Langford was at least highly regarded in Boston, home of the abolitionists where a black person could rise above the crowd. Sam spent his money on fine clothes and fêted his friends at bars. He took a drink occasionally himself and once, before embarking for England, nearly missed the boat as he said his raucous farewells to wellwishers who danced to the pier as the gangplank was going up.

In one of his infrequent returns to Canada he was greeted in Weymouth, Nova Scotia as the hometown boy who made good. In the province that had the highest proportion of blacks in Canada but didn't always treat them too well, everybody turned out to greet him and they carried him down the street on their shoulders. At Cape Breton he was acclaimed by miners who came up from the pits to cheer the Nova Scotian who had built a world reputation in the ring.

When Sam was nearing the end of his long career he made his only appearance in Toronto where he met Young Peter Jackson on October 18, 1921. The *Toronto Star* carried this advance notice on October 14: "Nothing is too good for Sam Langford, the King of Smoky Swat, according to local colored folk. One grand reception has been arranged for Hon. Sam by Toronto people of his race ... After a downtown parade, King Sam Swat is going to dine somewhere but just where has not been decided. About every colored man in town who has a spare room and credit for a pair of chickens or a collection of pork chops wants to have Sam's knees under his mahogany."

On October 19, the story of the fight, in which Langford knocked out Jackson in the second round, appeared under the byline of Lou E. Marsh. "A pickaninny has as much chance in a rassling match with a gorilla as Young Peter Jackson had with Sam Langford ... They say Langford trained on pork chops. Well! if he did he done gobbled up Mistah Y. P. Jackson in two bites like any other pork chop."

Langford was reportedly in his 40s when he won that fight but as is the case with Jersey Joe Walcott, former heavyweight champion, and Satchel Paige, the venerable baseball pitcher, his age has always been a source of speculation. Some record books note his birth year as 1880 and others make it 1886. He once explained that his father just chopped a notch in a tree when a child was born, and that way kept track of the youngsters if not their birth dates.

On other counts, however, his memory appears excellent and he can sit by the hour in his dim upstairs room in Boston recounting the past, a smile on his broad flat features, his head tilted back, an occasional slit of the white of his right eye showing briefly through smudged sun glasses. He is totally blind, but cheerful.

Sam's father was a sailor on a windjammer, he recalls, and the family lived on a farm near Weymouth. Between voyages, his father cut trees and hauled them by oxen into town where he sold them. There were four boys and three girls and Sam remembers that early in his life his father taught him a lasting lesson.

"I had an accident," he grins. "I was running with some boys and we went and borrowed some eggs. I say we borrowed some eggs. Well, they arrested us and the bigger boys said that I gave them the eggs. The judge gave me a $15 fine or 15 days in the Digby jail.

"My father said, 'I can pay the fine but I'm not gonna. I'm gonna learn him some sense.'

"So they put me in a cell with some other fellows and I guess I was about 10 or 12. When I came out who should be there to meet me but the old man and he says, 'Sam, I guess there'll be no more stealin'.' There wasn't either."

Not long after, Sam's father sent him to town to pick up some groceries. He met some boys, got playing, and forgot all about the groceries.

"The old man gave me a lickin' and I decided I'd go somewhere. I got up in the morning, got my oxen ready and drove them toward the woods where I was supposed to be cuttin'. But I just tied them up and away I went toward Weymouth.

"I had nowheres to go, no one would take me in and I remember I slept in a chicken house. I don't remember eating much but I slept the next night in a hay loft and in the morning a man came along and he says, 'Do you want work?' And I said I did and then he asked me if I'd like to go to Boston. I said sure I would and he says, 'If you meet me in Yarmouth Saturday I'll take you.'

"So I board a freight to Yarmouth and goes to the Grand Hotel and asks for Dr. Blodgett — the man was a doctor in Boston at the Massachusetts General Hospital — and I got him his horse from the stable and away we went to Boston on the boat."

The doctor and his family lived outside Boston. Sam drove him to the train each morning and met him at the train each evening. Through the day he worked in the stables. He used to play with the doctor's three children, two boys and a girl, and he recalls with a chuckle that they used to call him a "herrin' choker."

He stayed with the family for three years, by which time he was "gettin' on toward 15 or 16 I guess." He went to work in the brickyards in North Cambridge where he stayed a year and then he went to New Hampshire to live with his brother Charlie, who had left home ahead of him. Then he headed back to Boston where he had a sister.

"I could find a room for 35 or 40¢ and I used to go to my sister for something to eat," he says. "Then one day I was walking past the old Glenbrook Saloon and I went in and asked the man if he needed somebody to clean up. The man's name was Mike Foley and he let me clean up in the morning and wash glasses and work around the place like that.

"One day Mike was out at the back and a fellah comes in and asked for a lager. So I went behind the bar and gave him a lager. He asks for another and I give him another. He asks for another and I give him another. Then he starts out.

"'You owe me 15¢,' I says.

"'You're a scab,' he says. 'You're not a bartender.'

"So over the bar I came and we went to it. I knocked him down, took my 15¢ and Mike comes running out from the back and he looks and says, 'Sam, you ain't got no business being broke; you can make money fighting in the amateurs. Here's a dollar. Go to Prospect Street and get yourself a licence.'

"Mike Foley got me some battered old tights and a pair of gloves and in my first fight there's me and a Scotch fellow. I knocked him out and I get a watch that I can hock for $30. I fight a couple more times and then one day Mike says, 'Sam, do you know a fellow named Joe Woodman?' I say no and Mike says this fellow's a druggist who's interested in fighters and wants to see me. So I go, and Woodman says, 'You got no business fighting amateurs. I know where you can get some money.' That's all I wanted to hear. I became a pro and Woodman became my manager."

The record book shows that the year was 1902, when Sam was probably somewhere between 16 and 20. He had four fights, all in Boston, and won them all in six rounds or less. He had 26 fights the next year and lost only one. Although still a lightweight (135 pounds) he fought two draws with a middleweight (160) pounds, Andy Watson, and in December 1903 he met Joe Gans, one of the ring's great boxers who had temporarily given up the lightweight championship to battle in the welterweight (147 pounds) division. Gans had been fighting for ten years and he was later to regain his lightweight title. He was a strong favourite to beat the newcomer Langford.

Sam was over-awed by Gans' reputation and in the early rounds Gans' swift jabs and left hooks had him in difficulty. A hook staggered Langford and as Sam reeled back Gans followed with a right cross to the mouth. The blows made Langford even more wary, but by the fifth round his confidence was returning. In the sixth he began crowding Gans and for the next nine rounds he was clearly in charge. He won the 15-round decision.

In his next outing, two weeks later, he proved he was on his way to the top by fighting a 12-round draw with one of the most scientific boxers in the game, Jack Blackburn, who later became Joe Louis' teacher. The pair fought four times in the next two years. The first was a no-decision six-rounder, and the next three were victories for Sam.

In April 1906 Langford met the man he was to pursue for the next ten years in a fruitless search for the world's heavyweight championship, Jack Johnson. Sam was barely more than a heavy welterweight at 151 pounds and Johnson was a tough established heavyweight, 35 pounds heavier and on his way to the world's championship.

In nearly 50 years since that fight, which Johnson won on a 15-round decision, the story has grown that Langford gave Johnson such a handful that Johnson was afraid to meet him again. But the files of the *Police Gazette*, a sort of boxing Bible, relate that "Johnson gave Langford a terrible beating and was awarded the decision."

Sam was so upset by the defeat that in his next bout

two weeks later he lost a decision to Young Peter Jackson. But the same year, in Rochester, he later knocked out Jackson in five rounds.

In the spring of 1907 he was having difficulty finding opponents. He visited a Boston fight writer, Doc Almy of the *Post*, and asked him if he could help scare up some fights. Almy had been in touch with an English promoter, Peggy Bettinson, of the London National Sporting Club, and he asked Langford if he'd like to go to England. Sam spent three months in England. There he knocked out Tiger Smith in four rounds and Jeff Thorne in six. On his return the *Boston Post* was distressed that he had not brought back moving pictures that were taken of the fight with Thorne.

"It happened," the *Post*'s yellowed clipping revealed, "that when the pictures were developed they showed a large number of royalty occupying ringside seats. The authorities then prohibited the pictures being shown in England or taken out of the country."

In 1908 Langford became a Pacific coast favourite when he knocked out Jim Barry and Jim Flynn in Los Angeles and San Francisco. His attack on Flynn was ferocious. He broke Flynn's nose in the second round and broke his jaw in the third. When he put him away with a right uppercut Flynn was unconscious for more than 20 minutes.

In England again he knocked out Ian (Iron) Hague, the British heavyweight champion, on Victoria Day 1909, and a year later, after his no-decision affair with the middleweight champion Stanley Ketchell in Philadelphia, Langford was summoned back to London to meet an Australian heavyweight named Bill Lang who weighed 196 pounds, which made a resounding thump as they landed on the canvas in a heap in the sixth round.

Sam was dismayed because it took him six rounds to dispose of Lang; he felt he wasn't getting his usual snap into his punches. One possible explanation, he felt, were the gloves provided for the fight. They were white. He reasoned that against the dark background of his body the punches had been telegraphed to Lang. He cut open one of the gloves. It was stuffed with rabbit fur instead of horsehair, which gave the gloves the resiliency of a down-filled pillow.

"I must say," Sam said to the promoter, an Australian named Hugh McIntosh, "I never realized how many ways there were of using a rabbit punch."

McIntosh, impressed by Langford, took Sam and the American black fighter, Sam McVey, to Australia where 18,000 people saw them fight under a broiling sun in Sydney on Boxing Day in 1911. McVey was awarded a 20-round decision that was roundly hooted. The fighters were rematched four months later. This time Langford won in 20 rounds. Then he repeated with another 20-round decision in Sydney. In Perth in a violent brawl, Langford knocked out McVey in 11 rounds and then, a year to the day after their first meeting in Sydney, Sam knocked him out again, this time in 13 rounds.

The next three years, in the opinion of his manager Woodman and ring historian Nat Fleischer, were the best of Langford's long career. Fighting everywhere from New York to Paris to Buenos Aires he fought 30 times and lost only two decisions, one to Joe Jeannette and one to Harry Wills.

In the midst of his running battle with Wills, Langford reached the turning point in his career. On June 19, 1917, when he was in his early 30s, or thereabouts, he went to Boston to meet Fred Fulton, a towering 215-pound Kansan. Langford was out of shape — a puffy 181 pounds — and for six rounds he took a dreadful beating that eventually cost him the sight of his left eye. In the sixth he was knocked down for the third time by a left hook to the jaw. He climbed to his feet, dazed and helpless, and Fulton swarmed on him, driving both hands to Sam's eyes, nose, jaw, and stomach, and Sam simply rolled along the ropes.

Somehow he weathered the round and as he stumbled to his corner his left eye closed completely. As the bell sounded for the start of the seventh round Sam did not rise from his stool. He sat there, tears slowly trickling down his cheeks, as he signalled that he could not continue. He never regained sight in his left eye.

"Sam should have quit fighting then," Woodman, a voluble spry man, told me recently at Stillman's Gym in New York. "I told him to quit while he still had his senses and one good eye.

"'Are you telling me you're through with me?' Sam said, and I said 'I'm telling you, you should quit.' But he wouldn't quit. We parted but he went on fighting for another six years."

Sam continued to fight until late in 1923 when he was in his 40s. He had three fights in Mexico City, and then quit. He stayed in Mexico "six or seven years and then I got sick and tired of it." In San Antonio, Texas, one night he sat watching a fight card.

"Both my eyes were bad then but I could see a little bit," he recalls. "I knew I could lick the whole bunch put together."

He asked a promoter for a fight. The promoter agreed. The old fighter doesn't remember the name of his opponent but he remembers thinking, "They're not teachin' boys to fight these days."

"When we got in there," Sam recalls, "he started swingin' that left hand and I blocked it and he swung again and I blocked it. Then I knocked him out."

Sam adds that punchline with a smile. He smiles a good deal these days, skipping lightly over the hardship he's suffered after his last fight, the exhibition in San Antonio around 1929. Ten years ago a New York boxing writer for the *Herald Tribune*, Al Laney, writing a series about old fighters, went searching for Langford in Harlem. He found him after two weeks "in a dingy tall bedroom on 139th Street down a corridor so dark you had to feel your way."

Sam by then was totally blind as well as broke.

Laney's story marked the beginning of a fund that enabled Langford to return to Boston where he lived with his sister until a year ago. Boston writers raised a few thousand dollars in a benefit boxing card. But the funds were just about dissipated when Sam's sister died a year ago.

Then Mrs. Grace Wilkins, a widow who runs a some-what forlorn rest home in Boston, agreed to look after Sam. Ordinarily, she charged $35 a week to look after old people but there is nothing like that in what remains of Sam's funds. The money, she says, arrives sporadically, an occasional cheque for $49.18 from the New York fund and an infrequent $60 from Boston.

"Mr. Langford uses just about that much in coffee and tobacco and doughnuts," she said recently.

Sam is an amiable guest in the dim room on the second floor of the 15-room house at 136 Townsend Street — a big old house from which the paint is peeling and the shutters are hanging at odd angles. But he spends many of his dark hours worrying about money. Mrs. Wilkins, who sometimes buys him pyjamas, underwear, and tobacco, says he often expresses deep concern that he is too much of a burden.

"I asked him one time," Mrs. Wilkins said, "I asked him, 'Mr. Langford, what would you like to do now if you could do anything in the world that you wanted?'

"And he replied, 'Missus, I've been everywhere I wanted to go, I've seen everything I wanted to see, and I guess I've eaten just about everything there is to eat. Now I just want to sit here in my room and not cause you any trouble.'"

(NOTE: This piece appeared in a slightly different form in Maclean's *magazine in the spring of 1955. Obviously, the racial references have changed over the past 40-odd years.)*

BOLIVIA IN THE SUN

Neil A. Campbell

On the B train, rattling along from the northwest suburbs into downtown Chicago, yesterday was the morning rush-hour from hell. There was the usual horde of commuters trying to get to work on time. Jammed in with them were hundreds of Bolivians, decked out in red, green, and yellow, carrying flags, desperate to get to the Cathedral Church on East Wacker Drive by 8:30 a.m.

"We can't be late," said Edgar Clavijo, who left one of South America's poorest countries four years ago and now lives in Silver Springs, Md. "It has been organized for a long time, this cathedral service. Many are going to pray for a draw with Germany. I am going to pray for only a one-goal defeat."

It was opening day of the World Cup, Germany versus Bolivia at Soldier Field, and close to a billion people around the world were expected to watch live. It was not a big deal for the Germans. They have been to the championship final of the past three World Cups, winning in 1990. They are used to the world's biggest sporting stage.

But for Bolivia, yesterday was a day nobody will forget. "This is to us what the man on the moon was to America," said Demetrio Carrillo, another Bolivian riding the B train to church. It was the ultimate clash of cultures under the streets of Chicago, commuters with their heads buried in the morning paper, Bolivians nervously clutching their flags. They all desperately wanted the Americans to notice, to care, to smile at them. But to the average Chicagoan the World Cup is just another irritation on a hot summer morning.

"I don't think any of them realize this is a day we have dreamed about," said Carrillo. Said Jaime Escobar, the Bolivian counsel in Chicago: "Today is possibly the greatest day in our history."

It is said that in most countries, soccer is life. But it is also geography. Four years ago, Cameroon was on the lips of a billion viewers when it defeated Argentina in the tournament opener. "I had never heard of Cameroon before that day," Carrillo says. "I did not know it was a country."

Xavier Azkargorta, the Spaniard who has coached the Bolivian team to new heights, said much the same about his new home. "People say that nobody knows much about Bolivia the football team," he said. "Nobody knows *anything* about Bolivia the country."

It is one of only two landlocked countries in South America. The population is close to seven million, most of them in rural areas and most of them incredibly impoverished. In 1985 the inflation rate was close to 24,000 per cent and although things have improved a bit — many say the gradual rise of the soccer team from South American punching-bag mirrors the gradual rise of the country — Bolivians have been leaving their country in droves. Escobar said there are nearly a million Bolivians living in Argentina and Brazil, and more than 400,000 in the United States.

"We have very little industry, it is very hard to find work," Clavijo said. "Our president (Gonzalez Sanchez de Lozada), who is going to the World Cup game today, he is a good man, a very smart man. Things are going to get better and maybe in a few years I can go back."

Clavijo works as a mechanic in Maryland. He watched at a local club when Bolivia defeated Brazil last summer to give its qualifying campaign a kickstart. When the team later gained a tie with Ecuador in the final qualifying match and earned one of the 24 World Cup spots, he celebrated all night.

When the draw was made in December, pitting Bolivia against Germany, he started putting away $50 or more a week. "I had to pay more than double face value for my ticket ($300 instead of $120) but it is worth it." He blew the bankroll on this one game. Television will have to do for Bolivia's other two World Cup matches, against Spain and South Korea.

Like most Bolivians, like most everybody outside North America, Clavijo loves soccer. So does Escobar and Sanchez de Lozada, who attended the opening game with U.S. President Clinton and Chancellor Helmut Kohl of Germany, and warned he would go bonkers if Bolivia scored, no matter who was next to him.

It is not easy being a soccer fan in a small country. There is so little to celebrate. Bolivia, for example, can never hope to compete with giants such as Brazil and Argentina. All that can be hoped for is the one day in the spotlight that will provide memories to last forever.

"We were in the World Cup in 1930 and 1950," Escobar said, "but that was because we were invited; we didn't qualify. This time we qualified and we got into the opening game when everybody is watching. Everybody says how crazy they are about soccer in Brazil. They have gone to every World Cup. We are crazy about soccer, too, but we never get to celebrate it like this."

They celebrated in style yesterday, cars and vans from all over the United States with the country's red, green, and yellow flag hanging from the windows. Escobar said almost 1,000 fans made the trip from Bolivia, but Carrillo said none of them would be seen on Chicago's subways or streets, that the average Bolivian could not afford a World Cup trip.

But on the sun-baked pavements around Soldier Field, the U.S.-based Bolivians did their country proud. There were as many of them as Germans. Clavijo proudly wore the official Bolivian soccer tracksuit on which he spent the rest of his savings. For $200 he had it imported from Bolivia.

Up in the private boxes and down in the corporate tents Bolivian government officials shook hands and tried to sell their country as a place to do business.

"We are using this as an opportunity to market the country for investment and tourism, to show what a poor but developing country has to offer," Escobar said. "We've had an advance team in Chicago and we've connected with Ameritech, AT&T, Quaker Oats to awaken them to Bolivia.

"If we don't win on the football pitch, we want to make sure we win some off the pitch."

(Reprinted with permission from *The Globe and Mail*)

BOXING CROWNS A CHAMPION

Stephen Brunt

There must be foreplay. Big fights, like no other sporting events, rely on the ritual of mounting excitement, artificial or otherwise. Its form is as predictable as a Latin mass. Press conference. Weigh-in. Undercard. The great John L. and Gentleman Jim would recognize the routine.

George Foreman shouted hallelujah and talked about his urge to hurt people on Wednesday, while Michael Moorer remained inscrutable. On Thursday, they stepped on the scale, Foreman stripping off shirt and tie before revealing his relatively lean 250-pound physique, Moorer looking powerful at 222.

Then the day of rest, the long wait, and the long walk, until finally, two men, stripped to the waist, stand alone in the light.

It seems, and it is probably true, with the sport of professional boxing in precipitous decline, that each big fight lacks the atmosphere of the last. Part of the problem this time is the locale. The MGM Grand, home of the most spectacular indoor boxing venue in the world, is that great oxymoron, a "family casino," a den of iniquity with a theme park stuck on the back.

At Caesars Palace, or the Mirage, or even in Atlantic City, there was always a slightly shady veneer. The parade of women in slinky dresses, men smoking fat cigars, rent-a-dates and mobsters and Runyonites who strolled through the perpetual twilight made it all seem just a little dangerous. At the front door, rubberneckers would stand ten deep as the limos pulled up, disgorging movie stars and famous athletes, imported as ringside adornments.

Here the lights are too bright, there are too many children running around. The celebrities are mostly down-scale — Tom Arnolds instead of Frank Sinatras. It all reeks of side-show, and not just because former Partridge Family member and transvestite prostitute aficionado Danny Bonaduce is scheduled to fight an exhibition bout on the undercard.

But then again, given that the challenger for the heavyweight title is closing in on 46 years old, is better known to the public as a genial burger pitchman than as a boxer, then maybe the veneer is as it should be. The Home Box Office network is leading into the fight with a showing of *Mrs. Doubtfire*. That and big, cuddly George: what a great excuse to let the kids stay up late.

By the time the sound of Sam Cooke singing *If I Had a Hammer* rings through the arena, it is the dinner hour in Las Vegas. The undercard, which began four hours before, has been mediocre. Most of the paying customers don't bother taking their seats until just before the main event.

Foreman enters the ring in a well-worn black-and-white robe — no sequins, no tassels — a hooded grey sweatshirt that covers his shaved-bald head, and a pair of shabby red trunks with a faded purple waistband.

They are the very same trunks that he wore in Kinshasa, Zaire, that morning in 1974.

The ovation for him is utterly unanimous, 12,000 people standing and cheering, and as much as you can credit that to sitcoms and fat-man humour, it is also the reaction to a genuine folk hero.

When Moorer follows, as is the title-holder's prerogative, he is booed in a way you'd have to figure no heavy-weight champion has been booed before. His sin is that he is here to wreck the old man's dream, and for the tra-ditionalists in the audience, his sin is also that he would apparently rather be doing something else.

Great fighters have a purity of purpose. Their entire being is boxing. Moorer says he doesn't particularly like the business, that he'd just as soon be a Navy Seal or a police sniper, or something equally sinister and ridicu-lous. But you can't really play at being a boxer, because it's not really a game. The great ones — think of Mike Tyson — are never so conflicted. That Moorer can hold the greatest title in sport and still be ambivalent is considered sacrilege.

There are moments of almost unbearable anticipation in sport: the start of the Kentucky Derby or the Indianapolis 500, the kickoff of a significant football game. But noth-ing compares to the minutes before a big fight, and espe-cially nothing compares to the moments before a bout for the heavyweight championship of the world. All of the prognostication, all of the informed speculation, can never really anticipate what happens when the two fight-ers finally meet, alone. And with the big men, big punch-ers, there is also the sense of menace, of foreboding that comes with the knowledge that something wonderful and terrible could happen just as soon as the bell rings.

This time, the fight begins slowly, deliberately. Those trying to understand Foreman's strategy can see small developments as the rounds pass. He starts by throwing only the left jab, and harmless rights that are all arm, no power. Moorer, a left-hander, lands his right jab at will. Every time Foreman connects with a punch of any signif-icance, he fires back two or three. His handspeed makes Foreman look, by contrast, like he's boxing underwater.

Three rounds have gone by before Foreman throws his first left hook. The next round he adds his first uppercut. Then, a few exploratory shots to the body. Two rounds — the sixth and eighth — are keepers, with one fighter, then the other, taking control.

The fight is competitive, it is entertaining, and Foreman's performance is more than respectable. But it is also not close. Through nine rounds, few if any at ringside observers have given Foreman more than two. (Although it will turn out that one fight judge, inexplicably, has Moorer ahead by only a point). The champion's financial backers, a glittery group occupying a front row, are confident and congratulatory, and with good reason.

Foreman can't win a decision now. And only once before in his long career has he knocked anyone out as late as the tenth round. That was Gregoro Peralta in 1981.

And so it seems, the die is cast.

The punch is short and perfect and unexpected, one of the few that Foreman has thrown on the night when he has also turned with the blow, putting his force behind it.

"Giving it a little body English," as he describes it afterward. Boxing is not what they show in *Rocky* movies. At its best, it is a subtle art of timing and distance, not of brute force.

The blow lands on the side of Moorer's chin, and the champion is frozen, unconscious before he hits the ground. Those who have seen a few *petit morts* before can tell by the way he falls, and the way he lies on the canvas, that he is unlikely to rise. Moorer stares up at the distant ceiling, blinking his eyes, making a movement to get up, and then falling back.

How to explain the feeling in the crowd, in front of the millions of televisions, even in the press section, where stoic cynicism is the measure of objectivity? It is like a building, wondrous release, that climaxes at the moment when referee Joe Cortez reaches 10:2—03 of the tenth round. He waves his hands over Moorer's prone form, the pantomime that tells all it is finished.

But it is also the pure, innocent glee of childhood as well, the satisfaction of watching a big, dumb, sentimental movie where you can see the ending a mile away, but still can't help but be moved.

Foreman is expressionless as he watches the count. When Cortez signals the finish, he turns to the corner post and kneels in prayer. In an instant, he is swallowed up by the celebrants and mourners who spill through the ropes.

George Foreman at age 45 years and ten months is the oldest man to challenge for a professional boxing title in any division, eight years older than Jersey Joe Walcott — the next oldest champion — was when he captured the crown. It is 20 years and six days since he lost that same title to Muhammad Ali in Africa.

It is like Arnold Palmer winning the Masters now by chipping out of the bunker for an eagle, like Joe Namath coming out of retirement to lead a team to the Super Bowl, like Jimmy Connors — no, make that Rod Laver — winning next summer's Wimbledon. Like Nolan Ryan throwing that final no-hitter after coming back from ten years of retirement. Like Reggie Jackson being Mr. October next October.

It is, quite simply, a moment unprecedented and unparalleled in the history of modern sport.

The final act, the post-fight news conference. Moorer arrives first, surrounded by his suddenly less-ebullient entourage. He is gracious to a fault. "Boxing is a sport where you have a winner and a loser," he says. "Unfortunately, I lost. What can I say? I did my best." He didn't see the punch coming. "From what I can remember, it was just one punch — a right hand." He called his toddler son afterward, and the boy was crying — that, he said, was the source of his only real pain.

About his future in boxing, Moorer is ambivalent, not surprising since he was ambivalent about his present as well. He'll have to think about it. His words are almost drowned out by the introductions for the Bonaduce fiasco, which is obscene.

Moorer is gone by the time Foreman arrives, wearing a suit and tie and sunglasses to hide his swollen eyes. Colin Hart, the veteran British boxing writer, looks on and says he has felt this way only once before, when he feared for a fighter's safety, when he desperately hoped that he would survive, and then miraculously watched him win. Zaire, of course. With Foreman playing the other part.

"Don't let anybody tell you what you can't do,"
Foreman says, and suddenly the cornball rings true. "Don't
let people talk you down." He pauses. "And don't go to
Las Vegas and bet against me."

He is asked what comes next, and is noncommittal.

"Do we keep dreaming," Foreman asks, "or do we go
fishing?"

Fishing, you'd hope, since there could be no higher
high, but when people start talking about Mike Tyson
and a $100-million gross, it will be hard not to listen.

Still, now is not the time for dread.

The MGM Grand is decorated with images from one
particular movie produced by that studio before even
Foreman was born, a story of perseverance and hokey
optimism and wishes that come true.

As he prepared to depart for Houston, where yesterday
morning the Reverend George Foreman would lead his
congregation in prayer, the new, very old heavyweight
champion of the world recites the lyrics from its sound-
track, a familiar, secular hymn.

> *Somewhere over the rainbow*
> *Way up high...*
> *Bluebirds fly over the rainbow*
> *Why, then, oh why can't I?*

(Reprinted with permission from *The Globe and Mail*)

WANTED: SIX GO-GETTING MIDGETS

Ralph Allen

Wanted: *Six to twelve go-getting, clean-living midgets to work in sports department of established metropolitan newspaper. Maximum height 3 feet six inches, maximum weight 35 pounds. Knowledge of English grammar, hockey, baseball and football an asset but not essential. Here is a real opportunity for the midget of vision and ambition to enter a career with a genuine future. Interested midgets should apply, giving waist, chest and calf measurements, to Personnel Dept.,* The Evening Telegram, *Bay Street, Toronto.*

There has been a great deal of talk around town, some of it true, about the streamlining of this journal, so in one respect it is still the same old *Telegram*, only more so. Always notorious for its cosiness and intimacy, even in the days when Mr. Fitz was putting out the pages with the help of one rather undernourished cub, the physical habitat of the sports department still maintains the pristine dimensions conferred on it by the late John Ross Robertson. These, by actual measurement, are: length 22 feet; width 18 feet. The normal population of same, by actual count, now consists of 11 adult males, not counting such floaters as publicity men, office boys, bill collectors, fight promoters, angry wives, inventors of new systems for making racetrack selections, insurance salesmen, meddlesome employers, printers, and other traditional links between the sportswriter and civilization at large.

In addition to these human occupants, the enlarged telephone booth into which they are fitted contains the following items of furniture and literature: ten large-sized desks, ten large-sized chairs, one large wastepaper basket, three small wastepaper baskets, ten glue pots, three coat racks, one medium-sized ashtray, three old overshoes, four wall calendars, two record books, 113 empty Coca-Cola bottles, and two copies of last night's pink edition.

You might think this is impossible, and you would almost be right. Actually, if everybody who is supposed to work here showed up at one time, it would take a hydraulic press to squeeze us all in, even in theory. Mr. Robert Hewitson, who is in charge of the seating arrangements, has worked out a complicated diagram purporting to show that if all 11 of the nominal residents appeared at once, we could just make it by having a masseur come in to have a fast, last-minute go at Bunny Morganson, jettisoning our coats and vests out the window and inducing the last man through the door to lie down on the floor.

Despite Hewitson's show of confidence, I believe he is living in a fool's paradise. Already I see signs of a crack in his nerve. The weekend before last he sent a writer named Reeve to Florida. Last weekend he sent a writer named Frayne to Florida. God knows whose turn will be next. Every now and then I see him glancing my way, his eyes glinting speculatively like the man in charge of a lifeboat with the water running low. Just let him try that Florida ruse on me and see how far he gets. They promised me a chair and a desk all to myself when I came here, see, Hewitson, and I don't care if you offer to fly me to Tahiti in a sarong, I'm standing on my rights.

So far Hewitson has had a pretty good run of luck. One day a couple of weeks ago, before he started driving his loyal colleagues off to Miami, we actually had nine sportswriters in here all at once and it looked pretty dark. Just then the phone rang. Hewitson got to it by crawling on his hands and knees and chasing a couple of intervening authors under their desks with a copy spike. He listened for a minute and then a radiant smile broke over his face.

"Johnny Fitzgerald is sick," he said.

When Hewitson extricated his foot from my mouth, I spat out a couple of teeth and mumbled a few words of anxious inquiry.

"Heart!" Hewitson said happily.

Three days after that, Hewitson announced that another of the field hands, Bob Hesketh, was sick too.

"Medical science is baffled," Hewitson said, rubbing his hands. "It may be weeks before they even get the case diagnosed.

"Poor old Hesketh," one of his fellow swinkers sighed. "I'll borrow his desk."

"One of nature's noblemen," another colleague murmured while the tears streamed down his face. "As long as he won't be needing it I might as well carve my initials on that chair."

So for the time being, the pressure is off. Just the same, I shudder to think where we'll be if our comfy little group ever runs out of winter resorts or diseases. I still think the far-sighted, permanent solution would be to import a plane-load of pygmies and teach them to spell.

(First appeared in *The Toronto Telegram*, March 7, 1949)

NOBODY'S FIFTEEN FEET TALL

Kenneth Whyte

By any measure, Wayne Gretzky is a superb athlete. He has played 11 years in the National Hockey League, the first nine with the Edmonton Oilers, the last two with the Los Angeles Kings, and throughout he has monopolized the two principal currencies of on-ice excellence: silverware and statistics. He has won four Stanley Cup championships, seven Art Ross trophies as the league's top scorer, nine Hart trophies as the most valuable player in the regular season, and two Conn Smythe trophies as the best performer in the playoff, and has tied or broken 51 NHL records.

As a hockey player, Gretzky stands with the game's all-time greats — Gordie Howe, Rocket Richard, Howie Morenz, Bobby Hull, Jean Beliveau, Bobby Orr — and perhaps a little beyond them. No other player has dominated the game so completely and for so long. He has also distinguished himself in the manner of his achievement, playing with a degree of skill that verges on artistry few thought possible in a sport often celebrated for its breakneck brutality.

Yet Gretzky's greatness couldn't be fully appreciated until after August 9, 1988, the day Edmonton Oilers owner

Peter Pocklington traded him, with two others players, to the Los Angeles Kings in exchange for two players, three first-round draft choices, and $15-million cash (U.S.). In Edmonton Gretzky had been surrounded with exceptional talent. Suddenly he was a member of a team renowned for an enduring commitment to marginality. It was predicted a talent of Gretzky's calibre might subvert the Kings' status quo, but no one was prepared for the upheaval he excited. The Kings climbed from 18th place among 21 teams to fourth and upset the league champion Oilers in the first round of the playoffs.

Success, in the end, is a simple thing, particularly in professional sport, where it can be reduced unambiguously to rankings, records, box scores, championship games, award ceremonies, and highlight packages. But the means to it are invariably complex, especially in the case of so unconventional a specimen as Wayne Gretzky. He has managed to master the game of hockey without bearing the slightest physical resemblance to any familiar image of a hockey star. His arms, neck, and torso are slender, almost delicate, and he remains without the hind-quarter bulk that distinguishes so many in his profession. His playing weight is 171 pounds, although he's still listed as 175. A month after he was traded to the Kings — a move as difficult for him as it was unsettling for Canadians — he checked into training camp at 159. If published statistics are any indication, that made him one of the lightest players in the league.

His meager stature encourages the misconception that he is by some miracle extorting virtuosity from a body poor in athletic resources. In fact, Gretzky takes tremendous physical advantages to the ice. He has outstanding eyesight, balance, and hand-eye co-ordination. His cardiovascular system is just short of tireless. He possesses a high degree of kinaesthetic awareness (the ability to sense a change in pressure or weight, which allows an athlete to develop his touch). And there are some, including John Muckler, the Edmonton Oilers coach, who believe he is the quickest player ever to grace the NHL.

Bernie Nicholls and Dave Taylor, two talented Kings veterans, had played against the Oilers and Gretzky for the better part of a decade before he joined their team. They were familiar with his renowned play-making abilities but surprised by his physical skill, particularly his skating. "I always knew he was fast because you never see him caught from behind," says Taylor. "You don't know how quick and agile he is until you skate with him every day. His moves are so quick and his turns are so tight it's really hard to stay with him."

Experts on skating divide hockey players into two basic categories: those who skate with the ice, and those who skate against it. The second category includes the majority of NHL players, and the most striking example is Oilers captain Mark Messier. He relies on strength to skate, cutting harshly into the ice with each stride, bending deeply at the knee and fully extending the leg for maximum power, hardly gliding at all before grinding into the next step. It doesn't allow for great agility, and it is an inefficient technique — Messier makes a terrific noise when he's winding up, as though he's skating on cement. But it can produce a hellish combination of power and speed, and a player as strong as Messier is virtually unstoppable in full flight.

Less common are those who skate with the ice. Audrey Bakewell, a skating instructor who has worked with the Oilers and a number of other clubs, says there are usually only three or four on any NHL team, and none is better than Gretzky. He skates lightly, letting the ice work for him, sometimes taking short, quick strides, sometimes long and deep ones, but always with his blades whispering along the ice. Even on a tight turn he produces a slicing sound, seldom a crunch. Efficiency enables him to be in constant motion, to glide and circle and sweep over the whole ice surface, to dodge in and out of the play, make instant turns and shifts without wasting speed, momentum, or energy. What he lacks in power and sturdiness he makes up in quickness and agility.

Bakewell says one style is not inherently better than another; what counts is how the style suits the individual. She places Gretzky (along with Messier) among the three or four best skaters in hockey. Gretzky has the additional ability, she says, to "skate from the hips down and play hockey from the hips up," something most hockey players find very difficult. While moving forward, he can turn his head, even his shoulders, to look behind him or to reach back for a pass, without breaking stride. A player with more upper-body bulk trying the same move will usually shift his centre of gravity enough to throw himself off balance; he has to quit skating to do it.

Hall of Fame goaltender Glenn Hall, now a coach with the Calgary Flames, has also noticed this ability in Gretzky: "He skates with a lot of shoulder action and head motion. It's like he puts a deke in every stride." This upper-body mobility sometimes makes Gretzky look as if he's working against himself, elbows and knees shooting out at odd angles, and it has led some to criticize his skating, mistaking dexterity for awkwardness.

Midway through the fourth game of last spring's playoff series against Edmonton, Gretzky and Nicholls approached the Oilers blueline at full stride. On the other side of the line were Oilers Charlie Huddy and Esa Tikkanen. Nicholls' role was straightforward — slip between the two defenders to the net, keeping his stick on the ice to receive Gretzky's pass. Normally Tikkanen or Huddy would have checked him just inside the line, breaking up the play. But Gretzky, with a dazzlingly quick series of moves, opened a hole for himself.

Three feet short of the line, skating straight at Huddy, Gretzky turned his shoulders to the outside, towards the boards, faking an end run. It was only the ghost of a move, but it froze Huddy for an instant. Next Gretzky lunged forward with the puck, pushing it over the blueline ahead of Nicholls to avoid an offside call. He then cut hard, at a 90° angle, right along the line behind Nicholls to Tikkanen's side of the ice, which forced Tikkanen to play him.

All three moves — freezing Huddy, avoiding the off-side call, the turn to attract Tikkanen — took a second of time and six or eight feet in space. Gretzky's skates were actually turning towards Tikkanen while his shoulders were decoying Huddy. Nicholls passed easily between the Oilers, Gretzky found him with a pass, and Huddy had to take a penalty, hooking Nicholls to the ice to prevent a goal. The opportunity was a direct result of Gretzky's ability to skate and play hockey simultaneously, and he does it not in spite of but because of his physical nature.

Later in the same game Gretzky and line-mate Dave Taylor broke into Edmonton territory with three Oilers separating them and all the other skaters some distance behind. Gretzky, with the puck, charged deep into the zone, keeping tight against the boards, while Taylor dashed to the net. The Oilers stayed between them, hoping to block Gretzky's threatened pass. When all five players approached the end of the rink, Gretzky finally let go of the puck. Without turning to look, he floated it waist-high, not in the direction of Taylor, but back towards the blueline, into empty space. It appeared aimless until it landed, right in front of L.A. defenceman Tim Watters, who had been trailing the play and who now had an open path to the net. Watters missed his shot, but Hockey Night in Canada commentator Harry Neale was astounded at the setup. Gretzky, he marvelled, "sees out of his ears."

Neale, the colour man, is being colourful, of course. There is no magic to it. As Peter Gzowski noted in an 1980 article about Gretzky, what appears to be his sixth sense or intuition is actually a product of his superior knowledge of the game. He understands the action on the ice not as most players and fans do — a whirl of motion punctuated by remarkable individual plays (goals, scoring opportunities, hits, whistles). Rather, he has played hockey for so long and studied it so closely that he sees its larger rhythms, sequences of action, and repeating patterns. They are second nature to him. He can read a configuration of players on the ice, anticipate what is likely to develop next, and react to it instantly, without pausing to think.

Gretzky knew as he crossed the blueline that it would be difficult to beat three Edmonton defenders, so while skating forward he took a quick look over his shoulder, noted the alignment of skaters following the play, spotted Tim Watters in the lead, and gauged his speed and direction. Hatching a strategy on the spot, he dragged the Oilers deep into the zone, clearing a space for his trailing teammate. Finally, he threw the pass back, without looking, to the place he estimated Watters would be if he had followed through on the play. And there he was.

Neale gives Gretzky deserved credit for finding Watters and making the pass, but as usual he gets no recognition for his full contribution. He not only read the situation, he manipulated it, creating a new configuration to his advantage, just as he did when he parted Huddy and Tikkanen and sent Nicholls in alone.

Gretzky's mental approach to hockey is part of what makes him great, but it is not in itself enough to set him apart. Unless his body keeps up with his mind, it doesn't matter what he sees on the ice. His physical and mental skills are complementary. Constant motion enables him to be forever arriving in new situations, viewing the action from fresh angles, and increasing his opportunities exponentially. His head and shoulder action, his quickness and agility, his deceptively hard shot and unfailingly accurate passes allow him to take full advantage of whatever openings he finds.

Every bit as impressive as what Gretzky does on the ice is how often he does it. Between exhibition, international, regular-season, and playoff competition, with his average of 30 minutes' ice-time a game (most players see 15 to 20), Gretzky has probably played more hockey in the 1980s than any other professional. Through it all, there has seldom been a shift when he hasn't carried all his talents onto the ice and given them a full workout. "You marvel at how he can hold his level of play so high every night," says Dave Taylor. "His intensity is incredible."

Gretzky's performance in the first three games of last year's playoff against the Oilers was by his own standards only adequate, and the Kings lost twice. But in the fourth game, the one in which he set up both Watters and Nicholls, he seemed to be everywhere, always with the puck, always making something happen. He created seven good scoring opportunities in the second period alone and could have had ten points on the night had his teammates been luckier or sharper.

As it was, he counted three assists; the Kings lost 4-3 and fell behind the Oilers 3-1 in games. Still, he carried his determination into the fifth match, and by then his teammates were picking up on it. They went on to win the last three games and the series. Only when it was all over did Gretzky account for his change of pace. "Mr. Pocklington said that after Game Three people in Edmonton had told him that it was a good trade. Now, we'll see what they say tomorrow."

It is a familiar story line. In 1981, a young, talented, but unproven Edmonton Oilers squad led by 20-year-old Gretzky squared off against the venerable Montreal Canadiens in the first round of the playoffs. Before the first game, Montreal goaltender Richard Sevigny predicted his team would have little trouble in the series and that hockey's reigning superstar, Guy Lafleur, would "put Gretzky in his back pocket." Gretzky scored once and assisted on five others goals as the Oilers won the opener 6-3. Lafleur was invisible, and Edmonton went on to win the series in consecutive games, becoming for the first time a serious Stanley Cup contender. "I don't know what makes me like that," says Gretzky, "but when someone says I can't..."

Pride is a large and sustaining motive for him, but it is hardly his sole source of animation. Gretzky still loves to play hockey, to be a member of a team, on the ice and in the dressingroom. He derives sheer joy from his own talents and the opportunity to exercise them in competition. He has always been among the first to arrive at the arena on game day. He buzzes around the dressing-room, talking up a storm, not nervous but exuberant, sweating through his shirt.

A 1987 hockey documentary, *The Boys on the Bus*, catches Gretzky and Mark Messier in the midst of a discussion of motivation. Messier insists Gretzky is driven by pride, a desire to be the best, and the challenge of staying on top. Gretzky counters that he plays for the pure pleasure of "what I do when I'm on the ice." And they are both right.

Most great athletes are similarly driven. What distinguishes Gretzky is the power of his propulsion and his ability to control it. He can be breathtakingly ruthless with his emotions. The Edmonton–L.A. series was especially difficult for Gretzky. He must have felt closer to many of the Oilers than to his new teammates in Los Angeles. Earlier in the season, on his first visit back to Edmonton as a member of the Kings, he confided to Bernie Nicholls that he would have preferred sitting in the dressingroom to skating against the Oilers. "You know," says Nicholls, "that night in Edmonton was the first time I ever saw him miss with his passes."

Yet on the morning of the seventh game of the Edmonton–L.A. play-off, Harry Neale watched Gretzky at the morning skate and reported, "He was very excited at the possibility of eliminating the Oilers tonight. His smile, the sparkle in his eyes, reminded you of your little children the night before Christmas... It was really a beautiful sight to see pro sport's truest superstar that excited about a hockey game."

After the game, Gretzky talked of how difficult it was to see his old friends, whom he considered true champions, go down to defeat, and how the series had been no fun at all for him. Gretzky always says the right thing, but in this case the contradiction is probably an honest one.

Gretzky's fierce and impassioned performances inspire his teammates with devotion and enthusiasm — which is charisma in its purest form — by endeavour. Detroit coach Jacques Demers believes Gretzky's presence on a roster automatically makes every player on it 20 per cent better. Nicholls confirms the judgement: "He's out there playing his best, and you don't want to disappoint him."

His leadership extends to the club's off-ice activities as well. He dotes on his teammates — sharing their triumphs, defending them vigorously against critics, even helping them negotiate their contracts.

"The guys on the team," says Oiler defenceman Randy Gregg, "always knew Gretz would be there if they needed him. I remember when Marc Habscheid first came up to our team from Saskatoon. Marc was glad just to be in Edmonton, and perfectly happy to stay in the hotel, but Wayne opened his penthouse apartment to him. Habscheid was thrilled. His first time up, and he's living with the greatest player in hockey."

There are still many more levels of Gretzky's game. A treatise waits to be written on the million things his stick can do with a puck. ("I could hang a nickel in the net," one former Oilers goalie has said, "and he could hit it every time.") And his hockey intelligence is much more comprehensive than is generally supposed. "He knows the technical parts of the game better than anyone I've ever met," says Bernie Nicholls. "Including coaches." Adds an Edmonton sportswriter: "He has an owner's understanding of the NHL. He's been around the league a long time. He has friends and contacts on every team. He hears all the rumours, knows everything that's going on behind the scenes, where all the bodies are buried."

All of it points to the same conclusion. What most separates Gretzky from the one-season wonders, the occasionally great, the forever adequate, is his completeness. "You can't explain a talent like Gretzky in terms of any one thing," says Ted Wall, chairman of the physical-education department at McGill University. "All the truly great ones have all these things going for them: they are very knowledgeable about their disciplines, they have great physical skills, they have learned to control their own learning and their arousal levels. And they can bring it all together instantly to deliver precisely the performance demanded by the moment. That's what makes them great."

Twenty minutes after the final buzzer, there is no air left in the Los Angeles Kings' dressingroom, only a hot, sticky, suffocating fog, loaded with banter and eye-watering odours. Some 20 individuals are resting on benches or milling around the training table in the middle of the room, stepping over piles of damp equipment and towels. Many of them are still breathing hard, flushed with exertion. It's a long climb down from the press box. Finally, a few players wander out from the showers. Minicams roll and notebooks flip open.

The Kings are winners tonight, beating the Edmonton Oilers in the second game of the first round of the 1988 Stanley Cup playoffs. The first crowd develops around Chris Kontos, a 25-year-old winger who was called up to the team just before the series began. He squirms on the bench, naked but for a towel, trying hard to appear unaffected by the commotion about him. The reporters, ringing him three deep, want to know how he scored three goals in one game when they have never heard of him before, why a former first-round draft pick was playing in Switzerland all winter instead of in the NHL, and exactly what kind of personal problems he was having.

About five minutes into the interview, enter Wayne Gretzky from an adjoining room. The throng backs up and turns away from Kontos without warning or hesitation. Gretzky is fully dressed — dark slacks, white shirt, rich but subdued tie, wing tips — and he's fiddling with a cuff. He takes two steps before lifting his eyes, and in a single sweeping glance takes in everyone taking him in. He somehow discerns that the only unoccupied stretch of bench in the room is behind a crowd to his right. He moves there, sits down still working his cuff. A light beer in a plastic cup materializes on the bench beside him and the reporters clamber into position, crawling over each other, trading jabs and elbows, waving microphones a half-inch from Gretzky's mouth but never coming close to hitting him. Kontos watches him from across the room, looking spent, more naked than Adam.

Gretzky lifts his eyes again and the questions start. Have he and the Kings taken control of the series? What of his little shoving match in front of the net with Esa Tikkanen? What of the heat in the arena tonight? Did it make a difference having first-string goaltender Kelly Hrudey back in their lineup instead of back-up Glenn Healy? (Hrudey was out sick the previous night.)

He answers: "This series has got a long way to go yet. We won one game, we haven't won anything... He's trying to win. I'm trying to win. I expect to get hit... Sure, it's hot in there, but both teams have to play in it... We played tight last night. It wasn't Healy's fault..."

The reporters come and go in waves, the questions seldom vary, and Gretzky is glimmering. Composed, confident, gracious, glib, apparently unstudied. When a question is obviously stupid — are you pleased to have won tonight? — he flashes exasperation, brings it under control, then gives a better answer than is deserved. When a writer he knows and trusts insists on useful information — really, what difference did it make having Hrudey back in goal? — Gretzky turns ever so slightly from the others and says into the writer's notebook, "Kelly handles the puck so well, he's like a third defencemen out there. We know Edmonton's a pretty disciplined team, they're going to dump the puck in a lot, and we got a lot of confidence we can stand up-ice and Kelly's gonna get the puck and move it out." When the photographers come around, as they invariably do, he throws them a quick pose without waiting for the request or interrupting the dialogue, and if it weren't for their flashes you wouldn't notice they were there.

He finds occasion for a tirade against fighting in hockey. He sees familiar faces across the room and bestows little gifts of attention on them — a nod, a wink, a smile, a few words. It is impressive and disarming, an almost majestic performance, and people who have met him often, people who have watched him closely, say he is almost exactly as he seems.

"He is a superb athlete," writes Gary Wills. "I wonder why that is not enough. It isn't, of course… Sheer physical beauty, of unusual degree, seems to become different in *kind*, to call *complementary* significance. That can be bewildering to the beauty's possessor, who feels his or her power over others and recognizes that they want such power to include something *more*. More than mere animal glow. The magnetic 'star' tries to supply something extra."

Wills is referring to Muhammad Ali, who answered the demand by reciting float-like-a-butterfly doggerel and the Muslim catechism, flashing his fist at the camera, shouting "I am the greatest!" Wayne Gretzky takes a different tack. His is Galahad in short pants, a whisper of self-effacing virtue that carries far above the din of professional sport and makes a welcome counterpoint to the bellowing and bullying of Mike Tyson, Brian Bosworth, and the many other sons of Milo. He is forever excusing himself into the public eye, feigning a blushing reluctance, protesting "I'm just a hockey player."

Gretzky's is an act that has played particularly well in Canada, where, as the nationalist mavens tell us, to be polite, responsible, understated, and inoffensive is to be an irreplaceable delight. And its appeal reaches far beyond the hockey crowd. When Gretzky was traded to L.A., people who had little interest in the game, who knew him primarily for his celebrity, professed to feel the loss deeply. His move became a national issue. Some of the country's better political and cultural commentators made rare forays into the sporting world, sweating to put Gretzky and his accomplishments in proper context and to find appropriate expression for the collective grief.

Novelist and social critic Brian Fawcett wrote in *This Magazine*, the nation's leading leftist journal, that while he loathes that "horrible, violent game," and thinks that it should be banned, he considered Wayne Gretzky an exceptional person. He confessed that on hearing news of the trade he had contemplated obscene and violent acts against "slime scuppered" Edmonton owner Peter Pocklington, who had treated this symbol of all that is good in Canada as grist for the capitalist mill.

Over at *The Globe and Mail*, which Fawcett considers right-wing, reactionary, and a symbol of all that is evil in Canada, Ottawa columnist Jeffrey Simpson adopted an elegiac tone to vent similar sentiment. "In a sport dominated by bimbos and hucksters, where the average IQ of the players barely stumbles into the three figures, you had intelligence and dignity. In a country starved for heroes, you were Him...You had grace in how you played and in what you said. You were the model every parent in every two-bit rink in every two-bit freezing town, could point his son towards. You never embarrassed us. Not once, in all those years, no matter how bad the pain, no matter how stupid the question, no matter how thuggish the assault on ice."

Uncritical adulation of sports celebrities is not uncommon in the sports pages, but to find pundits who routinely approach the utterances and performances of public figures with scatological scepticism, embracing Gretzky's public persona wholeheartedly and unquestioningly — indeed, straining to enhance it for him — is curious. Yet Simpson and Fawcett weren't alone. Similar responses appeared on editorial pages coast to coast, sharing their basic theme: Gretzky, the national treasure, was lost, leaving us only with this outrageous game, this crass and shameful spectacle of overpaid louts clubbing a puck and each other around a cold arena to put millions in the pockets of barbarous hypesters.

The implicit assumption is that Gretzky transcends his sport, that he is above the grasping, the bluster, and the brutality. It is a pretty thought, but it doesn't make a lot of sense. After all, Gretzky's image, however bright and shimmering, is just an image, and Gretzky could no more live up to these perceptions of it than he could see out his ears. The man behind the public mask has been training for and living in the hockey world since the age of three, to the virtual exclusion of all else. The greater part of his knowledge and experience has been filtered through a prism of Plexiglas. He is both part and product of his game.

The predominant ethic in hockey, as in most professional sport, is expediency, an unwavering insistence that the only worthwhile measures of performance are results, and that whatever achieves results — skill, strength, intimidation, cheating, excessive violence — is laudable, or at least tolerable. In the 1972 Canada–Russia series the commanding player through the first four games was the great Soviet star, Valery Kharlamov. In the fifth match, certain that his team would lose so long as Kharlamov was on the ice, the leader of Team Canada, Bobby Clarke, aimed a vicious two-handed slash at the Soviet's ankle, breaking it. The Canadians won the next three games and the series. "It's not something I'm really proud of," said Clarke, now the general manager of the Philadelphia Flyers and a member of the Hockey Hall of Fame. "But I can't say I was ashamed to do it."

Gretzky has never been guilty of so blatant an offence as Clarke's, but he is guided by the same desperate light. He has always maintained that, for him, "winning is everything," and he insists that he is prepared to do "whatever it takes" to win. He is expert at taking dives to draw penalties, a skill he defends as useful for discouraging opponents from crowding him on the ice, and he's been known to fake an injury to the same end.

Asked once if he would go so far as to use drugs to enhance his performance, he answered no — but not because using drugs would constitute cheating and perhaps break the law. Rather, he believes they would prove damaging to his career in the long run. Around the time of the last NHL strike, he was asked his position on unions in sport. He said that if the NHL Players Association struck he would feel obliged to make a clear stand of solidarity with his peers. Asked if he would show a similar respect for unions if players on the junior hockey team he owns in Hull, Quebec, were to organize and strike, he answered, "I'd want my best players to cross [the picket line]. It's as simple as that. I'm not stupid."

Much has been made of Gretzky's opposition to the fighting that goes on in NHL games, but there is no altruism to his stance. (He has in fact dropped his gloves once or twice, but he fights like a kitten.) His primary reason for it, stated at the Kings training camp in Hull last September, is his firm belief that the American television market will never accept the game so long as it is viewed as a frigid variety of roller derby.

Violence and intimidation are ineffective tools to a player so fragile as Gretzky, but it's not unlikely he would take advantage of them if he could. His idol is Gordie Howe, a player of rare skill whose additional talent for discriminate brutality discouraged opponents from crowding him on the ice. (He once, in a moment of savagery as notorious as Clarke's, smashed his elbow into the face of New York Rangers forward Lou Fontinato, crushing the man's nose and causing his eyes to swell shut almost instantly.)

And while Gretzky is not equipped to answer the bell himself, he is careful to keep himself surrounded by those who will. A sports reporter was told by Gretzky's manager, Michael Barnett, that during a crucial juncture in the negotiations of the trade, Gretzky listened in Bruce McNall's office while the L.A. owner talked over a speaker phone to Edmonton owner Peter Pocklington, who thought the call was private. On Gretzky's advice, McNall asked that Marty McSorley, an Oilers enforcer with decent hockey skills and a history of being quick to Gretzky's defence, be shipped to L.A. as part of the deal. Pocklington said he couldn't approve such a move without first talking to his general manager, Glen Sather. Gretzky began waving his arms and McNall put Pocklington on hold. Gretzky explained that if Sather learned that such a deal were even under consideration he'd hit the roof. After a brief discussion, McNall went back on the line and said, "Peter, you're not going to hold up a $15-million deal over some fucking thug, are you?" And McSorley was back by Gretzky's side.

In addition to the thuggery, critics like Fawcett and Simpson also object to and attempt to isolate Gretzky from the hype and hucksterism, the naked fame-and-fortune-seeking so endemic in pro sport. They front his name with adjectives like "shy," "unassuming," "decent," and "gracious." These words do in some ways fit Gretzky, who can be quite a gentleman, and who next to many of his boorish peers often seems modest and pedigreed. All the same, he has been a celebrity since grade school — he was virtually incubated in a spotlight — and it continues to nourish him.

It was gospel among the Oilers during the Gretzky era that the weightiest certificate of celebrity one could possess was an invitation to guest on Johnny Carson's "Tonight Show," and they needled Gretzky, early in his career, that his accomplishments lacked legitimacy until he took a seat beside Ed McMahon. When the inevitable invitation came, he blurted to the Oilers defenceman Kevin Lowe: "Have I made it or have I made it — I'm going on with Carson!" When his commercial flight was snowed in the day of his scheduled appearance, Gretzky, a white-knuckle flyer at the best of times, phoned the NHL offices, advised officials there of the public-relations potential of his impending performance, and insisted they split the cost of a private jet to get him there on time, damn the storm. Unfortunately for Gretzky, the NHL offices did not see it the same way and he had to settle for a rescheduled appearance.

This was the same person who broke into the NHL speaking of himself in the third person and wearing on his back not the number 9, which had been good enough for Gordie Howe and Bobby Hull, but the audacious 99. Last summer he was a guest on "Late Night with David Letterman," hosted "Saturday Night Live," and put in an appearance at Cannes. The summer before, he invited the prime minister and Hugh Hefner to witness his marriage in Edmonton to *Playboy* cover girl and B-movie starlet Janet Jones, a spectacle that drew almost as well as the average Oilers homegame. Hardly the retiring type.

His public declarations are often as self-serving and politic as those of any other public figure. When a statue of him was unveiled at Northlands Coliseum in Edmonton last August, he listed for reporters the many things he missed about the city: his fans, the great hockey atmosphere — even the winters. A few weeks later at the Kings training camp, he was asked again what he missed about Edmonton. "Aside from my friends there," he answered, "nothing."

Absolutely nothing?

"Nothing at all."

Furthermore, he has always been among the most heavily marketed athletes in sport, fronting for a dizzying array of products from breakfast cereal to running shoes to antifreeze. He knows how to take care of those who take care of him. While he was still playing in Edmonton, the manufacturers of Ebel watches presented him with a bejewelled sample of their wares, worth five figures, presumably in appreciation of his talents. At a photo shoot for a magazine story the next day, Gretzky sported a variety of clothes and poses, managing all the while to keep the watch front and centre for nearly every shot. Explained his manager, Michael Barnett, "He didn't go to school just to eat his lunch."

If Gretzky is much less than his public image, he is also much more. He plays his role not only for fun and profit but also out of a sense of obligation. He is genuinely concerned about the example he sets for young people and is constantly aware of his responsibilities as his sport's most visible practitioner and chief spokesman. It is for these reasons, as much as for self-aggrandizement or marketability, that he is forever careful to keep his postgame beer carefully out of camera range and to tell people what they want to hear. One of the reasons his image is so successful is that the man behind it is a decent human being with many good intentions. The characterizations offered of him by Simpson and Fawcett are not so much wrong as highly exaggerated.

As the end of the 1986 season, a losing one for the Oilers, Gretzky began talking for the first time about his eventual retirement. He said that it would come sooner than most people expected and that he was certain he would leave like Hemingway's bullfighter, punctually, never to return.

For the moment, Gretzky is busy enjoying southern California. He says he loves L.A., loves the people, and intends to continue living there long after he has retired. His friends say he feels appreciated now, and that's understandable. For a number of years in Edmonton, he was remarkably underpaid. (In 1985, he was only the fourth- or fifth-highest-paid player in hockey.) He currently earns $2-million annually, unsurpassed in the NHL, and his opportunities for endorsements, which made him around $1-million a year in Edmonton, have quadrupled. Moreover, the Oilers deemed him expendable, whereas the Kings' organization revolves around him. Last spring, coach Robbie Ftorek was fired and replaced with Gretzky-friendly Tom Webster and, at training camp this fall, Gretzky was made team captain. (The honour was rather unceremoniously stripped from veteran Dave Taylor.)

The city of Los Angeles, too, has shown its appreciation. It may not understand hockey, but it has a keen eye for a phenomenon, and it respects, in an abstract way, Gretzky's achievements. It has launched him into an elite circle of North American sports celebrities, alongside the likes of Carl Lewis, Magic Johnson, Bo Jackson, Mike Tyson, John McEnroe, Orel Hershiser, Eric Dickerson. That is something Gretzky has always wanted, and something that was unlikely to happen so long as he played in Canada.

His fame is at its zenith. His talents, however, are no longer keeping pace. Even though last October he surpassed Gordie Howe's mark of 1,850 career points, establishing himself as the most prolific scorer in hockey history (and needing only half as many games as Howe to do it), there are signs of decline. Over the past three years, he has averaged 166 points a season, compared to 207 over the five previous years, and if the first 25 games of this season are any indication, he is again on target for 160. He has lost the scoring title the last two years running to Pittsburgh's Mario Lemieux, and while he was named the league MVP by sportswriters last year, his peers, voting on a separate ballot, gave the honour to Detroit's Steve Yzerman.

Gretzky may remain one of the dominant players in hockey for a few years to come (slow as his scoring pace may be this fall, it still tops the league), but his best days are past. And as his talent dissipates, his star, too, will begin to fade. Its spell will lift. And when he finally leaves the game, it will become increasingly apparent that what he really had to offer his public he gave at the arena. His greatness, after all, is entirely within the context of his sport. It is ice-bound.

Our tendency to loose our best athletes from the bonds of mere physical brilliance and celebrate them in so many other ways is perhaps a reason why sports heroes are usually tragic ones. We expect them, and they expect themselves, to meet with similar success in all avenues of endeavour, but their talents are nontransferable.

They have practised tirelessly for a world that, for all its seeming chaos, is quite simple and well-ordered. Everyone runs by the same clock, plays by the same rules towards the same goals, always knowing who is on whose side and who isn't. At the end of every night and at the end of every season there are winners and losers. Throughout their adult lives, they have seldom, if ever, known a time when their services weren't in demand, when making money wasn't easy, when people weren't clamouring for their favours and attentions.

The very best athletes appear invulnerable in their prime, but the illusion never lasts. Most outlive their good fortune and wind up looking quite ordinary, if not pathetic. Some, like Guy Lafleur or Muhammad Ali, hang around their games long past the point of dignity, or to the point where they do permanent physical damage to themselves. Others, like Gordie Howe or Joe DiMaggio, retire to an endless cycle of pre-game ceremonies and sportsmen's dinners. Still others, like Bobby Hull and football's Jim Brown, turn the aggression and violence that made them famous against their loved ones. The idea that the great ones withdraw from their noble battles to some jockish Avalon is for the most part a cruel joke.

For these reasons, perhaps the most appropriate of the many tributes paid to Gretzky in the wake of his trade was the city of Edmonton's. It has erected a statue on the grounds outside Northlands Coliseum. It is a bronze likeness of Gretzky in a most familiar pose: chin up and chest out, face triumphant, Oilers sweater tucked into his hockey pants at one side, and the Stanley Cup hoisted over his head. It is, in its own way, a grand overstatement. It stands 15 feet tall. Nobody is 15 feet tall. But it is at least an image of a hockey player and it is hard to begrudge Gretzky heroic cast when he is on skates.

(First appeared in *Saturday Night*)

A DAY AT THE RACES

Don Gillmor

The PPG Molson Indy Toronto car race looks like the future. It is loud and chaotic and nobody walks anywhere. They move through crowded alleys in battery-powered flatbeds, motor scooters and golf carts. Everyone has an identity card with their photo and status clearly marked. Hundreds of mutants stand guard. Countries have been replaced by corporate zones: Marlboro controls the largest bloc; Budweiser and Miller Genuine Draft are rival fiefs. Snap-On Tools is a developing nation. Every square inch of space is used to advertise a product; every shirt, car, wall, helmet, and shoe. Giant television monitors loom, and the quotidian scenes exalted by the sheer scale. The air smells like scorched rubber. After the apocalypse the only survivors are beefy men with sunglasses and a handful of former cheerleaders with blonde highlights.

Toronto is the ninth stop on the 16-race PPG Indy circuit, which is named for a Pittsburgh chemical and paint company in the U.S., and sponsored locally by Molson. Car racing is more popular than baseball in the U.S. and Toronto has embraced it gamely; 161,399 people will come to the temporary track at the Exhibition grounds over three days. The three-member Marlboro Penske team is dominating this year with "Little" Al Unser in first place overall, Brazilian Emerson "Emmo" Fittipaldi in second, and 25-year-old Toronto native Paul Tracy in sixth. Tracy won the Toronto race last year and he's anxious to repeat in front of the home-town crowd.

Talking to Tracy for half an hour is like watching a rerun of "The Andy Griffith Show," amiable and uneventful. He has a boyish face, prematurely grey hair, and carries within him the primitive gift of speed. His aggressive driving style began with dirt bikes at the age of five. He switched to go-karts at six and began racing them at seven. At 15, he finished sixth at the World Karting Championships and one year later, when he got his driver's licence, he became the youngest Formula Ford champion. He is married and lives in a Toronto suburb not far from where he grew up. His wife, Tara, drives a BMW, Tracy drives a truck. Their daughter, Alysha, was born on Carburetion Day at the 1993 Indianapolis 500.

Financed by his parents, Tracy worked through the Can-Am series and the Indy Lights circuit, eventually coming to the attention of racing mogul Roger Penske. On his first Indy race on the Michigan oval, Tracy got caught in turbulence, slipstreamed sideways and hit the concrete wall at 214 m.p.h., breaking his leg. He thought he'd be fined but Penske had him back on the track three days after the cast was off. In 1991 Tracy earned six points on the Indy circuit. In 1992 he had 59 to finish 12th; last year he was third with 157 points.

The Penske cars, dominant over the season, are listless in the qualifying heats. In the pit, Tracy zips up his red Marlboro suit, adjusts his glasses, and roars out in a high whine that deepens as his Ilmor recedes around the concrete bend. A 30-foot antenna picks up a signal from Tracy's car and feeds it through two IBM ThinkPad computers in the pit. The program monitors temperatures, pressures, suspension, fuel mixture, lateral G-force; some of this information is relayed back to him as he drives. A graphic of the course illustrates Tracy's progress. The orange-and-white Penske comes around corner No. 11, its 1,550 pounds and 740 horsepower arguing with physics, that low-slung thrilling velocity. Marlboro uses orange on its cars instead of the trademark red because it photographs better; red bleeds or turns a muddy brown on television. Reality is transitory but images linger.

When Tracy comes in for a pit stop 15 men in headsets swarm the car. It rises evenly on a pneumatic jack; wing panels are replaced to provide more down-force for the corners, tires changed, pressure tinkered with, the engine laid bare, alien and efficient-looking. Tracy is handed a computer printout that shows all the qualifying times. He is running fifth. Desperate information is exchanged. The crew hover like doctors, massaging the organs, watching the monitor for signs of life. Tracy moves back out into the traffic but can't improve his position. He will start in fifth place tomorrow.

Afterwards he sits in the pit running his hand through his hair. His father leans towards him while his mother checks the qualifying times on the monitor.

"I drove my ass off out there," Tracy says.

"He won't like being fifth," his mother says.

"New tires don't change the balance?" his engineer Nigel Beresford asks. Tracy shakes his head. They discuss suspension and down-force. The car has to be adjusted for each race and it has been sluggish and vague. Tracy and Beresford go back to their jerry-built garage and deconstruct the run as the car is quickly stripped to an ecoskeleton, gears lying in trays of clean oil.

On race day there are 66,503 fans stretched along the course in bleachers built on scaffolding, here to watch the home-town boy clean up. After two days of qualifying, dozens of adjustments and several sets of tires, man and machine are ready. The fans can see 150 metres of track, about four seconds of each car as it sprints past. The announcer's voice is lost in the engine noise, the over-sized monitors are bleached in the sun, and the race becomes a cyclical abstraction.

In one of the previous days' qualifying heats a crash on the monitor prompted nervous queries. Villeneuve? Mansell? Ghoulish *frissons* of death flit through the stands. The fans content themselves with speed, noise, and hot dogs. The track below looks smooth and claustrophobic. A breeze comes off Lake Ontario. A rock star sings the anthem.

The turbulence caused by 30 cars going 200 m.p.h. in a semi-enclosed space creates dangerous, ephemeral microclimates, alarming winds and sudden vacuums. "It's like if you've ever been in a snowstorm behind a transport truck," Tracy said before the race. "A bad, bad snowstorm and the car is sliding all over the place and you can't see where you're going."

The other 32 drivers complicate the analogy, their unquiet ids revealed on the track. "There's guys you can trust and guys you can't trust," Tracy says. "A lot of the guys, you've got to be very, very careful around them. There's guys that you can stick a car on the inside of them and they'll give you some room, race with you. Other guys, you even think about it they'll try and chop the front of your car off."

Some are perennial also-rans who limp around the track each week, dragging their sponsors' logos and trademarks like encyclopedia salesmen, hoping for a few minutes on the networks. There are talented drivers stuck with stingy sponsors or inferior cars. "A lot of guys racing are just doing it for the pay cheque," Tracy says. His career earnings to date are $2,121,951. He still hums with ambition, the hunger to go faster.

Before the race, Tracy's crew are dressed in black Marlboro fireproof suits, loose, talking about cars and girls.

"Watch that water temp *real* close..."

"The brake balance looked good this morning."

"Smell my finger."

The race begins in a mad roar; on the first lap Little Al Unser blows the engine of his car and he's out. There is a small pile-up and Tracy's steering rod is clipped by Michael Andretti's Ford. Tracy hobbles back to the pit and watches his chances disappear. Sixty seconds into the race a sense of anticlimax grips the crowd.

After 40 laps the field has been winnowed; Copenhagen chewing tobacco's Brian Herta is in St. Michael's Hospital in serious but stable condition. Hawaiian Tropic Tan and Craftsman Tools are both out with electrical problems. Comptech has been submarined by transmission woe. K-Mart and STP are moribund. Tracy comes in for another pit stop and the crew jump to it, replacing four tires and refuelling in 14 seconds. His remaining teammate, Emmo, hits a bump and accidentally turns off the ignition switch, shutting down his engine. Tracy spins out and whines in neutral briefly, losing seconds. Pole-sitter Robby Gordon misses a turn and rockets through the Princes' Gates like a missile. After 80 laps Tracy has gone from 31st to sixth. Sixteen drivers are gone from the race, technology failing them.

Tracy finishes fifth in a remarkable display of predatory instinct, moving through the pack repeatedly, seeking the leaders but finally running out of time. Michael Andretti wins. To accommodate ABC network demands the race was five laps shorter than last year's, a fact that worked against Tracy today. Without the networks, the advertising and sponsorship would shrivel, the sport wouldn't exist. At the post-race press conference Tracy smiles for the cameras, straightens his Marlboro hat, and says he is looking forward to the challenges ahead.

(First appeared in *Saturday Night*)

DEAD END

Steve Simmons

On a morning ride on a Jersey bus Terrance Alli thumbed through a sports section and found out he had killed someone.

Momentarily he froze, stared at the words, then turned the page.

"I refuse to let it bother me," the fighter said, two weeks after his fight, two days after learning his opponent died in hospital.

"We choose this way to live. It's our choice. It's our job. We know about the possibilities...

"You know, it could have been me."

It was two Saturdays back, in a sold-out Paris arena, that David Thio boxed for the final time. He was young, French, unbeaten, on the way up, until a right uppercut ended the fight, and ten days later, his life. A cerebral contusion, the men of medicine called it.

Admittedly, Terrance Alli had thrown better punches. Admittedly, he stood in the ring, waiting for David Thio to get up.

"They kept yelling at me, 'You've got to take this guy out. You're not going to get a decision here. You've got to knock him out,'" Alli recalled yesterday. "I knew what I had to do. I hit him pretty good in the eighth round. He staggered back to his corner. I thought it could have been stopped then... I don't know... there was so much pressure, everyone wanted him to win."

The bout ended in the ninth, in a blur of confusion, commissioners, doctors, and panic.

Alli never thought about the knockout in life-or-death terms. After the fight, he raised his own arm and waited for David Thio to get up. "I wanted to talk to him, to tell how tough he was. You knock a guy down, you expect him to get up at the end, to shake hands. But he never moved."

Later that night, while in his hotel room, Alli was told his opponent was in a coma. "Even then I didn't think I hit him that hard. It never crossed my mind I could do this to somebody."

Hurting people never mattered to Terrance Alli. Winning was all important. He is, what he calls, a professional fighter. A sweet scientist. And that he has been for his entire life — from the time he left Guyana for Toronto seven years ago.

He was Terrance Halley then; young, promising, on the way up himself, when he trained in Tony Unitas' gym and thought it would be neat to change his name to Alli with an extra L. He fought three times in Toronto, but left the gym on Augusta and Queen after losing a bout with Canadian immigration. Once, four years ago in an Atlantic City casino, he even fought for — and almost won — the world lightweight title. With that opportunity lost, he fights now because it is his job.

"No fighter I know thinks about death," said Alli. "A countryman of mine, Cleveland Denny, died in a fight in Canada. I felt that. But then you forget about it. Your hear about it. You know it happens. It's in the paper. You just don't think it'll happen to you.

David Thio has become another statistic, another pointed argument for those who advocate the banishing of boxing. His was the 14th ring-related death of the 1980s, the 362nd since 1945. Thio's name will soon be forgotten, like the Brian Baronets and Victor Romeros before him; past victims who lapsed from canvas to coma to death.

Thio had a wife and a four-month-old baby girl and Terrance Alli is aware of the scars he left behind in Paris.

"I've gone over this fight so many times in my mind," he whispers. "Why did it happen? Could it have been different?

"I'm sorry. I feel sorry, but I don't really know what I'm sorry about.

"I can't sit and mope. I can't cry. If I cry and mope, my career is over. I'm a professional fighter. This is what I do. I've got to keep going."

On the morning ride on a Jersey bus, 28-year-old Terrance Alli learned of the damage he had done and kept going. He folded the newspaper, left it on the bus, and went back to the gym to train.

"It's the game," he said without apology. "It's what I am."

(First appeared in the *Toronto Sun*)

FAREWELL TO THE OLD CFL

Scott Taylor

At some point the Canada versus United States angle will get tiresome. Frankly, who cares if Baltimore wins the 82nd Grey Cup game? It's just another football game, right?

Well, maybe.

The giant life-of-its-own issue that won't go away simply won't go away. The Yanks have invaded and they're here to stay. This three-down football that once held Canada together like some kind of sporting glue is now about something completely different. This game marks the passing of an era, the end of the Canadian game as we know it.

This is not the football of the 1940s any more. It's a '90s game now — brash, loud, trash-talkin' and very, very fast.

Watching the Baltimore receivers and the B.C. defensive secondary is a lot like watching a full-contact track meet. There are no slow, sure-handed, Canadian-born slotbacks or fullbacks in that Baltimore offence. It is now the sprinter-as-target in the CFL. Baltimore receivers give quarterback Tracy Ham as much speed outside as the U.S. track team had in Barcelona.

The CFL is different now and we can't change it back.

American ingenuity and the free-market mentality own the CFL now. Everything is for sale and the quaint Grey Cup celebrations of the '50s are as old-fashioned as the single wing or the drop-kick field goal.

The CFL changes for good in this Grey Cup game. It ain't the War of 1812 but even 'way out here in Vancouver it has some cultural significance. Not everyone is sure what that significance is but they'll be able to buy the T-shirt, video and official Spalding J5V game ball (and yes, the game ball changes next year, too) in order to cherish the memories for years to come. Now, does that sound like a TV commercial? Or does it just sound a little more American?

So okay, Mr. Commissioner, let 'em play. Don't lessen the Canadian influence on the CFL. Don't even consider a name change. That's right, Larry Smith, don't touch the ratio unless you're going to force the American-based teams to use 20 Canadian players, too.

For in this game on the cushy turf at B.C. Place Stadium, ten Canadian starters plus a 40-year-old kicker sent a message to those American-born coaches of Canadian-based teams who think using Canadians is a burden.

Thanks to the play of folks like Rob Smith, Jamie Taras, Sean Millington, Tommy Europe and Lui Passaglia, the B.C. Lions beat the Baltimores 26-23 to halt the southern flow of precious metal.

The silver-plated Grey Cup will remain in Canada after one of those football games that ought to be the topic of heartwarming discussion for years. Brilliant play after brilliant play turned what started as an embarrassment into the best Grey Cup since Saskatchewan beat Hamilton 43-40 in 1989.

Of course, until the second half things didn't look good for either the Canadian player or Canadian football. The Baltimores took a 17-10 halftime lead, in no small way due to the horrible play of an American — B.C. quarterback Kent Austin.

Austin was six for 16 for 69 yards with three interceptions. Still, thanks to the play of the Lions' all-Canadian offensive line and their all-Canadian defensive line, B.C. hung tough.

It was a marvellous football game underscored by a season-long debate on the merits of the import: non-import ratio. Can Canadians compete in professional football? Do they need a boost by forcing American-born and trained coaches into keeping them on the league's rosters?

The answer is "Yes." To both questions.

For in this Grey Cup contest it wasn't the Canadians who screwed up. Baltimore's Tracy Ham was horrible and Austin was as bad as he's ever been. They say he had a partially-separated shoulder and it certainly looked that way. When he reinjured the shoulder with seven seconds to play in the first half, Baltimore coach Don Matthews should have fined the two defensive linemen who hit him. With Austin running the B.C. offence, Baltimore had a chance. With Danny McManus in it, the Lions suddenly had new life.

However, it wasn't so much McManus as it was the brilliance of that all-Canadian B.C. defensive line which, late in the game, made it possible for the Lions to pull out a last-play, winning field-goal thriller, the clincher supplied by the 40-year-old Lui Passaglia. Naturally, a Canadian.

The precise, all-American, four-down, technologically-advanced game of NFL football is fine — if you want to put hyperactive children to sleep. But if you want heart-pumping, wide-open, crazy-to-the-max excitement, then it's the Canadian variety — complete with Canadian players, Larry — that you crave.

And you can just ask the 55,097 delirious nutbars who sat through that magnificent piece of work at B.C. Place yesterday.

THE BEST?

Jack Batten

Imagine Fred Astaire on skates and you've got Max Bentley. Like Astaire, he was slim, quick and graceful. Swift of foot, he was a dancer on the ice, master of the stutter step, the feint, and the shift. Of course, one shouldn't carry the Astaire comparison too far. A key point of difference is that, for all of the appearance of spontaneity in Astaire's dance routines, every glide and tap was rehearsed and practised. Bentley, on the other hand, was an improviser in his movements, in his hockey. While he had certain set patterns, he was more often skittish and unpredictable, a couple of qualities that confounded linemates who had less talent for free-form play than he. But Bentley and Astaire were alike in character, both decent, shy and modest. And, for what it's worth, both were small men who wore their dark hair in the same slicked-back, elegant style.

Bentley was born on March 1, 1920, in Delisle, Saskatchewan, a farming community 25 miles southwest of Saskatoon. He was the youngest son in a family of six boys and seven girls. The closest brother in age to Max was Doug, four years older. Doug made it to the NHL with the Chicago Black Hawks in 1939. Max followed to the same team a year later. When the two brothers were combined with another little guy, Bill Mosienko, the NHL had one of its most creative lines of all time: Max at centre, Doug on left wing, Mosienko on the right.

To all appearances, these three players plugged into one central nervous system. They moved themselves and the puck in ways that seemed uncanny and instinctive. A large part of that perception was true. They did have amazing anticipation for one another on the ice. But they also used orchestrated pieces of business. Mosienko preferred that Max — who was possibly hockey's most elusive stickhandler — pass him the puck before Mosienko hit the other team's defence, whereas Doug liked Max to dump the puck between the two defencemen, allowing Doug to swoop around the defence and pick up the puck.

"We used to talk about all kinds of ideas," Max once explained. "Mosie was very conscientious for talking. I had to keep all the ideas in my head, but I knew I'd be all right because those two, Doug and Mosie, were the best and fastest I ever saw."

The three men had enormous personal success. Doug led the NHL in points in 1943, Max in 1946 and '47. Mosienko finished in the top ten in points in four consecutive seasons. Doug was a First Team All-Star in three different seasons. Max was the All-Star centre in 1946, the same year he won the Hart Trophy as the league's most valuable player.

Alas, their individual success didn't translate into team success. Chicago finished out of the playoffs three times in the early 1940s, and in the only year they made a respectable showing, 1944, the Montreal Canadiens swept them in four games in the Stanley Cup final.

Max Bentley thought he knew the reason for Chicago's failures. "There was no ice to practise on in Chicago," he said many years after he retired. "Most of our guys couldn't get in good condition. We'd be ahead at the end of the first period or second period in games, then we'd fade right out and lose. The only guys who were okay for condition were me and Doug and Mosie. That's because we played at least half of every game all by ourselves."

All of which helped to explain why Chicago's president, Bill Tobin, agreed in November 1947 to a trade that, for sheer stunning impact, probably wasn't equalled until

Edmonton peddled Wayne Gretzky to Los Angeles in 1988. Tobin reckoned that he couldn't have all his eggs in one basket, all the good players on one line. He needed more bodies, and he was willing to sacrifice Max Bentley to get them. Conn Smythe had designs on Bentley for two reasons; it would give him strength on all three forward lines, and it would protect him against the day fast approaching when Syl Apps, 32 years old going into the 1947-48 season, chose to retire.

So the trade: Max Bentley plus an obscure winger named Cy Thomas (who played six games for Chicago and would play eight in Toronto) for one complete forward line — Gaye Stewart, Gus Bodnar and Bud Poile — and one defence pair — Bob Goldham and Ernie Dickens. These were no stiffs that Smythe was giving up. The players included two Calder Trophy winners (Bodnar and Stewart), three certified goal scorers (Bodnar, Stewart and Poile) and a strong, intelligent defenceman (Bob Goldham, the guy in the trade Smythe hated most to lose). The five produced splendidly for Chicago, particularly Poile and Stewart, who were Second Team All-Stars in the year of the trade. What the five couldn't manage was to yank the Black Hawks out of the cellar. The team finished in last place in four of the next five seasons and didn't make the playoffs until 1952-53. That's why Bill Tobin came to regret the trade; last place was better with Max Bentley than without.

In Toronto, Bentley felt lonesome for a couple of months. He missed Doug. That was both on and off the ice. His Leaf linemates were Joe Klukay, a hard-working if unimaginative right-winger, and, as Max put it, "umpteen rookies on left wing." Sid Smith was one of the umpteen that first year, and he later explained the sense of disarray an ordinary man could experience playing alongside Max Bentley.

"I was a straight, driving sort of skater," Smith said. "But Max was different. He'd go dipsy-doodling. He'd head out of our end, then all of a sudden he'd whip to one side of the ice, and by that time, I'd be all the way down the rink."

Nevertheless, especially after Bentley got over his lonesomeness off the ice — Turk Broda, he always said, was the biggest help in that department — he brought a dimension to the Leafs that Toronto never had before. Even in the relative straitjacket of Hap Day's defensively-oriented system, he presented the team with invention and brio. He glittered. As strategy, Bentley playing the point when Toronto had a man advantage meant the Leafs had the most effective powerplay in the league. Even with rookies and other pedestrians on his wings, he remained a consistent 20-goal scorer in his six Leaf seasons. Max Bentley kept the game alive and magical. He was an original. Others skated, he danced.

(Reprinted from *The Leafs*, with permission from Key Porter Books)

EAGLESON DEFEATHERED US

Roy MacGregor

Innocent and proven guilty. That, regardless of the outcome of the Boston grand jury indictment of Alan Eagleson on 32 counts of embezzlement, fraud, and racketeering, is the verdict we must deliver today on ourselves, the Canadian sports media.

Eagleson, of course, is innocent until proven guilty. But we who should have been asking questions based on possibility instead of losing ourselves in the fantasy of games should have known better; our innocence, our naivety did not serve us well.

And Canadians have questions to ask. Could it be that an entire country was blinded — by vanity, by ambition — to the point where, for years, no politician ever wondered what was happening to taxpayers' money being spent on proving to the world we were best at one thing, anyway?

And how could it be that this story, whatever becomes of it, has been unfolding in an American court, with Canadian police only checking after American police came to check again and again?

In time, Alan Eagleson may be cleared completely. But that will not clear the rest of us. Even if the questions have answers, the point is: we failed to ask them.

Nearly a quarter of a century ago, the late *Globe and Mail* sports columnist Dick Beddoes said his profession was "burdened with hacks who make tin-can gods out of cast-iron jerks." I believe there is still a tendency among sports reporters to slant news in favour of the home team, to defer to local sports management for the sake of maintaining cordial working relationships, and to accept publicity handouts in place of digging for their own stories.

Beddoes was then a bit unfair and it is also fair to say that sports reporting has improved immeasurably since he spoke, but the continuing Eagleson saga shows just how far we all still need to go.

Almost everything the Boston grand jury has examined during the past two years, from NHL players' pensions to the Canada Cup tournaments, concerns events that took place on Canadian soil, not American.

And the questions that will now be asked in court might never have been asked at all were it not for a mild-mannered sports editor whose first love is race cars, not hockey, and whose small paper, the Lawrence, Massachusetts *Eagle-Tribune*, is not available in this country.

In the fall of 1991 when Russ Conway published his first investigative report on Eagleson, his discoveries stunned the hockey world. He was named runner-up for the Pulitzer Prize yet his work was ignored in hockey's main country and Conway was ridiculed by his Canadian peers.

When, over time, others joined Conway in his investigations, they, too, were often cold-shouldered by the sporting press. Since it became impossible to ignore, it has all been catch-up.

This story has, at times, been a reminder of the unnatural relationship that persists between sports journalism and sports. A century ago it began cockeyed — teams often carried the press on the payroll — and though much of the early damage has been repaired, sports figures still fail to fathom the difference between journalism and promotion.

Today's media are also to blame, having allowed the hysterical agenda of sports — games every day — to control budgets to the point where there is neither money nor time left over to do the sort of investigative work Conway has been pioneering.

But says Conway, "I do it for the love of the game, for what the game deserves to be."

Strange sentiments to hear from an American.

Particularly strange at a time when Canadians are bemoaning the loss of our national game to the Americans, and on a day when an American court decides to hold up our national sport so everyone can take a long look at what it has become.

(First appeared in the *Ottawa Journal*)

SOME STUD

Muriel Anne Lennox

Northern Dancer was waiting impatiently on a cold and grey February morning for Harry Green to lead him outside. Ever since he had arrived back at the farm, each day was much like the one before: Harry and his assistant arrived at 6:30 a.m. and the stallions were fed and turned out in their individual paddocks. On this day, however, Harry had not taken Northern Dancer out.

Northern Dancer's obsession with food in his racing days had been replaced by a yearning to be outdoors, free to roam. No matter how deep the snow or how severe the cold, outside was where he wanted to be. A disruption in his schedule made Northern Dancer anxious and angry.

Finally, at about ten o'clock, Harry arrived at the volatile stallion's stall. Northern Dancer reared up, slammed his right hoof on the floor and glared at Harry through the stall bars.

Harry approached him cautiously. Once he won Northern Dancer's confidence (and no doubt regained his own) he clipped the lead shank on Norther Dancer's halter and led him into the wide aisle. Out in the cold, blustery air Northern Dancer bounced and bucked happily, but instead of going to the paddock they headed down the path towards the indoor arena. Northern Dancer was about to be bred — or attempt to breed — his first mare, Flaming Page.

Flaming Page had been chosen with good reason: she was an exceptional racehorse, the best filly bred in Canada yet. Second to three-time U.S. champion Cicada in the Kentucky Oaks, Flaming Page won the Canadian Oaks, and a week later trounced the country's top colts in the 1962 Queen's Plate. (For students of divination, Flaming Page was also the seventh foal of the mare Flaming Top and from the seventh crop of the stallion Bull Page).

Equally important, Flaming Page was tall, nearly a full hand taller than Northern Dancer. While there could be no doubt now that Northern Dancer was exceptional, people continued to see his height as a problem. No one wanted foals to be built like him (not yet, at least). By matching Northern Dancer with Flaming Page it was hoped that the foal might have Flaming Page's height and body type.

Halfway down the path to the indoor arena Northern Dancer began to sense Flaming Page, and that she was in season. Once they were inside the arena, Harry could hardly restrain him. But there was a serious logistical problem. Try as he might, Northern Dancer was simply too short, and Flaming Page got so fed up she kicked him smack in the ribs.

"A very scientific solution was found," Peter Poole, the farm manager at Windfields, said, laughing.

Poole had his staff dig a shallow pit in the middle of the arena's dirt floor for the mare to stand in. They poured a concrete base, surfaced it with asphalt, and blanketed the entire area with non-slip matting. Northern Dancer was then able to consummate his relationship with Flaming Page.

Northern Dancer took to his new vocation with enthusiasm. Such was his commitment that he was prepared to service each and every one of the more than 100 mares on the Windfields property. Much to his displeasure, he had to share stallion duties with eight others, including his own sire, Nearctic.

Indeed, when another stallion was led past Northern Dancer's stall en route to the arena to breed a mare,

Northern Dancer flew into a rage. Rearing, bucking, hollering and slamming around in his stall, he kicked over water buckets and demolished feed tubs. The problem was that Northern Dancer considered all the mares on the farm to be part of his herd and, as such, he was prepared to breed each and every one of them. The sight of another stallion going toward the breeding arena made him crazed.

Putting him out in his paddock wasn't the answer — he would simply gallop himself into a lather and possibly get hurt.

Finally, the crew at the farm resorted to tying him up in his stall in these stressful situations. Since he had shown he could snap the strongest hemp, they secured him with a thick metal chain. They looped the chain round one of the vertical metal bars at the front of his stall and clipped it to the metal ring of his halter, under his chin.

Confident this would do the trick, Harry Green, Peter Poole, and the crew dispersed to tend to their other farm duties.

Seconds after they left the barn, they were startled by a crash from the direction of Northern Dancer's stall. When they rushed back to the barn the astonished horsemen found Northern Dancer hanging upside down by the chain. It seems that, chain or no chain, Northern Dancer was determined to get to the breeding arena and had attempted an escape over the top of the partition. When the men unclipped the chain he fell to the ground with a great thud.

That first season, however, he danced and pranced down the path to the arena to breed 35 mares. Northern Dancer's legacy had begun.

(From *Northern Dancer: The Legend and His Legacy*)

HAROLD THE TERRIBLE

Earl McRae

Dorothy Higgs
Beloved wife of
Harold E. Ballard
"Walked with God"
Dec. 2, 1969
Mother of Mary
William and Harold Jr.
The Lord is her shepherd
— Cemetery stone

Even now, more than ten years later, he visits her grave almost every day, arriving alone in his midnight-blue Lincoln Continental with the tinted windows, a fresh wreath on the seat beside him. In the fall and winter he removes broken twigs from the site and kicks away the dead leaves; in the spring and summer he plants fresh flowers and waters the grass. On hot summer nights when sleep won't come easily and the loneliness for her becomes a rage in his heart, he'll come after midnight, set up a lawn chair next to the stone, and sit there for hours in silent communion.

From all accounts Dorothy Ballard, whom he affectionately called "Jiggs," was a jewel of a woman, and when she was buried on that black December day after a lingering death from cancer, buried with a diamond-encrusted heart necklace — her favourite gift from him — around her throat, he returned to the big house they'd shared, locked himself in the sun room she loved so much, collapsed in a chair, and wept until the tears would come no more.

He was 65 then, and she was four years younger, the mother of his children, the hub of his universe. He'd had it all planned — the retirement from ownership of Maple Leaf Gardens and the Leaf hockey team, the world travel, tending to the flowers at their country home, easing gracefully together into a pink and pastoral twilight. But it was not to be, and there, in that sun room, a part of Harold Ballard died too, and another part took its place, an ugly growth on his psyche. It had always been there, but for her he'd kept it hidden from the public. And now, like a weed, it flourished, a defect that would later drive him to dark moments of anger and bitterness at the injustice of her death and which he would vent by striking out at the world with bullying insults and senseless cruelty, only, in the end, to lose the most important remaining treasures he had: his children.

He would come to worship at the shrine of power and greed, consumed by a lust for that icon of our national religion, the Stanley Cup, and the total redemption of sin the cup would deliver. What enemies he had to slay on the odyssey mattered not. Ballard didn't care, or if he did he couldn't help himself.

Evil forces, he was convinced, were conspiring to shatter his kingdom. Dorothy's death; the charges of tax evasion and misuse of Gardens money against him and his partner and dearest friend, Stafford Smythe; the death, only days before the trial, of Smythe (after which, on the night before the funeral, Ballard slept on a couch next to the casket, sometimes weeping, frequently getting up and opening the casket to see if Smythe was truly dead); the conviction in 1972; the one-year prison term. The humiliation. The stigma. The subsequent resolve: *Bastards! They won't break me. I'll show them.*

The terrible and inflexible pride. As if to atone for the hurt and guilt and shame he felt, he deliberately curried dislike, even hatred, flagellating a tortured soul. He trotted out the venom under the pretence of showbiz hucksterism, but as an excuse it failed. Harold Ballard became one of the most despised public figures in Canada, the recipient of hate mail and verbal crucifixion for his callous and intemperate behaviour.

For the public knew only one Ballard. The Ballard who, when the revered legend Gordie Howe scored his 1,000th career goal, refused to flash the news on the Gardens announcement board, because "a blind man can score in that [WHA] league." The Ballard who, when the Gardens press area was recently renovated, sent Foster Hewitt's famed and fabled gondola to the incinerator rather than to the Hall of Fame. The Ballard who labelled Czech defector Vaclav Nedomansky "a traitor to his homeland" for fleeing tyranny to play in North America. The Ballard who, on the CBC Radio current affairs show *As It Happens*, called host Barbara Frum a "dumb broad," told her to "shut up," and snarled that women were "only good for lying on their backs."

The Ballard who publicly questioned the ability of some of his Leaf players, the intelligence and competence of some of his coaches and general managers. The Ballard who sought a court order to prevent two of his players, Mike Palmateer and Darryl Sittler, from performing on the NHL-approved series *Showdown* and, when that failed, vetoed the telecast during Leaf games. The Ballard who, as owner of the Hamilton Tiger-Cats football club, cast the vote that vetoed the sale of the Toronto Argonauts to broadcasting mogul John Bassett for no other reason than that he hates Bassett. The Ballard who bragged on a weekend pass from prison that life on the inside was like "a high-priced motel with steaks every day, swimming and golf." The Ballard who called John Ziegler, the president of the National Hockey League, "a know-nothing shrimp," certain NHL governors "hebes," and certain black ball players "niggers."

And there are the private stories. Ballard refusing to attend the wedding of his youngest son, Harold Jr., because he didn't approve of the bride, an older divorcee with two children. Ballard kicking his oldest son, Bill, out of the

Gardens and his vice-presidency, claiming the son was plotting to overthrow him. Ballard refusing to give away his daughter, Mary Elizabeth, at her second wedding, because he didn't approve of the husband. Ballard walking in on Bill and friends at a private reception for equestrians in the Gardens Hot Stove Lounge, shouting for Bill to get out; Bill storming into his father's office, breaking down the door, overturning furniture and ripping pictures off the wall in his screaming demand to know why the old man had humiliated him. Ballard asking Harold Jr., who was employed at the Gardens box office at the time, to fake the father's signature on some 7,000 Christmas cards to be sent out to friends and business colleagues, which the son did — and then didn't receive a card from the father at Christmas. Ballard telling the children not to visit him in prison. Ballard cutting the salary of his longtime scout Bob Davidson by two-thirds to make him quit, which he did.

Ballard refusing to speak to a *Toronto Star* sportswriter, Frank Orr, because he didn't like a particular column and then calling the heterosexual Orr "a queer" behind his back. Ballard, during a minor fire in a Montreal hotel where the NHL governors were meeting, shouting, "Too bad that goddam Snider wasn't in it," in reference to the Philadelphia Flyers owner, Ed Snider, whom Ballard detests for his support of an NHL merger with the WHA. Ballard refusing the delivery of a new Lincoln, done up in Maple Leaf colours, by telling the salesman, "Looks like a bloody circus wagon — take it over to the sheenies on Spadina Avenue."

Friends, family and enemies have searched for explanations for the squalls in the Ballard bloodstream and have come up with creeping senility, maybe, or the poison of absolute power. "He's the crudest, rudest person I've ever known," says Frank Orr. "The way he treats his players, the way he runs the show. And yet he's a loser. He hasn't won a thing since he became the sole owner of the club." Ed Snider says, "Ballard is a disgrace to hockey. His racism, his bully tactics. I have no time for him."

Harold Jr., 32, an artist now selling cars, says, "We've never measured up to his expectations. My wife, my girl-friends before, Bill's girlfriends, they never measured up to our mom in his eyes." Harold Jr. accepts the notion that Ballard wears the death of his wife and the prison sen-tence like a crown of thorns. "He's our father and we love him, but he makes it hard sometimes." Says Bill, 33, a lawyer turned concert promoter, "He can't understand my world, nor does he want to." Mary Richards, the sister of his late wife, says, "He hasn't been the same since Dorothy died. He'd never say the things he says or be the way he is if she was alive today. He's a wonderful man, Harold, but he's lonely. With Dorothy gone, he just decided he doesn't care anymore, nothing can hurt him."

Red Foster, 75, an advertising executive and old friend, says, "You never saw a closer, more loving family when Dorothy was alive and the kids were younger. He seemed a man at peace with himself. There was none of this vin-dictiveness." And from Munson Campbell, another long-time friend and a former NHL owner: "I think he'd love to reconcile with the kids. I know he does love them, but he just doesn't know *how*. It's that damn pride. It's a tragedy, really."

"Children," snaps Harold Ballard, "are like dogs. They come up, sniff your crotch, you pat 'em on the head, say 'Nice Fido, now screw off.' My kids don't bother me, I don't bother them. I don't understand them or their friends, they don't understand me. I don't want to be a burden on them."

It's 5:30 a.m. and Ballard is in his apartment in the Gardens, making breakfast of peanut butter on toast. He had the apartment built not long after Dorothy's death; he could no longer live in the big house with the memo-ries of her presence, her perfume. When Mary Elizabeth innocently removed her mother's slippers from beneath her bed — three months after her death — Ballard went wild with anger and had them put back. To this day the house is exactly as Dorothy left it. And so it will remain.

Ballard is 76 but looks much younger. He doesn't drink

or smoke. He does sit-ups and push-ups and lifts weights in the Leaf training room when the players aren't around. He sleeps no more than two hours a night. He sits up most of the night answering his mail, the good and the bad. He loves the mail. It's the payoff. Proof that he matters. Ballard enjoys good health, but he is diabetic. He injects himself with 40 units of insulin a day, 25 more than prescribed. "That," he chortles, "is because I love eating ice-cream and chocolates every day. Doctors don't know how I'm still alive. I say it's all in the head anyway, diabetes." He wears a copper bracelet for a touch of arthritis in his right hand. And his office chair is fitted with a vibrating device for his back, which is sometimes sore. "Never use it. That's all in the head, too."

Ballard is a vain man. A huge portrait of himself hangs on a wall overlooking his bed. He carries a stack of picture postcards of himself in his jacket pocket at all times to give out to autograph seekers. He has his hair styled once a month, his fingernails lacquered, his teeth cleaned. Ballard swears a lot, laughs a lot, and likes telling dirty stories. Nude centrefolds from girlie magazines plaster one of the doors in his apartment. He has, he says, lots of girlfriends. "Just like the players, I got 'em in every city," he roars. "And I can still handle 'em too. The one in New York's a real beaut. When I'm horny I fly down for a quickie."

He admits he's an ultrachauvinist. "Goddam right. Can't stand those feminist broads. Bunch of frustrated old maids. You should have heard them phoning me after the Barbara Frum thing. I had all the calls put right through to me. I'd say, 'Hi, honey, whatsamatter, can't get a man today? Y'after my body?' Boy, they went nuts. Loved it. *Loved* it." He's not, he says, a racist. "Look, I'm liable to say anything. It means nothing. People are so goddam thin-skinned today. Call a Jap a Jap and you're labelled a racist, and all kinds of human rights groups and academic types are out for your hide. Christ, you call a Chevrolet a Chev, don't ya? As for the Nedomansky thing, I just said it to get the ink. Look, I hate Commies. When I was in

Moscow for the '72 series, I slapped a Leaf sticker on that Commie Lenin's tomb. That's what I think of those jerks. Why do you think I won't let the Leafs play them?"

Finally, there is another Harold Ballard, the one he strives desperately to hide for fear it will unravel all the bad will he feels it necessary to foster. Alan Eagleson, the executive director of the NHL Players' Association, the agent for several Leaf players and Ballard's arch enemy in the hockey wars, puts it best: "If I ever needed $100,000, Harold Ballard would be the first to give it to me. Privately, we're great friends. Harold's talk is just that. He loves stirring up things. But what the public gets is not the *real* Harold Ballard."

The real Ballard is also the man who, when Eagleson's parents celebrated their 50th wedding anniversary, sent them 50 red roses, a warm letter praising their son and a wish that he and Dorothy could have celebrated theirs, too. The man who, when a black man was brought aboard a plane in Chicago, his feet amputated due to frostbite, had the stewardesses give the man $250 but not say what seat it came from. The man who, when a Jewish friend recently went bankrupt, gave him money to start up again. The man who loads his car with gifts and food at Christmas and has a driver deliver them to Toronto hostels and missions. The man who, when John Bassett Jr., the son of his hated foe, was in the hospital with cancer, visited him every day. The man who, when a little old lady had to pay a $25 food bill at a supermarket checkout counter, signalled the cashier to give the bill to him, instead. The man who for Christmas gives his players TVs, radios, microwave ovens and airplane tickets to anywhere in the world. The man who gave Darryl Sittler an $8,000 antique silver tea service for scoring ten points in one game. Who gave Paul Henderson shares in the Gardens for scoring the winning goal against the Soviets in the 1972 series. Who every year cries at the sight of wrestler Whipper Billy Watson carrying the little crippled boy at the sportswriters' banquet for charity. Who gives more than $250,000 a year to societies for the deaf, the crippled and the retarded. The man who, when the late Leaf Tim Horton needed money to start his doughnut business, provided it.

"You know," says Ballard. "I'm not really that bad a guy. It's just that if you mention those things every leech in the country will be on me. But you couldn't be married to Dorothy and not be that way. God, she was wonderful. The best thing that ever happened to me. I see all the parasites and bums in society, giving nothing, sponging, and they just seem to coast right along. Then I remember Dorothy, that lovely woman who did only good and..." Harold Ballard can't finish the sentence for the tears.

Four a.m. Maple Leaf Gardens. All is silent. All is still. A chunky figure suddenly appears on the ice, ghostly in the cathedral-like glow from the surface. He skates up and down, as he often does at this hour, firing a puck into the net, against the boards, echoing in the dark and hollow void. He is utterly alone, but in his mind the Gardens is filled and the crowd is cheering and waving and calling his name, and then, in triumph, in glory, the Stanley Cup is brought to centre ice and placed in his hands. He touches it, strokes it, and smiles his beautiful smile, and at that moment all the guilt, all the hurts, all the wrongs are forever vanquished. Harold Ballard is a winner at last. He will think of Dorothy. And look for the children.

(First appeared in the *Ottawa Sun*)

CANADA FROM EH TO ZED

Alison Gordon

We're pretty excited about the World Series up here in Canada, home of the Arctic mass. From Kamloops, British Columbia, to Come-By-Chance, Newfoundland, fans are putting aside their traditional loathing of trendy Toronto to wave the Blue Jay banner and the maple leaf flag. (By the way, we traditionally do the latter with the leaf pointy-side up.) We've abandoned our usual national chant — "We're Number Two! We're Number Two!" — for a coast-to-coast chorus of "OK Blue Jays! Let's Play Ball!"

Reports filtering north lead us to believe that you Americans welcome the internationalization of the Fall Classic with the enthusiasm you would normally reserve for a plague of locusts. We're sorry you feel that way. Really we are. Maybe you would change your mind if you learned a little more about your neighbours north of the world's longest undefended border.

We're only trying to help, eh?

A is for AMERICANS, which all the Blue Jays are, all the ones who aren't from Puerto Rico, Jamaica, or the Dominican Republic. There are those who would make a big deal out of this, but we haven't noticed how many Atlanta Braves were born in Georgia or, for that matter, have aboriginal blood in their veins.

B is for BUNTING. In the United States it's red, white and blue. In Canada, it's our favourite offensive weapon. Just ask Jimy Williams (he who learned how to spell his first name from Dan Quayle).

Williams, the Atlanta third base coach is, of course, a former Blue Jay manager. In the winter before taking over as the Jays skipper, he was trotted around the annual banquet circle to rally the fans. At a dinner in Ottawa, Williams was asked, not for the first time, if he planned to use the bunt more than his predecessors had. "What is it with you Canadians?" he asked, clearly exasperated. "You all think the bunt is God Almighty."

Well, why not. Bunting is a very Canadian thing to do: obedient, modest, self-effacing, efficient, polite. As a baseball tactic, it practically screams out, "Excuse me." The home run is American; the bunt is Canadian, and when the bunter is done he trots politely to the dugout, embarrassed by the applause.

C is for CUSTOMS, which you have to clear before you can come here to watch the World Series. You must have some identification — a passport if possible — but there are no skill-testing questions.

You have to leave your weapons at home if you want to come north. Our gun-control laws are stricter than yours, so handguns are not welcome. This week border guards are probably confiscating tomahawks, too.

D is for Dominican Republic, the other nation with a significant rooting interest in this Series. Dominican fans figured to be rooting wholeheartedly for the Blue Jays, what with pitching sensation Juan Guzman being a national hero in the Dominican Republic now, and Manuel Lee and Alfredo Griffin being not far behind. But then, of course, Francisco Cabrera, another Dominican, did his ninth-inning number for the Braves against the Pirates, becoming an instant celebrity and creating some confused loyalties down on the island.

E is for EXCUSE ME, which is what a Canadian says when you step on his foot. Apology is the Canadian way, part of our national inferiority complex.

F is for Jane FONDA, last Friday's "Sunshine Girl" in the tabloid *Toronto Sun*. On its front page the paper ran a full-colour picture of Mrs. Ted Turner wearing a Blue Jays sweater, holding up her fingers in a victory sign. The *Sun*, known mainly for its pinup photos, right-wing views and bite-sized articles, explained in fine print that the photo had been taken a few years ago, when Ms. Fonda was not yet a baseball wife. Which didn't stop Torontonians from posting it on every fridge door in the city.

F is also for the folks at FITNESS ONTARIO, who lead the exercises that make up the seventh-inning stretch at the SkyDome, a quaint custom of which we are sure Ms. Fonda will approve.

G is for Cito GASTON, who has so far brought three division championships and one pennant to Toronto in four seasons as the Blue Jays' manager. And every night on the phone-in shows, someone says he should be fired. Go figure. The players love him because he leaves them alone and lets them do their jobs. The know-all fans hate him because they can't see his wheels turning. That he is also one of only two black managers in baseball is something Canadian fans stopped noticing a long time ago.

H is for HANLAN'S POINT, in Toronto, where Babe Ruth hit his first professional home run. You could look it up. H, therefore, is also for baseball HISTORY, which I bet you didn't think we had.

I is for IGLOOS. There are very few of them in downtown Toronto. Ditto bobsleds, beavers, grizzly bears, and moose. How can you tell an American tourist? He's the one who brings skis along for a holiday in July.

J is for Peter JENNINGS. Did you know he's Canadian? So are Paul Anka, Anne Murray, Oscar Peterson, Michael Myers, Alex Trebec, Robert MacNeil and Donald Sutherland. We may be an alien nation, but we're a bigger part of your culture than you know. Watch out.

K is for KILOMETRES, kilograms, litres, and degrees

Celsius. It's 100 metres from home plate to the left-field corner at SkyDome. Like most of the civilized world, Canada is metric, so our measurements may seem a bit strange to you. Don't worry about it. We'll translate. (You may have noticed already that we spell like the British: Devon White labours in centre field.)

L is for LANGUAGES, of which we have two official ones, English and French. Atlanta right-fielder Dave Justice thinks he knows all about it. In a pre-Series interview, he described a visit to Toronto. "I didn't go walking around much," he said, "because if I got lost and I encountered someone speaking French, I knew I had no chance. So I just kind of stayed in my hotel room."

He needn't have worried. In Toronto he would have been more likely to encounter someone speaking Italian or Portuguese. But American fans should perhaps learn a few French phrases in preparation for next year's all-Canadian World Series, when the Montreal Expos will represent the National League. A strike is a *prise*, an out is a *retrait*, and a home run is a *circuit*.

M is for funny MONEY: our two-dollar bills are pink, our five-dollar bills are blue, and our ten-dollar bills purple. We haven't got any dollar bills, just coins we call loonies. This is because they have the image of a loon on the flip side of the portrait of Queen Elizabeth, although these days a lot of us think that it's because anyone who believes the dollar has any real worth is ready for the loony bin. Over the years, Blue Jay players have been known to laugh at our money all the way to the bank.

N is for the NETWORKS. Not that we want to point any fingers. That would be rude, and Canadians are never rude, but we wish some of the television commentators in the U.S. would do their homework and get some basic facts right. Excuse me, CBS, but Toronto is on Lake Ontario, not Lake Erie. And CNN, for your information, Duane Ward and Tom Henke are not a "lefty-righty tandem." They both pitch from the right side. And very well, too. This kind of thing drives us bonkers.

O is for O CANADA, the Canadian national anthem,

never before played at a World Series game until now. It's easier to sing than yours.

O is also for OK BLUE JAYS, the irritating song played during our seventh-inning fitness break.

P is for the PRIME MINISTER, Brian Mulroney, who is in almost as much trouble as your President, and also for the PREMIER of Ontario, Bob Rae. He's a socialist (that's allowed up here) and a real baseball fan. The son of a diplomat, he rooted for the Washington Senators when his family was posted there. He was also Richard Nixon's paper boy, and some analysts assume a connection between the size of the tips Mrs. Nixon gave him and his eventual leftward leanings.

Q is for QUEEN ELIZABETH II, who is Canada's head of state. There has been some confusion about what will happen when the Blue Jays win the World Series. Will President Bush invite them to the White House? Why should he? They're Canada's team. We think they should be invited to Buckingham Palace ("Will that be milk or lemon with your tea, Mr. Alomar?")

R is for the ROYAL CANADIAN MOUNTED POLICE. You'll see their scarlet tunics and flat-brimmed hats during the opening ceremonies, but don't expect to see them directing traffic in those getups. The Nelson Eddy paraphernalia is strictly for the tourists.

S is for SEAGULLS, which you won't see inside SkyDome, for which Toronto slugger Dave Winfield is grateful. When the Blue Jays played in Exhibition Stadium on the lakefront, sea gulls were natural outfield hazards. In 1983 Winfield, who was then playing for the Yankees, astonished everyone, including himself, by killing one when he tossed a warmup ball toward the bullpen. He was arrested by an overzealous member of the local constabulary and charged with cruelty to animals.

Whenever Winfield returned to Toronto, seagulls with long memories gathered in right field and dive-bombed him, anxious for vengeance. This year he's mobbed only by adoring fans.

T is for TORONTO. On October 26 Canadians will

be voting in a referendum on national unity. The measure is complex (suffice it to say you vote either Yes or No), but it's sort of like your upcoming election: Each alternative is as distasteful as the other.

Some of the tall foreheads in political office hope that the presence of the Blue Jays in the World Series will make all Canadians feel so warm and fuzzy that we will vote Yes. Others feel that this is wishful thinking and that the Yes team must be pretty desperate to be looking to the ball diamond for salvation. Still others believe that since the referendum is non-binding, it's nothing more than an extremely expensive opinion poll and we might as well forget it and enjoy the ball game. You can see why the World Series is a welcome distraction.

V is for VELEZ, an original Blue Jay and part of the small tradition we have scraped together in 16 years in the big leagues. Longtime fans took a moment to remember him and all the others who had the misfortune to be Blue Jays at the wrong time.

W is for the WAR OF 1812. We won. You lost.

X is for X-RATED interludes. There haven't been any since May 15, 1990, when an amorous couple in one of the stadium-view hotel rooms at SkyDome found an original way to pass the time during a boring game against the Mariners. After the love-birds were spotted in their window by a killjoy columnist who blew the whistle on them, all guests checking into those rooms have to sign an indemnity agreement not to make whoopee with the curtains open.

Y is for YANKEES, the hatred of whom is the only thing fans in Atlanta and Toronto have in common.

Z is for Z. We pronounce it Zed. You wanna make something of it?

MIRACLE KID

Cam Cole

My hero takes the long snaps and pins the ball for the placekicker of the Edmonton Huskies. I have never seen him play.

He is the No. 2 quarterback of the Huskies and unless the starter, Cory Pradine, gets hit by a bus my hero may not get to play a down at the position of his dreams this season — his first and last as a junior football player.

But that's OK with me. He doesn't have to be the quarterback to be my hero. He just has to keep on being Olwen Lepps. He just has to keep on being.

Olwen Lepps lost his right eye to retinal cancer at age five. He had two more bouts with cancer, glandular tumours on the left side of his neck when he was 12 and again when he was 18, and he just kept going. Chemotherapy, radiation, surgery, rehabilitation... and sports. He loved sports so much he willed himself past all the obstacles.

"I don't deserve this," says Olwen Lepps, self-consciously submitting to an interview while his teammates walk past, kidding him.

"Hey, O.J., make sure to mention my name!" they say, and he laughs. O.J., that's what they call my hero. As in Olwen Junior.

"I feel kind of bad for the guys," he says. "A lot of players on the team really deserve this kind of attention. They're good players and they're working so hard and what can you write about me? That I have really great pin-ning techniques? I don't think I deserve to have a story written about me. If we won a championship and I was an integral part of it, that's when I'd say, 'Hey, now I've really done something!'"

Well, maybe it's just me but I have an idea he already has done something. Something harder than anything Wayne Gretzky or Warren Moon or Jari Kurri or Brian Kelly ever did — or any of the other athletes I've covered and thought of, in their way, as heroes.

Olwen Lepps got past the cancer to become, by the end of his senior year at Bonnie Doon, the school's Haliburton Trophy nominee as the outstanding player in Edmonton high school football, and was asked to sign a letter of intent to play football at the University of North Dakota.

Then he began having heart problems. Serious prob-lems. He tried twice to make the Huskies, in 1988 and again in 1989, and failed the medical examination both times.

"His heart output was only 12 per cent of what it should have been," says head trainer Shirley Fell. "He could have suffered a heart attack walking down the street, never mind playing football."

Olwen Lepps was crushed. A coach remembers him leaving the medical room in tears when he was told he could never play football in his condition.

"The second year, I was a little more prepared," he says. "I mean, I kept talking about how I trained harder and was in better shape but I knew I was getting progres-sively worse. You know, shortness of breath, chest pains."

The coaches kept him around awhile, hoping he would be satisfied with keeping statistics, but that's not what Olwen wanted and eventually he just faded from the scene.

"I'd kind of lost track of him until this spring when we had our minicamp," says Fell.

One day in early May Olwen Lepps, aged 22, walked into Huskie House in the river valley and said, "You told me I had a bad heart. Well, I got a new one." And smiled a brilliant smile.

"Just like that," said head coach Norm Brown. "It was the damnedest thing."

Olwen Lepps had never let illness stop him. Not ever. Sometimes he did ridiculous things. He had been hospitalized more than once with what amounted to heart failure and yet last New Year's he went on a ski trip. When he returned he had his worst attack yet. The 12 per cent heart was not going to make it.

On January 5 Dr. Dennis Modry removed Olwen Lepp's heart and transplanted a healthy heart into his body at the University of Alberta Hospital. Twelve days later Olwen walked out of the Heart and Lung Transplant Clinic and five months after that he was throwing footballs and taking hits and doing the thing that only he truly believed he could do: playing quarterback in the Prairie Junior Football Conference.

"I have to say I was a little tentative about taking that first hit," says Olwen. "I mean, any time you're stitched up you're a little nervous about busting it open, I guess. But the first hit — I played a quarter and a half in a pre-season game in Calgary — was straight on the chest, almost as though the guy meant to test it. And it was fine."

"We talked about whether it was safe but there is always risk with this sort of edge-of-the-envelope stuff," says Dr. Terrance Montague, one of a team of specialists who supervised the rehabilitation of their most remarkable patient. "The thing is, if we can't get the patient back to this sort of lifestyle you have to question whether the whole damn program is worthwhile. But Olwen is a pretty remarkable fellow irrespective of his heart problems."

"He's got an indomitable personality," chuckles Dr. Modry. "He reminds me of that fellow in the Monty Python movie, the black knight who's defending the bridge and keeps getting parts of his body lopped off by a swordsman but refuses to admit he's hurt. Olwen just won't give up."

"Olwen took us [the transplant procedure] to the moon," said Dr. Montague. "If you've seen pictures of the early spacecraft you know that technology wasn't the only thing that put man on the moon. It was the guys who were willing to sit inside those things and extend the envelope."

Olwen Lepps wanted to play football. He would do anything, try anything, take any chance. The danger was not a factor, although it was for his mother, Mavis, a child-care worker, and his father, Oliver, who owns an automotive shop.

"Right now, I'll tell you, my mother is not loving what I'm doing," says Olwen. "But they're both behind me."

Mavis speaks slowly in a voice that carries a light accent of Guyana where the Lepps family moved from when Olwen, the fifth of six children, was 16 months old.

"I wish he would be careful but it's hard to play football and be careful," she says. "He's pretty headstrong, yes, but I guess he has to be to cope with everything that's happened."

She would love to be told that her son is going to make it now, that his troubles are behind him at last, but...

"The doctors really can't say that. They're not God. But God has spared his life so far and if this is what he wants, if it's the only thing that will make him happy, we have to let him go. He's an adult now."

In truth, Olwen Lepps is not out of the woods yet.

"When you've had a heart transplant your automatic nervous system doesn't work properly," says Shirley Fell. "Normally, when you run your heart beats faster. O.J.'s doesn't. So he has to warm up slowly."

A more serious problem is that the drugs used to ensure that the body accepts the new heart suppress the body's immune system. The patient, explained Dr. Montague, becomes like an AIDS victim, susceptible to infections. The immune deficiency is not caused by a virus but by drugs. In a case like Olwen's, medication might allow cancer an unimpeded return.

But if Olwen Lepps were going to worry about cancer he'd have given up long ago.

"You get to the point," he says, "where they come to you and say, 'You have cancer,' and you go, 'OK, OK, let's take care of it and go on from there.'"

That was his childhood, that and radiation treatments every morning before classes in junior high school. He was 12 then, confronting the first serious roadblock to an athletic career.

"I've been faced with controversy from Day One," he says. "In bantam football they said, 'Listen, kid, don't you know you've got one eye? Get serious. You can't play.'"

But Brendan Doyle, now an assistant coach with the Huskies, was his coach in bantam, and went to the Edmonton Eskimos for help. Equipment man Dwayne Mandrusiak fitted a mask to Olwen's helmet, the same contraption middle linebacker Dan Kepley had used the previous season when he played with a broken jaw.

The mask and a signed waiver from his parents satisfied the league and Olwen was on his way. Today he wears a clear plexiglass visor over the top half of his facemask.

But it has not all been smooth sailing. The glass eye and the scar from cancer surgery are impossible to miss. Olwen is unmistakably "handicapped" in the eyes of those who see him for the first time, and it has been his lifelong struggle to eliminate that mind set.

"I've been the one-eyed quarterback forever, so that's no big deal," he says. "It's good on this team that we've got to the stage where the guys joke about it. I'd rather that than have everybody tiptoe around and whisper, 'Ooh, that's the transplant guy; don't crack any heart jokes.' I had to make sure nobody had reason to say, 'Hey, what's he getting special treatment for?'"

Clearly, he has succeeded. He is the No. 2 quarterback on merit and gets as much abuse as everyone else.

"He throws a good ball, he's a leader and in the huddle the guys respect him," says Coach Brown. "That's why he's on the team."

"O.J. is so smart and so conscious of where everyone is on the field," says Brendan Dolan, the assistant coach. "He adjusts for that eye. He can throw the long ball, then come right back and throw the short one perfectly. I've seen him roll the wrong way, wrong for his good eye, and then turn and throw back to the opposite side and I'll say, 'How the heck did you see the receiver?' and he'll say, 'I knew he'd be there.'"

"There's a lot of timing and memorization for me," says Olwen. "I count on the receivers to run precision patterns and knowing where they are."

The coaches marvel at his ability to compensate for his lack of depth perception, which should be a killer for a quarterback.

"I played basketball in high school and became not a bad outside shooter," says Olwen. "But then what else could I be? I'm only 5-foot-8."

He has a self-effacing sense of humour and is smart. His doctors, Modry and Montague, agree that he is a spectacular advertisement for heart transplants and have enlisted his help in talking to patients waiting for new hearts. He provides inspiration.

Olwen has been building an immunity to fear since he was five. He looks ahead in life the way any young man pondering university might.

"I hope this doesn't sound conceited, but I don't see a limitation," he says. "I mean, I probably would never be a doctor — for one thing I don't have the brain capacity. I'm an above-average student but that's with a lot of hard work. For another reason, I'm not sure I want to spend any more time around hospitals. If I go back to university, who knows, maybe I could make the Golden Bears and finish my career there even if it meant sitting on the bench."

"I guess O.J. doesn't have any problems, just challenges," says Coach Brown. "He's an inspiration. When I see guys going into the ice room with an owie on their arm or a twinge in the groin, and then I look at O.J. and what he's overcome…"

The heart surgeon, Dr. Modry, doesn't worry about Olwen. "We told him that as long as he's in good shape he shouldn't hurt himself. People have run marathons, triathlons, and climbed mountains with new hearts. That's pretty remarkable when you think they've gone from death's door to elite athlete.

"I'll tell you one thing: if I were that starting quarterback I'd worry. Once Olwen Lepps sets his heart on something there's no slowing him down."

Olwen Lepps is alive and well and living in Grande Prairie, Alta. After finishing up his junior career, he made the University of Alberta football team and spent four seasons with the Golden Bears. He graduated with a Bachelor or Education degree in May 1995, and now teaches high school in Sexsmith, Alta., where he is also the head football coach. At 27, his heart is still in the right place, and works just fine.

(First appeared in the *Edmonton Journal*)

RUSSIAN DAWN

Jim Proudfoot

Five of the Soviet Union's greatest players could be competing in the National Hockey League a year from this fall.

Victor Tikhonov, coach of the Soviet national team, confirmed last night that there is an excellent chance two defencemen and a complete forward line will be given official permission to emigrate after taking part in the Olympic tournament at Calgary next February.

The NHL wasn't specified but it would be the logical destination for defencemen Vacheslav Fetisov and Alexei Kasatonov, centre Igor Larionov and his wingers, Sergei Makarov and Vladimir Krutov. This quintet is the starting unit for the Red Army, Soviet champion the last 11 seasons, and for Tikhonov's highly successful nationals. They have worked together since Larionov's arrival in 1981.

This signals a complete change of thinking in the Soviet Union because, previously, a man like Tikhonov would have ridiculed the very suggestion that one of his players would go abroad and become and out-and-out professional. Now he is saying nothing could be more reasonable.

There are those who contend that Fetisov is the best defencemen anywhere hockey is played. Fetisov himself doesn't dispute the proposition and, as a matter of fact, wouldn't mind having an opportunity to furnish further evidence to support it. He, too, has reason to believe this very thing is about to happen — possibly in time for the 1988-89 NHL season.

Fetisov definitely thinks he can see the day quickly coming when Soviet veterans will be permitted to go abroad to complete their careers — in the NHL, obviously. And he hopes such a policy will be enacted before it's too late for him. At 29, he is about the begin his 11th season with the Soviet national side, and his eighth as captain.

Fetisov would never defect, though. Oh, no. This subject was broached in conversation here in Stockholm while the redshirts of Moscow were in town for some Canada Cup rehearsals. Some notable fugitives were mentioned, like ballet dancers Rudolf Nureyev and Mikhail Baryshnikov. Why not a hockey player? Fetisov thought it a reasonable question.

"I am aware I could earn a great deal of money in the NHL," Fetisov said. "And yes, there have been offers. I won't say where from. Also, I don't suppose it would have been very difficult, during some of the tours we've made.

"But hockey players grow up with a strong love of the motherland. It is part of us. There is a bond that none of us would ever break. To go away, with no chance of returning — that is impossible to imagine."

Still there is a new mood afoot in Soviet society. Rules once held sacred are being relaxed under the Mikhail Gorbachev regime. And Fetisov feels the climate may be favourable at last for an exodus of hockey talent at the highest international level. Czechoslovakia did it with standouts like Miroslav Dvorak, who spent three years in the NHL with the Philadelphia Flyers, and Jiri Bubla, a Vancouver defenceman for five winters. Basically, they were just exported for limited periods, and in exchange for hard currency. Fetisov would be delighted to be the first Russian shipped overseas under similar circumstances.

Tikhonov took matters a step further after last night's exhibition victory over Sweden. "This has been discussed by our federation," Tikhonov said, "and I believe it is at least a possibility that is open for negotiation."

The skaters mentioned, of course, are five of the best

players ever to represent the Soviet Union internationally and for them, emigration could only mean the NHL. If
they really did become available, you would see the
wildest scramble in NHL history. Each would have to go
through the yearly NHL amateur draft or, because of their
sheer magnitude, some special distribution process.

Fetisov didn't specify which NHL uniform he'd want
to wear if the possibility were to arise next winter but
only agreed he would welcome a chance to test his skills
on a regular basis in North American rinks.

"Playing for both the Army club in Moscow and also
on the national selection has been a difficult life and I am
beginning to feel tired," he admitted. "Here am I, only 29,
and this could be my last season of international hockey.

"For example, we began training on dry land at the
end of June. I was on the ice with Army July 10, and with
the national side July 25. Now there is the Canada Cup
and after that our normal season, except that the Olympic
tournament is coming too. The pace is always hectic, and
I can now understand what Vladislav Tretiak meant when
he said he was worn out and couldn't continue.

"That is what I admire about Wayne Gretzky in
Canada. He maintains such tremendous quality in his
hockey year after year, no matter how difficult the schedule becomes. For me, he is the best of the present players,
although there could never be one like my countryman,
the late Valery Kharlamov. He was our greatest star."

Fetisov would be the perfect person to spearhead a
Soviet invasion of the NHL. He is like Denis Potvin, cruel
and efficient in his own zone and utterly dynamic on the
attack — possibly Russia's first genuine big leaguer.
Kasatonov is almost a duplicate. The trouble with an NHL
draft is obvious. It would separate Makarov, Larionov and
Krutov. They have toiled collectively as a forward line
since 1981. Makarov, the 29-year-old right wing, is exceptional. He has been a Soviet allstar in each of the last
nine seasons. Fetisov and Kasatonov are next with eight
selections. Krutov and Larionov are only 27, you see. They
haven't had as long to dominate.

The Soviets presumably would have to pass through the NHL amateur draft, as did the Czechoslovakian veterans when they were exported. Though each of the Soviet Union's so-called Big Five has been taken in previous drafts, those commitments have evidently expired. So Fetisov, Makarov, and the others would become the big prizes of 1988.

"A draft?" chuckled Igor Dmitriev, who is expected to become Soviet national coach after the Olympics. "I have an idea for you, my friend. Take the whole five home to Toronto. Then the Maple Leafs will never lose again."

(Jim Proudfoot filed this story to his paper, The Toronto Star, *in August 1987 upon learning that the Soviets, in the early stages of* glasnost, *were considering exporting hockey talent. This was a giant breakthrough, though the story was denied everywhere. In fact, Fetisov and the others weren't allowed out until 1989, so Proudfoot was more than a year early with his scoop.*

A STAGGERING MARATHON

Milt Dunnell

Canadian amateur sport had its greatest day and its darkest moments in front of the biggest crowd that ever paid to see amateurs play in this country.

The fondest hopes had been exceeded when both Dr. Roger Bannister of England and John Landy of Australia broke the four-minute mark in Saturday's miracle mile, highlight of the British Empire and Commonwealth Games. The paid audience of 32,500 and millions who watched via TV elevated amateur sport to a lofty pedestal. And then it happened.

Over the PA system it was announced that the first marathon runner was approaching the stadium. The announcer added: "He looks in bad shape." The press box snickered.

The sports writers knew the leader was the veteran Jim Peters of England, a noted showman, whose running style copies the agonies of the great Emil Zatopek.

But one look at Peters convinced the most hardened cynic that this was no case of showboating. Peters wobbled through the gate at the north end of the stadium on legs that might have been licorice sticks. He looked wildly around the packed park, which suddenly was hushed.

There's a graded runway from the gate to the running

track at that end of the stadium. Peters couldn't navigate it. He sprawled in the dust, rolled over, got up on one knee and finally struggled to his feet again.

He took maybe half-a-dozen drunken steps. Then down he went again. It took longer to reach his shaky pins this time. Spectators in the rush end began pleading with him to quit. Peters looked at them stupidly.

Finally, he reached the track. Instinct made his feet go. He travelled a few yards, then crumpled in a heap. To make a sordid story short, he was down a dozen times in 120 yards. Among those who watched the sickening show was the Duke of Edinburgh.

In the end, Peters was disqualified when he apparently thought he had reached his goal. He fell into the arms of the English masseur, Mick Mays, after crossing the finish line of the mile for the sprints and relays. But it wasn't the finish line for the marathon.

By this time, women were being hauled from their seats in a dead faint. Men were screaming, "Is this what you call sport?" There were folks in the stands who looked as white as Peters. Seldom in the history of Canadian sport has there been such an outcry against a single incident.

But it's old stuff for the marathoners. Another English favourite, Stanley Cox, ran into a lamp post after 23 miles of Saturday's race and knocked himself cold. They carted him off in an ambulance.

The very first marathoner of all time dropped dead after carrying the news of the battle of Marathon to Athens.

In 1908 at the Olympics in London there was the closest thing to what happened here Saturday. The favourite, Dorando of Italy, collapsed near the finish line. Some of his supporters carried him over the line and raised his hand in victory. But it was no dice. John Hayes of the U.S. was declared the winner.

Maybe it isn't sport, as the townfolks are screaming here, but you certainly have to agree that it isn't a profession.

(Reprinted with permission from *The Toronto Star* Syndicate)

BRAWL IN THE FAMILY

Gare Joyce

Behind the trademark reflecting sunglasses, bedecked in his pink and black tights, beneath the glare of television lights, Bret "The Hitman" Hart — 235 Calgary-born pounds of the stuff that heroes are made of — is set to take on the world wrestling champion, Rick "Nature Boy" Flair, the lasciv-ious peroxide blond regarded by the *cognoscenti* as the greatest wrestler of his generation and by all fair-minded folks as a real rotter. Flair could have scratched out of this title match at Saskatchewan Place in Saskatoon last October. He apparently suffered an inner-ear injury a few days before and has been advised by doctors to take a month off the circuit. A wrestler, however, wins the respect of his peers by his willingness to get into the ring with injury, to avoid the no-show. Flair has the respect of his fellow pros but the sympathies of the generally unwashed crowd are summed up in three words: "Flair, you suck."

The old industry joke goes: Q. What has 100 legs and 40 teeth? A. The first two rows at a wrestling match. To this loyal throng — pubescent fantasists, bikers, loud, round women who drink at the Legion, working stiffs, and a few slumming semiologists — a world-championship match involving a true Canadian is the Stanley Cup, World Series, and Olympics rolled into one.

Wise guys will always deride pro wrestling and call it "phoney," "fake," or "just theatre." Of course the nay-sayers have never attended a live show and scrutinized the action. "They've probably never taken a shot in the squash either," Hart says. For those in attendance, the matches shock because of the quantity and the degree of contact. In the first minute of this showdown, Hart suffers a severely sprained ankle. His punches raise welts on Flair's face and compound the champion's vertigo. After five minutes of action Hart notices that one of his fingers is jutting out at an odd angle. Recognizing this as a simple dislocation, he pulls the finger back into the socket and goes back to work.

Stu Hart, the father of The Hitman, sits in the stands, wringing his oft-broken hands. A former promoter and wrestler himself, Stu Hart still has some celebrity in Saskatoon. He has been brought in from his home in Calgary and introduced to the crowd for the sake of nostalgia, a remembrance of eye-gouges past. Watching the action in the ring, seeing Bret take the fight to Flair, Stu recognizes moves he taught his son. And though the game has changed a lot, Stu knows you can't fake a dislocated finger.

Two hundred and fifty nights a year, Bret Hart slams into turnbuckles, jumps off top-ropes, kisses canvases, lets blood, and peers out into unsightly mobs. Hart broke into the pro game 16 years ago, working on small regional wrestling circuits before a few hundred fans. Today he plies his trade in arenas throughout North America, Europe, and Japan. He has performed before as many as 93,000 fans at one live card and millions more on pay-per-view television. *Western Report* calls him "almost certainly the best known Albertan on earth." The Hitman would accuse that august publication of thinking small. He operates on the assumption that the Harts are Canada's first family of sports and that he is nothing less than the nation's greatest athlete. Camp it ain't.

In a demimonde populated with caricatures, Bret Hart is simply a character, the closest a wrestler might come to The Everyman. "I'm basically good but I can be as bad as I have to be," he explains. The wrestling crew divides evenly between baby-faces (sugar-coated goody-two-shoes) and heels (evil incarnate). Matchmakers and promoters draw heat (create fan interest) by shooting angles (developing story lines and conflict between wrestlers). Surrounded by a comic-book cast that includes a catwalk-obsessed GQ fashion plate, a sword-wielding Viking, a Ugandan cannibal, an unscrupulous billionaire, a heartless tax man, and other broadly drawn no-goodniks, Hart provides relief in both substance and style. Hart has no shtick. His nickname, The Hitman, connotes nothing other than the finality of his finishing moves. Though he bears the stamp of the common man, it is in no way the imprint of mediocrity. For more than a year, Hart owned the Intercontinental Belt, the second-most prized not to mention bejewelled accessory in the World Wrestling Federation. Only the WWF's world-title belt ranks higher. The championship is perhaps not the best measure of Hart's excellence; it is his longevity that truly impresses. In a business with weekly turnover, the 35-year-old Hart has been a staple in the WWF for 11 years, longer than any of the federation's stars except for Hulk Hogan and Mexican baby-face Tito "El Matador" Santana.

Bret Hart's ring skills are unique these days. He has mastered hundreds of holds, reversals, and throws. The majority of wrestlers on the circuit today are larger than Hart and a number of behemoths dwarf him. Yet few have command of more than a couple of signature moves. Hart does nothing particularly original — there really isn't anything new under the ring lights — but rather he pays homage to the past and borrows from wrestling styles from around the world.

"I resent being called 'just an actor' or 'just a body-builder,'" Hart says. "There's a lot more to what I do. I was a provincial champion as an amateur wrestler in high school. I've watched the best wrestlers in the world since I was a kid and I've worked with Japanese and European champs. The only [WWF wrestler] out there that's close to me technically is The Rocker, my little brother Owen."

No one is born to wrestle but no one more than the Hart kids was born into it. Their father, Stu, wrestled for more than four decades and, until his retirement two years ago, was the promoter of Stampede Wrestling, a Calgary-based circuit renowned for its gothic violence and gore. Stu's career dates back to the sport's dark ages — before television broadcasts — practically, as his wife, Helen, describes it, "to the invention of the headlock." Stu and Helen's eight sons have all been engaged in pro wrestling, if not in the ring then in promotion. "At six I had my first job, selling programs," Bret says. "Then I worked my way up to ring crew, then to music."

The Hart *kinder's* exposure to pro wrestling wasn't limited to the arena. For many years Hart House, the family's 20-room home on the outskirts of Calgary, served as residence for wrestlers working Stu's shows or for those training at his wrestling school. It is no coincidence that the four Hart sisters married pro grapplers. Ellie married Jim "The Anvil" Neidhart, with whom Bret twice won the tag-team title. Diana married Davey Boy Smith, "The British Bulldog," who deposed Bret as the WWF Intercontinental champ before 80,000 fans at Wembley. With an angle of unprecedented verisimilitude, their match was billed as "The Battle of the Brothers-In-Law."

The Hitman maintains that he is an excellent athlete although not "a natural." Still, he says his understanding of wrestling feels almost preternatural. "Sometimes in the ring I feel like I'm tapping into the past, maybe something I saw on a card when I was six or practised in our back-yard ring. I'll do something instinctively, and it will work before I realize what it was." Bret Hart usually avoids false modesty. He'll tell you that, when he arrived in the WWF 11 years ago, he was already as skilled a wrestler as there was on the circuit. But when he can tone down the braggadocio, he'll admit that he cannot take full credit for his greatness. Wrestling was the Hart legacy, something imposed on him, as inescapable as a hammerlock.

"What you should know about Stu," Helen Hart tells me conspiratorially, "is that he never got enough to eat when he was a child and he's been trying to make up for it ever since." Mrs. Hart is sitting at a table in a Calgary steakhouse while her husband defoliates the salad bar. "Stu has a healthy appetite," she says, "for a wrestler, that is. For normal-sized people, the amount of food he eats would be dangerous, but in his business there were always big eaters. We had to cook for Andre the Giant — he's 500 pounds — and the McGuire twins — they were over 700 pounds each. Stu is no trencherman compared to them."

As wide and as thickly-set as the door to a bank vault, Mr. Hart returns to the table with a plate loaded six inches high. "Oh Buff," Mrs. Hart says, "you can make two trips up there, oh really." For the amusement of onlookers, she goes through the motions of being appalled by her husband's lack of etiquette.

He teeters slightly on his cowboy boots before wedging himself into the booth. "What was that?" he asks. "You'll have to forgive him," Mrs. Hart advises me. "Stu's hard of hearing."

Stu leans across the table. "Here, feel my ear," he says.

"Stu, the young man is trying to eat," she says.

He turns his head to left profile and waits for me to work up the nerve. I touch the calcified membrane that few would mistake for an ear. It has the shape and texture of petrified cauliflower. "If wrestling was all fake," he says, "I'd have ears that look like yours."

The waitress arrives with Stu's dinner, the second-largest prime rib on the menu — the largest is a promotional eat-two-sixty-four-ounce-steaks-and-we-rip-up-the-bill. "I'm not complaining about my ears," Stu says, as he carves. "If I didn't wrestle I wouldn't have met Tigerbell."

"The young man's not interested in ancient history," says Helen.

Stu continues. "I was a fair athlete back in the late Thirties," he says, punctuating every pause in the story with a forkful of rare meat. "Played for the Eskimos in football, played and coached hockey and baseball. When I was just a youngster on leave from the navy, I made it to Philadelphia and met up with Toots Mondt, who was one of the most famous wrestlers around in those days. He took a liking to me and started me into pro wrestling. While I was down there I made a trip to New York and met Tigerbell. Her father, Harry Smith, had been a miler at the 1912 Olympics. Harry was a big celebrity in New York, had lots of famous friends."

"I don't know what my family thought about you and me," she says.

"She read a lot of books," Stu says, "and was dating a teacher. She had her choice of a lot of suitors and she picked me and we got married."

"It wasn't quite the noble savage and Fay Wray story," Helen says. After almost a half-century of practice the Harts have developed their own style of repartee. They trade the floor and work in flurries, like good tag-team partners trading places in the ring.

"I started up Stampede Wrestling back in '48 with 15,000 bucks," Stu says. "Our best years we took in a million dollars a year at the gate from shows all across the prairies."

"If it sounds the least bit glamorous," Helen tells me, "You should ask him about driving hundreds of miles to cards in small towns in the dead of winter, six huge wrestlers crammed in one car to save gas money."

"Had them all here. Killer Kowalski. Sky Hi Lee. Harley Race, now there was a great worker." Stu rhymes off names for ten minutes. The best of them he calls "great workers," investing the words with the distinction worthy of "artists" or "craftsmen." Stu makes it clear that Stampede Wrestling's best worker was its most unlikely candidate. "Tigerbell here put together the programs and press releases and handed out the pay cheques while I was cooking up meals for the wrestlers and the kids."

The conversation halts for a moment as Stu tucks into his meal with renewed seriousness. Helen reaches into a manila envelope and pulls out a stack of photographs. She shows me a recent shot of their sons and daughters and their spouses at a family gathering. "That's what Bret looks like without his hair slicked down," Helen says. "The WWF wants all the wrestlers to do something with their hair but Bret's isn't flattering."

"That's Jim Neidhart there," Stu says, pointing to a huge man with a billy-goat Vandyke. "The bastard."

"If Stu calls him a bastard that means that he likes him," Helen says. "Bret's career only took off after he became The Anvil's partner." Then Helen pulls out an eight-by-ten of their children posing beside Rocky Marciano, the undefeated heavyweight boxing champion from the 1950s. "That's from 1965," she says. Bret is a slight, angelic-looking eight-year-old with a brush cut.

"Marciano," Stu says. "I tried to shoot an angle with him one time. After he quit boxing, he came up here to make an appearance at the Stampede parade. On our float I set it up so that Waldo Von Erich [a pseudo Nazi villain] would take a shot at Marciano. I didn't tell Marciano about it though, just for the best effect. So Von Erich pulls Marciano's cowboy hat down over his head and Marciano doesn't react. 'Just clench your fist, anything,' I tell Marciano. We could have sold out the Corral the next week, the place would burn up. But Marciano didn't want any part of it. He was, I dunno, righteous, self-righteous, or something. He thought all this wrestling stuff was comedy — that is until a wrestler — I don't wanna say who — snatched him in the dressing room in Chicago one time..."

"When he says 'snatches' that means he jumped him and beat him up," Helen advises.

"Yeah, Marciano had a notion that all this stuff was fake but he got cured," Stu says proudly.

"Wrestlers," Helen says. "They're just a bunch of over-grown kids. And Stu wonders why I only went to two or three wrestling shows in all the years we've been married."

"Did you ever hear about the time Sika the Samoan got in a fight and bit off a guy's nose," Stu says. He puts down his knife and fork and goes after what's left of the prime rib with his bare hands.

Fifteen minutes into their match in Saskatoon, Bret Hart has Flair in a compromised position, flat on his sun-lamp-orange back with his hairless left leg in Hart's grip. Hart turns and whirls and suddenly Flair's face is being pressed into the ring floor. Hart is sitting on the small of Flair's back and has the Nature Boy's legs in a most unnatural position. This is Hart's signature move, the Sharpshooter, a combination of two submission holds: the figure-four leglock and the Boston Crab. Bret Hart is administering the coup de grapple, pro wrestling's most devastating submission hold. He knows that he'll win now, that he'll win the world championship, and waits only for Flair to give in.

In 1981, long before his transformation into The Hitman, Bret Hart was an anonymous greenhorn on the WWF circuit. He languished at the bottom of the cards, scratching out a living, just waiting, he says, "for that one big break to make a name for myself." Bret was sure that his break had come the day the Japanese wrestling office called. Bret was told that a British wrestler, The Dynamite Kid, had signed to fight the Japanese hero Fujinami for the world junior heavyweight title (under 200 pounds) at Madison Square Garden. But 24 hours before the bout, The Dynamite Kid was held up at the border because he didn't have a work visa. The Japanese official asked Hart to fill in on short notice. "The Garden was and will always be like Carnegie Hall," Hart says. "Once you perform there you know you're established." Hart flew to New York and appeared at a press conference for Japanese journalists the afternoon before the match.

After the press conference Hart went to his hotel room, took the phone off the hook, and went to sleep, dreaming of status that was soon to be his. At 6:15 he packed up his gym bag and set out to walk over to MSG. He got as far as the hotel lobby. An official from the Japanese office stopped him. "You're off the card tonight," he told Hart and handed him an envelope containing $200. Hart was dumbfounded and demanded an explanation. The official told Hart that the decision had been made by

Vince McMahon Sr., then the voice of God in the WWF and the most powerful man in wrestling. "The Garden is only for the biggest names in the game," the official told Hart. "Vince Senior decided you don't have a big enough name."

"I always wanted to get past that knock of not having a big enough name," Hart says. "I always wanted to get even for that. It was the worst experience I've had in wrestling, worse pain than all the injuries I've had." In Calgary and Western Canada, there had been security in the Hart name — a certain amount of baggage but also instant recognition. But the biggest name from one of the territories, from Stampede Wrestling, couldn't even get him in the door at the Garden.

After this disappointment, Hart was determined to make a name his own way. He rejected the suggestion of the WWF brass that he become Cowboy Bret Hart. "I told them I can't ride a horse and I don't sound like a cowboy," Hart says. "More than that, I didn't want to get typed as a cowboy for my entire career." Hart took on Jim Neidhart as a tag-team partner to create "The Hart Foundation," developed the Hitman persona, and became a heel in defiance of the conventional wisdom that he was too good-looking to be a bad guy. Soon after repenting his past sins Hart set out as a newly righteous soloist and won the WWF's Intercontinental belt. "Whenever I wrestle at Madison Square Garden, I think, 'They know who I am now,'" he says. "I'm pretty damn high up." With Rick Flair contorted beneath him, Hart is sitting on top of the wrestling world.

Now appreciate that an audience with The Hitman and The Rocket is not easy to secure. Three out of every four weeks they're on the road, utterly at the mercy of the WWF matchmakers. The only place to corner them is at the gym. On the road and at home they pump iron about two hours a day, five days a week. In Calgary The Hitman and The Rocket do their lifting at B.J.'s Gym, a body-culture emporium owned by one of their brothers-in-law and decorated with glossy photos and posters of pro wrestlers, most prominently The Hitman.

Also appreciate that a member of the media will be granted an audience with The Hitman and not necessarily Bret Hart. That is to say, Hart will show up in character. He arrives in the same attire he wears into the ring for an evening's simulated hostilities: a black leather jacket adorned with a Hitman logo on the back and wraparound reflective sunglasses. He has lacquered down his hair and adopted The Hitman's good-natured conceit. For The Rocket the occupational schizophrenia is less pronounced because, as a recent arrival in the WWF, he has yet to develop much of a character. "I'm just the all-American, clean-cut, high-flying wrestler," The Rocket says. "I don't have to paint my face." And to his mother's relief, he is blond enough that he doesn't have to slick down his bangs.

And also appreciate that The Hitman and The Rocket have their guards up. For the past year the WWF has been enduring a spate of bad publicity. In 1991 a doctor in Pennsylvania was sent to jail for illegally prescribing steroids to several WWF wrestlers. Though the Harts were never mentioned in the charges, Hulk Hogan, the long-time golden boy of the WWF, was implicated. Later the federation became the object of another scandal when former wrestlers and officials claimed they were the objects of unwelcome homosexual advances from high-placed WWF officials. "All the recent charges — and most of them are unfair — have put us on the defensive about our profession," The Hitman says.

Inconvenienced, in character, and on guard, the Harts still manage to charm. Their business requires a sense of humour as much as gym-built muscles. Bret and Owen talk proudly, lovingly, about their brutal and often cynical trade because it is, after all, the family business. "When I was just a little kid, I didn't have a real good idea of what wrestling was," Bret says, removing his shades and dropping The Hitman's arrogance. "Guys came up to me and said, 'My dad can take your dad.' I had to fight to defend the family honour and wrestling too. I was fighting for a just cause but I wasn't sure what it was."

Bret and Owen, the two most successful wrestlers of the Hart progeny, were originally reluctant warriors. "We were the two sons who didn't want to go into the business," Bret says. "I wanted to go to film school but after I started wrestling for my father I couldn't quit. I was better than all the other guys starting up. I had a gift."

Owen's account of his ring debut sounds like the confessions of a "father wound" at a New Age men's therapy group. "I wanted to be a phys. ed. teacher," The Rocket says. "I wrestled only to appease my father. I was compelled to get into the ring. Once I started there was the pressure of having the Hart name — I was expected to be good."

It wasn't merely the family name that gave The Hitman and The Rocket their shot. Back then, the organization of pro wrestling provided greater opportunities for novices. "Ten years ago you could find work all over the world," Bret says. "There were a bunch of regional shows or territories. The WWF was the main organization but the other outfits acted as feeder systems. Stampede Wrestling was just one of a whole slew of them."

The phenomenal growth of the WWF squeezed out the smaller shows and, in turn, led to a decline in the quality of wrestling. "Now any guy who works out in a gym wants to be a wrestler," Owen says. "Lots move up without learning the ropes and paying their dues." Bret cites the Ultimate Warrior, the heir apparent to Hulk Hogan, as a prime example of a star wrestler who can't wrestle. "I'd like to see the Warrior do three or four moves in the ring," The Hitman says. "He has a clothesline [a forearm to the throat] but that's it. WWF wrestling is fast paced and theatrical, but there has been a loss of skill. Owen and I definitely have a foot in the past as far as knowing the moves and I hope that we're part of a new wave of wrestlers, a return of old-fashioned amateur wrestling skills."

The Hitman also hopes that his sons will be part of that return to the Harts' family values. "I'd like my sons to be the first third-generation pro wrestlers," he says. "My oldest son, Dallas, doesn't quite understand what it's all about but he takes it seriously. He went into hiding when I lost my Intercontinental title. The youngest, Blade, is two years old and he goes crazy as soon as he sees me on TV."

In one of Stu's last matches — he was in his 60s — he teamed up with Bret. Neither Bret now Owen can foresee staying in the game long enough to enter the ring with their sons. "I keep saying one more year and that's it," Bret says. The Hitman's forehead, just below his hairline, is creased with scar tissue from gashes that were opened up by punches and sometimes sharpened fingernails. He probably never envisioned such a buildup of wounds. Owen seems even less inclined to hang on. "I can see wrestling until I'm 30, but then I'd like to get out and be with my family," he says. "I wondered whether it was all worth it when I was injured at the Survivor Series last year. I was doing an aerial move off the top rope and took a head butt in the groin. I had to finish the match because it was live TV but I spent a week in hospital. I almost had to lose a testicle. I had just got married and wanted to start a family. It put into perspective the risks that I was taking."

Though their older brothers, Smith, Keith, and Bruce, were once regulars on the Stampede Wrestling circuit, Bret maintains that his sisters Ellie and Georgia were his toughest and most frequent opponents for sibling scraps at home. "My sisters were rough enough for any of us to duke it out with," Bret says. "It was a no-win situation. My father was especially partial to the girls. If you were caught laying a finger on your sister, you had to deal with old Stu."

The Hitman fighting, maybe even losing to, a girl? Being put in his place by his father? Bret Hart perhaps realizes that he has strayed too far out of character. He stands up abruptly, puts on his shades, and assumes The Hitman's belligerent *hauteur*. "You *are* finished," he announces.

My eyes are watering, my neck has just cracked, and the well-appointed dining room at Hart House is starting to spin. The clenched right fist and thick forearm of Stu Hart has just bruised and almost crushed my nose. "You felt that did'ya?" he asks. "See I'm just shooting it across like this…" He does it once more, further loosening my tenuous grip on consciousness. Stu Hart is showing me a little ring-craft. I have said nothing to encourage this lesson. I have advised him that I'm late for an important appointment. He said that he'd rush through it. "I'm only showing you this 'cause you seem like a good guy," he says. His hand grips me near my right elbow. "See, I have you there," he says. I can see the pictures of the Hart family that hang on the walls around the long dinner table. I can see a vintage photo of Stu from his fighting days. His body then rippled and his dark eyes were piercing. Suddenly the pictures are upside down — or rather I am. I have hit the floor with a jolt, how I don't know. I can feel my head being pressed towards my navel. "Some people think this wrestling stuff is fake," he says. "they have no idea what goes on in the ring, how tough this stuff is." Stu — who I am now sure is the world's most dangerous, 77-year-old — leans his full body weight, about 260 pounds, onto my back. I free up my head but I can't draw enough breath to cry "Uncle." "It's a good thing I like you," he says without menace. I look into the living room and see studio portraits of the Hart children from the mid-60s. With my head ringing, my spine cracking, and the world fading to black, I can now understand that for Bret and Owen and the other sons the Hart name was sometimes a burden, one that, if you crossed old Stu, could collapse a lung.

Last September rumour had Bret Hart ready to leave the WWF. According to a few published reports, other wrestling circuits were interested in him, but a closed-door meeting with Vince McMahon, Jr., the owner of the WWF, sorted out the matter. The son of the man who ruled that Hart didn't have a big enough name, decided that The Hitman was worthy of a push, which explains the showdown with Flair in Saskatoon. Hart is ready to ascend to the summit: the WWF world championship. Flair is writhing on the canvas, struggling to escape the Sharp-shooter. This night Hart has his finishing move locked in and awaits only the ref to halt the proceedings. Flair submits. The ref calls for the bell. Hart lets loose the hold, grabs the championship belt, and holds it aloft. The fans give him an ovation and see in the match many things. Good guy vs bad guy. The decent Canadian vs the ugly American. Gel vs peroxide. These are the subtexts that the promoters invent and enact, the plot confections that the mat fans swallow whole. But the victor, the new champion, is playing out another story line that is closer to the truth. When Hart was starting out in the early 80s, trying to make a name for himself after working his father's promotions in Western Canada, Flair was already the best scientific wrestler and showman in the game. Now Hart has not only won the most important title in wrestling, he has won it in what was for four decades his father's territory. Bret Hart suffered indignity long ago but, for The Hitman, retribution is the only angle to shoot, the only sure-fire way to draw heat.

(Reprinted with permission from *The Globe and Mail*)

THE LEGENDARY HABITANTS

Mordecai Richler

I can remember exactly where I was on VE-Day, on the day John F. Kennedy was shot, and when the first man landed on the moon. If I can't recall what I was doing on the day Stalin died, I do remember that a journalist I know was in the elevator of the *Montreal Star* building the morning after. Ascending, she turned to a neighbour and said, "Stalin died."

The elevator operator overheard. "Oh my God, that's terrible," he said. "Which floor did he work on?"

The point I am trying to make is that on days that shook the world, or my world at any rate, I was never on the spot until the night of September 2, 1972, when Team Canada tested our belief in God, the free-enterprise system, and the virility of the Canadian male, by taking on the Russians in the Montreal Forum in the first of an eight-game series. A series, Tim Burke wrote in the *Gazette*, that the Canadian public viewed as something of a political Armageddon. Going into the contest we were more than overconfident — with pity our hearts were laden. The pathetic Russian players had to lug their own equipment. Their skates were shoddy. The players themselves had names appropriate to a plumbing firm working out of Winnipeg's North End, but otherwise unpronounceable: Liapkin, Maltsev, Mikhailov, Kharmalov, Yakushev, and, oh yes, Tretiak. Everybody but John Robertson, then with the *Montreal Star*, predicted that our champions would win all the games handily or, at worst, might drop a game in Russia. A matter of *noblesse oblige*. Robertson called for the USSR to win the series six games to two. On the other hand, Alan Eagleson, one of the organizers of the series, ventured, "Anything less than an unblemished sweep of the Russians would bring shame down on the heads of the players and the national pride."

After Ypres, following Dieppe, Team Canada and our very own belated St. Crispin's Day. Brad, Rod, Guy, Yvan, Frank, and Serge, once more into the breach, once more for Canada and the NHL.

> *From this day to the ending of the world,*
> *But we in it shall be remember'd;*
> *We few, we happy few, we band of brothers...*

We were only 30 seconds into the fray at the Forum when Phil Esposito scored. Some six minutes later, Paul Henderson, taking a pass from Bobby Clarke, scored again. But the final count, as we all know, was Communism 7, Free Enterprise 3. And our players were booed more than once in the Forum, ostensibly for taking cheap shots at the Russians as they flew past, but actually for depriving us of one of our most cherished illusions. We already knew that our politicians lied, and that our bodies would be betrayed by age, but we had not suspected that our hockey players were anything but the very best. If Team Canada finally won the series, Paul Henderson scoring one of hockey's most dramatic goals at 19:26 of the third period in the last game in Moscow, the moral victory clearly belonged to Russia. After the series, nothing was ever the same again in Canada. Beer didn't taste as good. The Rockies seemed smaller, the northern lights dimmer. Our last-minute win came more in the nature of a relief than a triumph.

After the storm, a drizzle. Which is to say, the endless NHL season that followed was tainted, revealed as a parochial affair, and the Stanley Cup itself, once our Holy Grail, seemed suddenly a chalice of questionable distinction. So, alas, it remains. For the Russians continue to be the dominant force in real hockey, international hockey, with the Czechs and the Swedes not far behind.

But when I was a boy, and the Russians were still learning how to skate, the major league was right here. And furthermore, the most dashing and aesthetically-pleasing team to watch, in the old vintage six-team league, was our own unrivaled Montreal Canadiens.

Les Canadiens sont la!

The legend began before my time, on the night of November 29, 1924, with Aurel Joliat, Howie Morenz, and Bill Boucher, the first of many fabled lines. On that night, their first night in the Montreal Forum, the line scored six goals, defeating Toronto St. Pats 7-1. "Of course," wrote sports columnist Andy O'Brien, "the line had a lot of ice time because the Canadiens carried three subs, while Georges Vezina (the Chicoutimi Cucumber) in the goal left back-checking superfluous."

Morenz was our Babe Ruth. Alas, I never saw him play; neither was I present in what must be accounted the most tragic night in hockey, January 28, 1937, when Morenz crashed into the boards and suffered a quadruple leg fracture. He was still in the hospital early in March, complications set in, and the Stratford Streak was no more. His fans, French Canadian factory workers and railroaders, had once filled the Forum's cheap seats to the overflow, and to this day that part of the Forum is known as the "Millionaires' section." "His body," wrote Andy O'Brien, "was laid out at centre ice and the greats of hockey took turns as guards of honour around the bier day and night. Then a sportswriter with the old *Standard*, I arrived at the Forum to find the front doors jammed. I entered by the furnace room and, as I walked toward the Closse Street entry, the stillness made me wonder — was nobody else in the building? But there were 15,000 fans, quiet and motionless in a tribute to a man — and hockey — that has never been matched."

Morenz played on three Canadiens Stanley Cup winning teams, but with his passing a drought set in. The Flying Frenchmen, or the Habitants, as they came to be known, a team that has won the Stanley Cup 21 times, more often than any other club, did not claim it again until 1943-44, with the lineup that became a golden part of my childhood: Toe Blake, Elmer Lach, Ray Getliffe, Murph Chamberlain, Phil Watson, Emile "Butch" Bouchard, Glen Harmon, Buddy O'Connor, Gerry Heffernan, Mike McMahon, Leo Lamoureux, Fernand Majeau, Bob Fillion, Bill Durnan, and, above all, Maurice "the Rocket" Richard.

To come clean, this was not the greatest of Canadiens teams — that came later — but it remains the one to which I owe the most allegiance.

1943-44. Cousins and older brothers were overseas, battling through Normandy or Italy, and each day's *Star* brought a casualty list. Others, blessed with a nice little heart murmur, stayed home, making more money than they had ever dreamed of, moving into Outremont. But most of us still lingered on St. Urbain Street, and we seldom got to see a hockey game. Our parents were not disposed to treat us, for the very understandable reason that it wouldn't help us become doctors. Besides, looked at closely, come playoff time it was always our pea-soups, which is what we used to call French Canadians in those days, against their — that is to say, Toronto's — English-speaking roughnecks. What did it have to do with us? Plenty, plenty. For, much to our parents' dismay, we talked hockey incessantly and played whenever we could. Not on skates, which we also couldn't afford, but on the streets with proper sticks and a puck or, failing that, a piece of coal. Saturday nights we huddled around the radio, playing blackjack for dimes and nickels, our eyes on the cards, our ears on the score. And the man who scored most often was Maurice Richard, once, memorably, with an opposing defenceman riding his back, and another time, in a playoff game against Toronto, putting the puck in the net five times. Then, in 1944-45, Richard accomplished what no other player had done before, scoring 50 goals in a 50-game season.

I only got to see the great Richard twice. Saving money earned collecting bills for a neighbourhood butcher on Sunday mornings, my friends and I bought standing-room tickets for the Millionaires' section. And then, flinging our winter caps ahead of us, we vaulted barriers, eventually working our way down to ice level. Each time we jumped a barrier, hearts thumping, we tossed our caps ahead of us, because if an officious usher grabbed us by the scruff of the neck, as often happened, we could plead, teary-eyed, that some oaf had tossed our cap down and we were only descending to retrieve it.

Among the younger players on ice with the Rocket during his last years was the consummate artist who would succeed him as the leader of *les Canadiens*: Jean Beliveau.

I was, by this time, rooted in London, and used to make a daily noon-time excursion to a Hampstead newspaper shop especially to pick up the *International Herald Tribune*, turning to the sports pages first, seeking news of big Jean and his illustrious team-mates, easily the best *Club de Hockey Canadiens* ever to take to the Forum ice. They won the Stanley Cup five years running, and such was their prowess on the power play that they were responsible for a major change in the NHL rule book. With Beliveau at centre, Dickie Moore on one wing, an ageing Richard on the other, the Canadiens, with the man advantage, could score as many as three goals in their allotted two penalty minutes. Consequently a new rule was introduced. It allowed the penalized team to return to full strength once a goal had been scored.

I didn't get to see Beliveau play until 1956 and was immediately enthralled. He was not only an elegant, seemingly effortless skater, but an uncommonly intelligent playmaker, one of the last to actually carry the disc over the blueline rather than unload before crossing, dumping it mindlessly into a corner for the others to scramble after, leading with their elbows. "I not only worry about him when he's carrying the puck," said Punch Imlach, then coach of the Toronto Maple Leafs, "but about where the fuck he's going once he's given it up." Where he was going was usually the slot, and trying to budge him, as Toronto's Bill Ezaniski once observed, "was like running into the side of an oak tree."

Ah, Beliveau. Soon, whenever I was to fly home from England, I would first contact that most literate of Montreal sportswriters, my friend Dink Carroll, so that visit might coincide with a Canadiens game, affording me another opportunity to watch big Jean wheel on ice. I was not alone. Far from it. In those halcyon days knowledge-able Montrealers would flock to the Forum to see Beliveau on a Saturday night as others might anticipate the visit of a superb ballet company. Big, handsome Jean was a commanding presence, and as long as he was on ice, the game couldn't degenerate into Ping-Pong: it was hockey as it was meant to be played.

Beliveau was truly great, and a bargain, even if you take into account that *le Club de Hockey Canadiens* had to buy an entire team to acquire him. In 1951, Beliveau, already a hockey legend, was playing for the "amateur" Quebec Aces, his salary a then stupendous $20,000 a year. The cunning Canadiens bought the Aces, thereby acquir-ing the negotiating rights to Beliveau. He received a $20,000 bonus and signed a five-year, $105,000 contract, which was unheard-of in those days for a 23-year-old rook-ie. Beliveau went on to score 507 goals for *les Canadiens*. He made the All-Star team nine times, and led his team to ten Stanley Cups in his 18 years with the club as a player.

If Beliveau was the leader of the best Canadiens team ever, it's also necessary to say that decadence, as well as grievous loss, characterized those memorable years. Deca-dence came in the unlikely shape of one of the team's most engaging and effective forwards, Bernie "Boom Boom" Geoffrion, who introduced the slapshot, wherein a player winds up like a golfer to blast the puck in the general direction of the net, sometimes scoring, more often watching the puck ricochet meaninglessly off the glass. Loss, irredeemable loss, came with a change in the draft rules of 1969. Until then, *les Canadiens* had call on Quebec's first two draft choices, but come '69 and expansion, that was no more. In practical terms this meant that Marcel Dionne and Gil Perreault, among others, were lost to Montreal. Sadly, if either of them had a childhood dream it was certainly to play with *le Club de Hockey Canadiens*, but when they skate out on Forum ice these days, it is as dreaded opponents.

A tradition was compromised in the dubious name of parity for expansion teams. For years, years and years, *les Canadiens* were a team unlike any other in sports. Not only because they were the class of the league — for many years, so were the New York Yankees — but also because they were not made up of hired outsiders but largely Quebecois, boys who had grown up in Montreal or the outlying towns of the province. We could lend them our loyalty without qualification, because they had not merely been hired to represent us on ice — it was their birthright. As boys, Beliveau and I had endured the same blizzards. Like me, Doug Harvey had played softball in an NDG park. Downtown had always meant the same thing to Henri Richard as it had to me. So the change in the draft rules meant that *les Canadiens* were bound to lose a quality that was unique in sport. Happily, however, the time was not yet. Not quite yet.

For one player promising true greatness did slip through the revised draft net. After Morenz, following Richard and Beliveau — Guy Lafleur. Lafleur, born in Thurso, Quebec, in 1951, was, like Beliveau before him, a hockey legend even before he came to *les Canadiens*. In 1970-71, still playing with the Quebec Remparts, a junior team, he scored a record-making 130 goals and graduated to *les Canadiens* under tremendous pressure. Universally acclaimed as Beliveau's heir, he was even offered Beliveau's number 4 sweater. "He asked me what he should do," said Beliveau. "I told him if you want number 4, take it. But, in your shoes, I would take another number and make *it* famous."

Lafleur chose number 10, and for his first three years in the league, helmeted years, he was a disappointment. Seated on the bench between shifts, he seemed a solitary, almost melancholy figure. Even now, having acquired some of Beliveau's natural grace by osmosis, perhaps, he is far from being a holler man, but then in the winter of 1974 he suddenly bloomed. Not only did Guy score 53 goals, but, eschewing his helmet, he was undoubtedly the most dazzling player on ice anywhere that year, leading old-style end-to-end rushes, splitting the defence, carrying the puck as if it were fastened to his stick with elastic, unleashing swift and astonishingly accurate wristshots, dekeing one goalie after another and coming back with the play, going into the corners. Once again the Montreal Forum was a place to be, the Saturday-night hockey game an occasion.

(From *Home Sweet Home* by Mordecai Richler. Used by permission of the Canadian publishers, McClelland & Stewart, Toronto)

SPRINGTIME IN THE DIVOTS

Lorne Rubenstein

The squishiness of the green, still-sodden ground beneath my spiked feet; the earthy scent of the now fertile soil and the spray of water as my club head contacts the ball; the flight of the ball towards the green; or, often, its helter-skelter path, wind-borne, clasped to the welcome breezes blowing spring warmth onto the course. These are some of my impressions of early games of golf each spring. Every year for 30 years I have taken to the game anew, wondering what the season will bring. Still, the passion remains for a game that Winston Churchill once derided as being like "chasing a quinine pill around a cow pasture."

Ah, but Churchill was misguided. What did he know of the energizing feeling that courses through a golfer's body when he contacts the ball on the sweet spot of the club face? How could he even dare to speak so maliciously of a game in which even the most horrible hacker can sink a long putt across the hollows and bumps of a tricky green, knowing for a moment that he or she is feeling just like Jack Nicklaus or Nancy Lopez? More golfers than ever are celebrating an illogical love of a game in which even the great Ben Hogan, master of the swing, said that he hits only a few shots each round that come off as he imagines.

Can so little success anywhere, on any field of play or in any walk of life, offer such rewards as a golf ball perfectly struck? Golfers know. And never mind the golfer's standard rueful lament. Asked after a round how he played, a golfer can quite rightly answer: "I didn't play my usual game today. Come to think of it, I never play my usual game."

But who needs usual games anyway? Golf, and especially late spring golf, when hope is still writ large in the golfer's mind, is about reaching for the unusual, the outer limits of what the golfer can do. We golfers are exhorted to "extend" the club head, to "swing to the target." Spring golf stretches our vision, pulls us out of our winter selves, huddled for warmth, at last. But winter also propels us forward for golf. The very hibernation it imposes makes the anticipation of a spring round keen indeed. Awakening, sensate again, we believe in ourselves. Against common sense, encouraged by thoughts sharpened over many a winter's night, the golfer believes that he can still play to his potential. That is the promise of the game, the lure that brings the golfer out spring after spring. An odd round down south during the winter does not count. That's a holiday round. Now comes the real thing, in spring.

But what is the real thing? With no apologies to Churchill, or to George Bernard Shaw, who sneered that golf is "a typical capitalist lunacy of upper-class Edwardian England," the fact is that golf is not some backwater foolishness where only the lightweight, the fat cat and the dopey participate. Many golfers are fit and more than a few read books, attend plays, keep up with the news and even make worthwhile contributions to society beyond advising fellow golfers where to place their elbows on the backswing. There is high art and bizarre science enough in striking the ball to satisfy most anybody, and even to capture the imagination of people who, mistakenly thinking they are politically correct, call golf "an old man's game."

No, no, a thousand scoreboards no. Think of something Brendan Gill wrote about his father in his memoir *Here At the New Yorker*. Gill's father was "a brilliant surgeon and physician ... He hunted, fished, hiked, chopped wood, planted trees and painted houses, barns, sheds and every other surface a brush could reach. But his favourite outdoor activity was golf. The game amounted to a passion with him."

Passion. Now there's a word often heard in connection with golf. Go figure. "Passion," used to describe a game in which nobody even hits one another or runs after a ball. The word means "strong emotion; outburst of anger; strong enthusiasm." Roget comes up with such synonyms as "desire, distress, eloquence, fervour, mania, torment, zeal." Golf does inspire these feelings.

It might seem crazy but there's a fellow who shall go unnamed here who has said that his self-esteem rises and falls with his golf. He's an orthopaedic surgeon whose family life and career are going along beautifully. But he can't figure his golf game out. He can't play his "usual" game.

This fellow, and millions like him around the world, know what a gentleman named Douglas Bertram Wesson meant when he titled his book, *I'll Never Be Cured And I Don't Much Care: The History of an Acute Attack of Golf and Pertinent Remarks Relating to Various Places of Treatment*. Exactly. Who cares? Life is fraught with problems so why should a golfer not be allowed the simple pleasure of an early evening on the course, alone or in company? How good it feels when a warm drizzling rain tickles one's head. The white flag on the green ahead may be barely discernible as it slaps the air in the dusk, but a shot hit just so will reach the green and perhaps cuddle up to the flagstick. Is this a dream, only a dream? These spring rounds can make the dream real.

But perhaps it does not matter if the shot is good. Maybe the walk is what matters, the opportunity for silence, for reflection. A round of golf can be a communion with oneself and with nature. Truly, though, the game is rarely played this way nowadays. Most public courses are jammed and buzz with carts. People accuse one another of playing too slowly. Golfers diligently add up their scores as if they are checking stock quotations; they are too concerned with their scores. The game becomes a sombre affair.

To care too much about score is to lose the rhythm of the game. Judging our shots, we can miss the essential pliability of golf, the way it bends us every which way. Golf is really not about judgement but about acceptance. The essence of the game is that a player drives the ball in the middle of the fairway and lands in a deep, ugly scar of a divot left by a golfer ahead. Accept it. This is the game; golf is played outdoors on grass. It is not possible to control the environment. Let the pliability of the game encourage a suppleness within yourself.

This is what the late George Knudson, Canada's deeply introspective and mightily gifted golfer, alluded to when he suggested that the golfer "give up control to gain control." That is, the player ought to stop thinking about what to do with the golf club at every segment of its route away from and back to the ball. Said Knudson, "Let yourself swing."

Perhaps that sounds too much like Zen golf. But we will risk any accusation of limp thinking because we know that we find almost an altered state when we bounce on the rolling turf, and when we are aware of the high grass swaying in the rough, and when we wrap our fingers around a velvety grip, and when we swing the club to and fro, and when we fall into the grace of the game, an outing that sends us inward.

If we play sensibly we can discover the sensuality that lurks everywhere on the course. Thinking about slow play, Knudson once said, "I don't know what all the concern is about. Slow play means that you're going to spend a longer time in a nice place." Take a book along on the course, then. Read a poem. Chat with your companions. Swing, swing, swing. Walk in the woods.

Knudson's comment can be a code for the game. Spring has been here for weeks but the season still feels fresh and we are renewed. As for me I have scratched the itch long enough. I want grass clippings stuck to the soles of my shoes, mud on my golf ball, dirt on my club face, the club in my hand while I turn it round and round until it feels right. Care to join me?

(First appeared in *Toronto Life*)

WENDEL CLARK UNMASKED

Rosie DiManno

Wendel Clark is a simple man in a complex world. This would not matter had be stayed on the farm back in Kelvington, Sask., threshing his wheat and driving his cattle and kicking up dust in his worn leather cowboy boots. Perhaps grunting the occasional folksy observation, with a grain husk protruding from between his lips.

But the self-professed yokel who continues to describe himself as "just a farmer" — a sentiment which is engraved on the brass buckle of a hand-tooled belt that holds up his low-slung jeans — is not, alas, the perennial country-boy of twangy song and heartland literature. No matter how much he wishes it.

He is the captain of the Toronto Maple Leafs in a town unrivalled in its hockey sophistication. He is, at 27, a veteran and a survivor of the Dark Age at Carlton and Church, having sacrificed his youth and his physical soundness to the blight of the Ballard years. He is a celebrity and, yes, a city slicker and a team spokesman — all designations which sit awkwardly on his shoulders and run contrary to his nature.

That is the conflict at the core of Wendel Clark: how

to take moral responsibility for the role in which he has been cast and of which he is justifiably proud, while having neither the desire not the deceit to reinvent himself.

How to be what he has always been, without disappointing those who expect more, something beyond his placid off-ice temperament.

"I'm not a talker," Clark was explaining a few days ago over a breakfast of ham and eggs, a milk moustache superimposed on the hairy one. "If you talk all the time I think it goes in one ear and out the other. But if you're not known as a talker maybe when you do have something to say other people will listen."

Whatever leadership qualities he can demonstrate, particularly as the Leafs prepare to host the Chicago Blackhawks in tonight's playoff opener, he prefers to do in the one venue where he can be eloquent without opening his mouth. "It's all out there on the ice. Especially in playoff time, just be ready to play with your game face on. Other players will see that. But we have a lot of players who can lead by example, guys like Dougie (Gilmour) and Bob Rouse."

Clark is, he will admit, "a shy guy," and it has always been thus, when he was a kid on the farm, when he first left home as a 14-year-old to play bantam hockey 100 miles away, and when he was selected first over-all by the Leafs in the 1985 entry draft. He was only 18 when he joined the parent club. "It was the game of hockey that brought me out of myself," he says. "All of a sudden people were asking me questions and I had to answer them."

He was just a boy, then. He has become a man, since.

It's been a sometimes painful and always public coming of age. Because Clark has been around for so long he has emerged as a kind of repository of memory, a walking annal of the Leaf fortunes over the past decade. He had become the Leaf of record even before he was named as the club's 16th captain in 1991.

It would appear by nature that Clark is a good soldier, not a commanding officer. But he took the "C" and that means he had to take the responsibility, always, and the blame, sometimes. He has responded, consistently, with an almost eerie calm, and the stoicism of a, well, farmer.

In last year's first-round playoffs against the Detroit Red Wings Clark was sharply criticized for his dismal effort in the first two games. Some of the harshest observation came from this writer and was, I still maintain, justly deserved. Clark didn't flinch, recoil or fight back. Instead, he strapped on his leg braces — the supports he wears on both limbs — and reasserted himself ferociously on the ice.

He verily flew through the subsequent games of that series and the later playoff encounters with the St. Louis Blues and the Los Angeles Kings. Here was the renaissance of Wendel Clark, as if he had stepped backwards in time; was young and strong and fearless. In fact, he had 20 points and ten goals in the 21 games the Leafs played over a heady 41 days, five goals over the final two post-season games.

But he never said, "I told you so."

What he'll say now is that coach Burns ordered him not to play hard-nosed, not to be drawn into fisticuffs with Bob Probert *et al* in those early encounters with the Red Wings. Most of all, not to take fighting penalties.

There was another, uncomfortable element to the war-of-words and the general feeling of hostility that surrounded that Detroit series. Clark's courage was questioned for his conduct on the ice. But his very manhood came into disrepute and his alleged lifestyle off the ice was even discussed on a radio show.

Clark smiles at this now and shakes his head. "I am not gay," he says, sounding neither defensive nor outraged. Just a simple statement of fact. There is no hint of homophobia in his attitude, only a genuine puzzlement.

"How the rumours started, I have no idea, not a clue. But yah, I've heard them," he continues, then addresses a few more of the persistent whispers that have long been repeated in this city. "I do not live with [figure skater] Toller Cranston. I do not live in Toller Cranston's house. I have never met the man."

Hockey players tend to marry early and sports celebrities, in general, have traditionally worn their sexual escapades on their sleeves. This is a macho indulgence of the testosterone-pungent sporting world. Clark is single and in his nine years as a Leaf has never revealed the intimate details of his life. That's his right. And, as Clark argues, there's not much to reveal anyway.

"My life is hockey, that's the best part of it, just playing the game. I don't really do much away from it. Just hang out, ya know?"

Why has Clark allowed the rumours to fester? Here, he shrugs his shoulders. "What am I supposed to do? And why bother? It won't get me anywhere. If I let the rumours bother me, then I would be allowing these people to get the better of me. So I'm not going to worry about it. The people who know me know that it's not true. And I'm not going to worry about the people who don't know me."

One incident in particular, though, he does want to set straight. In that series last April, Detroit's Probert was widely quoted as having referred to Clark as "Wendy," a ghastly insult in this sport and a remark which rekindled the gay rumours.

"With those Detroit guys, calling me Wendy would have nothing to do with my sexual orientation," Clark insists. "They did that because they thought I played tougher on home ice than I did on the road. You know: Wendel at home, Wendy on the road.

"But they never called me that name on the ice. The players know me. They understand that we all come under pressure of one kind or another. Every player goes through turmoil in his career."

The pressures these days, to Clark's relief, are strictly hockey oriented: trying to duplicate or surpass the team's astonishing playoff performances of last spring.

"Expectations are high and everybody has them, including the players," he says. "We want to do the same or better and we realize we have to work as hard or harder. Then we have to get some luck and some bounces and everything else it takes to win. I don't think that [the '93 success] has made the situation any harder for us. We just have to stay in the right frame of mind. You can't let the pressure weigh on you because then it becomes uncontrollable.

"If we go 0-2 to start the series, then we're in big trouble. If we go 2-0, they you're over-confident. And everyone will be on the bandwagon more than ever. You have to keep a level head, no matter what happens. Stick together and don't believe anything you hear until it's all over."

Sticking together is also why Clark recently called a team meeting in his hotel room during the last Leafs regular-season road trip, during which they played some abysmal hockey and were blasted by Burns. They were floundering, it seemed.

"It was as much Dougie's idea as it was mine," Clark explains. "We wanted to reinforce certain things to the players. We had lost a few games and I wanted to bring everybody back to square one, to doing the things we were doing when we were winning, and to restore our confidence.

"You don't want to go into the playoffs with people starting to hate each other or losing confidence in each other, getting mad at each other. You don't want to be fighting at playoff time, which is when you should be pulling together."

Whatever inner crisis the team had been experiencing appears to have been resolved. And they're keeping the details to themselves. "Did it work?" Clark wonders aloud. "Well, we're not separated as players. We're not pointing fingers."

They are, instead, pointing all in the same direction, embarking on a journey that they hope will take them one step farther than it did last time around.

And Wendel Clark, who plays out each of the games in his mind's eye long before he steps on the ice — sketches it in his head — has this one recurring image: a Stanley Cup held aloft.

(Reprinted with permission from *The Toronto Star* Syndicate)

GRANNY GOALIE

Jim Taylor

Paul Reinhart would have been 11 years old when Mary Gretzky leaned over the boards at the Brantford Arena and smacked him over the head with her purse.

He was playing defence for an Atom League team called the Kitchener Krauts and pinning her grandson against the boards in a manner that everyone in the rink deemed legal except Mary. She didn't hesitate. "Let him go!" she yelled, and began flailing away at Reinhart with her purse.

"Grandma," Wayne Gretzky says fondly, "was a competitor."

She was also a friend, a confidante, and the first goalie Gretzky ever faced, boucing rubber balls off her legs as she sat in the big chair in the farmhouse by the Nith River where, two months shy of his third birthday, he took his first, hesitant steps on skates. When she died Saturday at 85, No. 99 lost his No. 1 fan.

I met her first in 1993, out on the farm near Canning, Ontario, where her five children were born and raised and where Wayne and his sister and brothers did most of their growing up. We'd driven the 12 miles out from Brantford after lunch, but she insisted we sit down and have a little something, which turned out to be a huge bowl of home-made soup so thick with vegetables the spoon all but stood on its own.

"I don't think I can..."

"Eat," she said

We ate, and watched the pickup game in the yard — tennis ball, tennis racquet, over the trailer is out and into her vegetable garden, you deal with Grandma. The Gretzky kids played, and so did guests in town for the Celebrity Tennis Tournament, and Mary shook her head and told me stories about the way it was.

She always knew Wayne would be rich. "Hairy arms," she said, with a finality steeped in Polish folklore. "I told him, 'Hairy arms mean you will be rich someday.' And in the mornings he would come and ask me if he had any more hair."

The farm was where Gretzky built the high-jump pit after practising by jumping over the wire fence to feed her chickens. It was the place he first leaned to fish and, in later years, the sanctuary that was always there when the pressure of being Wayne Gretzky grew too severe.

It had been a working farm, and Mary kept her part of it that way to the end. Walter would bring her home from a hospital session she'd spent battling a heart problem or stroke, full of doctor's warnings to take it easy. She'd nod yes, and the next day she'd be in the garden harvesting potatoes. "This is my life," she said. "What else would I do?"

The other part of her life was watching Wayne. Once Frank Mahovlich had been her hero. Now it was the WHL, the Wayne Hockey League, and there was only one player in it. For years she squirrelled money away, bit by bit, against the day she'd be able to buy him a car. When he turned pro at 17 and bought one of his own, her first reaction was, "Now what will I do with the $4,000?"

She was in Edmonton when Wayne married Janet Jones, making the trip with a nurse by her side. "Nice," she said, looking around the hotel ballroom. Then she looked at Wayne and Janet. "Very nice," she beamed.

A couple of years ago technology came to the farmhouse on the Nith: a satellite dish so she and her daughter, Ellen — a Down's Syndrome victim — could watch more of Wayne's games, there in the room where he'd crouched on the floor beside her, watching Toronto Maple Leafs. "So many games," she mused. "So many things…"

Today the Gretzkys say goodbye to Grandma. Then Wayne jumps on a plane for Pittsburgh to join the LA Kings for another showdown with Mario Lemieux. Maybe, somewhere, she'll be watching. It's one she'd hate to miss.

(First appeared in *The Vancouver Province*)

BLOOD AND MONEY

David Macfarlane

It could make you mad, if you wanted to think about it, staring into the bottom of a bowl of chili in Brookings restaurant in Lexington, Kentucky, about two miles and a world away from the Keeneland auction arena. Charlene's gone to fetch another Michelob. The old fan hums, a fly drifts over the ketchup bottles on the counter. Outside, a drowsy southern evening closes in as ordinary folks sit on their wide, ordinary verandahs, and the sound of cicadas rises and falls in the trees.

He comes in and ambles past the cash and the candy rack, a hefty, pleasant-looking fellow with a country-and-western face, and a head of dark, carefully-groomed hair. He sits at the counter, hoisting his grey flannels to bend his knees. His black shoes are carefully shined. He's wearing a green Keeneland blazer — the blazer worn by the spotters and the auctioneers at the most illustrious horse sale in the world. It's a surprise to see him here, so out of context. It's an ordinary little restaurant, and there is nothing ordinary about Keeneland.

Earlier that day he was standing on the floor at Keeneland looking for bids, his green-blazered back to the auctioneer. His gaze passed back and forth over the crowd like a searchlight and, at one point, like an actor catching the eye of a friend in the audience, he gave a friendly smile to the president of Windfields Farm, a moon-faced, placid-looking gentleman in jacket and open-necked shirt, Charles Taylor. A few years ago, a friend of Taylor's — the woman he would marry in the spring of 1987 — had been sketching the horses led into the arena, and the spotter mistook her perpendicular pencil for a $1-million bid. Taylor, a respected Canadian journalist and author, is the son of E.P. Taylor, the man who, 26 years ago, bred one of the most influential horses in the history of the thoroughbred — Northern Dancer.

In 1965, when Northern Dancer began his stud career, fees for his services were $10,000 with a guarantee of a live foal. As the number of Stakes Winners among his offspring began to climb, it became apparent that Northern Dancer was what all breeders hope their sires will be: prepotent. A prepotent stallion passes on his own strengths as well as the strengths of his ancestry. It also happened that Northern Dancer's bloodlines were impeccable — both parents were descendants of some of the most distinguished thoroughbreds in history. And his strengths were remarkable — despite a height of just over 15 hands, he was well-balanced and finely muscled at the peak of his racing career, winning the Kentucky Derby, the Preakness Stakes, and the Queen's Plate in 1964. It also happened that Northern Dancer's stud career coincided with the escalation of thoroughbred prices. "The right genes in the right place at the right time," was how his jockey, Bill Hartack, put it.

In 1970, Windfields sold 23 shares in Northern Dancer while retaining control of nine shares itself. The syndication price was set at a then remarkable $2.4 million. George Gardiner, Jean-Louis Levesque, Garfield Weston, and D.G. Willmot became the Canadian investors. Even then, many Americans seemed to underestimate Northern Dancer. His popularity was called "fashionable", as if, once the hemlines dropped, he would disappear. But there were some who suspected that Northern Dancer was more than just a fad, and their names had a certain ring. Mrs. Richard du Pont, Paul Mellon, and Alfred Vanderbilt bought in.

Northern Dancer's first foal crop produced ten Stakes Winners from 21 foals. His second crop included the English Triple Crown winner, Nijinsky II. Then, by the mid-70s, as Northern Dancer grandchildren began to appear, a remarkable, almost unbelievable fact became apparent. Northern Dancer was more than prepotent. He was, it seemed, capable of passing on his prepotency. He had become the horsebreeders' equivalent of the philosopher's stone. He had, by an astonishing confluence of genetics, become the siphon through which three centuries of breeding for speed, stamina, and physical perfection passed. In the early 1980s, as European and Arabian money fought at Keeneland for Northern Dancer blood, his stud fees leapt astronomically. By 1987, when he retired from the breeding shed at the age of 26, he had produced 125 Stakes Winners and his stud fees had traded up to the $1-million mark, no guarantee. And at Keeneland, on July 23, 1985, it was perfectly clear that there was no ceiling on the price people would pay for Northern Dancer blood.

Charles Taylor puffed on his pipe, smiled back at the spotter, and made a note in his Keeneland catalogue. A Northern Dancer grandson, by Nijinsky II, was led into the sales arena. The one-year-old colt wore number 215 on its hip, and a cackle of excitement passed through the crowd. This particular yearling, a bay colt with Northern Dancer on his sire's side and Seattle Slew on his dam's, was, as yearlings go, about as good as they get. The crowd was ready for a very expensive fight.

Charlene comes back with the Michelob. "Charlie," she says, nodding to the spotter now seated at the Brookings counter.

"Charlene," Charlie replies.

"Saw you on TV," Charlene says. "Where that horse was bought."

"Yup," says Charlie. "Wasn't that something."

And it could, if you let it, make you mad. For the fact of the matter is this: that year, in the summer of 1985, ten days after the world, in a fit of guilt and then an

explosion of self-congratulation, raised $70-million for
famine relief in Africa, a roomful of people at the
Keeneland auction in Lexington, Kentucky, had, with
subtle, almost invisible nods and brief flicks of steely eyes,
spent more than twice that on a slate of one-year-old
quadrupeds with impeccable bloodlines, no names, and
I.Q.s slightly lower than the average pig's. Horse money.
There are few things stranger.

There had never been quite so much money in the air
as on the steamy afternoon of July 23, 1985 — not merely
the money of limos and Dom Perignon but quiet money,
unshakable money, the kind of money that won't go away,
that can't possibly be spent, that reproduces itself more
quickly than the wildest, most extravagant imagination
could ever dream up ways to take a poke at the principal.
And has a smell. Daisy's voice, wrote F. Scott Fitzgerald
in *The Great Gatsby*, was "full of money." At Keeneland,
so is the air. The scent is rich and thick and seductive,
and in the auction arena, where once a year the most
serious horse people in the world buy the most serious
horses for the most serious prices, the smell is easy enough
to identify. Noting the number of ravishing young women
on the arms of older, impossibly wealthy men, pondering
on an industry based on athletic prowess and blasts of
sperm, on rock-hard erections and the groans of mares in
heat, you might decide that the air at Keeneland is full of
the smell of sex. And perhaps it is: young girls, everyone
knows, fall in love with horses, and the old men with
money enough to own the most beautiful horses often
fall in love with young girls. Sometimes the girls grow
up to be rich old women, and one *grande dame*, described
frequently in the pages of *Town & Country* as "a socialite",
reserves two seats at Keeneland — not to bid but simply
to watch the shiny, muscular flanks of one-year-old blue-
bloods come and go, her gin-racked face held in a taut gri-
mace by surgery, her diamond-crusted fingers wrapped
tightly around the broad, tanned hand of the ageing boy
she keeps in Italian suits by her side. ("Firebird isn't a
horse," hissed wild, lustful Elizabeth Taylor to poor,

impotent Marlon Brando in *Reflections in a Golden Eye*. "He's a *stallion*."] Or perhaps, as the dignified gentry of the international horse set —long tired of jokes about studs and broodmares — would contend, the atmosphere at Keeneland has nothing at all to do with such base considerations. "In this modern day of the jet engine and the paved street," observed the American breeder Leslie Combs II in 1969, " the horse remains with us as a reminder of the graceful and leisurely life from which this country has sprung." But the smell at Keeneland, whether it stands for business or sport, beauty or decadence, sex or money, or complex combinations of all of these, can be reduced to what it actually is: perfume and manure, tobacco and horse-piss.

Such, more or less unchanged, has been the smell of horse money for 300 years.

There are always people who will tell you how to look at horses. They gather round the betting windows, beneath the stands of any track, racing forms in hand, snap brims pushed back on their heads. Or they sip chilled white wine in the dining rooms at Longchamp or Epsom. They will speak about bloodlines, the intricate maze of ancestral connections that trace a thoroughbred's lineage back to the 18th century. Or they will discuss conformation — the bone structure and musculature of a horse. They will say you have to analyze a horse's walking gait, the rhythm of its movements. You have to be able to see a horse's spirit, read the meaning in a horse's eye. And, on the basis of this, they will bet a week's wages on a race or spend a million dollars on a horse. But the strange thing about horses is this: there are lots of people who will tell you how to look, but there aren't very many who will ever see anything.

Of the few horsemen who have had the ability to see whatever it is that makes a great racehorse, perhaps the most influential of the century was an Italian senator, Frederico Tesio. At his breeding farm, Dormello, on the shores of Lago Maggiore, Tesio pursued his experiments in equine genetics from 1906 until his death in 1953, establishing a line that would eventually lead to Northern Dancer, Nijinsky II, and the yearling at Keeneland in 1985 called hip 215. Tesio, unlike many of his peers, was as interested in breeding as he was in racing. Indeed, judging from his writing, he was less interested in horses than in the complex genetic patterns that produced great thoroughbreds, less interested in racing than in measuring the success of his breeding against a controlled standard. Frederico Tesio, like E.P. Taylor, had an uncanny eye for horses but, in an odd way, the horses themselves were almost irrelevant. He might have been cultivating orchids.

From his study at Dormello, Tesio studied centuries of bloodlines, plotting his pairings carefully, always conscious that the wrong coupling could reinforce weakness rather than enhance strength. Speed, stamina, beauty, and the ability to pass on strengths were the qualities Tesio tried to produce in his stallions, and in 1935 he created his masterpiece. Tracing a complex route of inbreeding back to St. Simon, the winner of the 1884 Ascot Gold Cup and one of the greatest racehorses and stallions of all time, Tesio engineered the birth of Nearco. He bred Nearco by Pharos out of Nogara, and the pairing proved to be one of the most important in thoroughbred history. Nearco was an undefeated champion, a winner of the Grand Prix de Paris in 1938, and, as a stud, the sire of successful racers.

"Although we cannot reduce the number of a horse's ancestors," Tesio wrote in *Breeding the Racehorse*, "we can select his parents in such a way that one particular ancestor will occupy more than one place in his pedigree, thus ensuring a greater probability that certain desired characteristics will be inherited." The statement — bearing within it the role of chance, the possibility of compounding genetic superlatives, and the danger of overemphasizing unperceived weaknesses — is the craft and gamble of horse breeding in a nutshell. Tesio's approach was almost mystical: St. Simon, he noted, had 16 ribs and six lumbar vertebrae, as opposed to Touchstone, the winner at St Leger in 1834, who had 17 ribs and five vertebrae.

What this had to do with breeding racehorses in the mid-20th century, only Frederico Tesio knew.

Few horsemen could have differed more from Frederico Tesio than E.P. Taylor. A down-to-earth businessman, Taylor liked horses, especially horses that won races and, as far as he was concerned, winning races was what breeding was for. Sport was sport, and business was business, and through the 1930s and early 1940s E.P. Taylor's business was his Canadian Breweries Limited and Argus Corporation. His hobby was horses. But for Windfields, as indeed for many stables, the distinction would eventually disappear.

In 1950, Taylor purchased Colonel Sam McLaughlin's Parkwood Stables, a 450-acre farm near Oshawa, Ontario. The acquisition puzzled Canadian horsemen — Canadian horses had never been a force internationally, and the scale of Taylor's operation seemed, for want of a better word, international. Which was exactly what Taylor intended. In 1952, for instance, he purchased a mare for $35,000 at the Newmarket sales in England. The mare was called Lady Angela, and she was a descendant of the celebrated St. Simon. Then, Taylor did what Frederico Tesio would probably have done. In 1953, the year Tesio died, Lady Angela was shipped to Canada, carrying a foal by Tesio's greatest stallion, Nearco. The offspring, born in Canada, was Nearctic, and six years later, after a successful racing career, the stallion covered the three-year-old Natalma, a daughter of the 1954 American horse of the year, Native Dancer. The following May, Northern Dancer was born.

At the 1985 Keeneland sale, Robert Sangster was anxious to buy and 215 was the horse he wanted. He had his reasons. "Horseflesh," Sangster had said in 1977, "is an international currency." This may have been a disturbing observation to the coterie of aristocrats and millionaires who met one another at Epsom and Longchamp and Churchill Downs to swap the service of mares with a handshake and a clink of champagne glasses, but it was precisely the kind of thinking that the consignors — the owners of the commercial stables that breed and sell the yearlings — at the Keeneland select sale wanted to hear.

A multimillionaire who runs Britain's largest soccer pool, Sangster is one of a handful of men who, in the past decade, have irrevocably changed the economics of thoroughbred breeding and racing. In fact, that handful of men — Sangster; the Greek shipping magnate Stavros Niarchos; Sheik Mohammed bin Rashid al Maktoum of Dubai; the Texas millionaire Nelson Bunker Hunt; the chairman of Gulfstream Aerospace, Allen Paulson; a close advisor to King Fahad of Saudi Arabian, Khala Abdullah; and a Saudi businessman, Mahmoud Fustok — all have their seats at Keeneland. All of them wander the grounds on show day with their trainers and veterinarians and advisers, sipping the mint juleps and buck fizzes offered by the commercial stables. They chat with the sellers, their good friends from Claiborne and Gainsborough and Windfields, and catch up on the news from the celebrity guests, Priscilla Presley and Larry Hagman and Burt Bacharach. But mostly the serious buyers look, long and hard, at conformation, at bloodlines, at the look in a yearling's eye, at the way a horse moves as the grooms parade them on oval pathways in front of the abundant flower boxes of the peaceful stalls. And that year, beneath the shady trees of Keeneland, the big money was very interested in 215.

The colt's consignor, Warner L. Jones Jr., of Hermitage Farm in Goshen, Kentucky, knew he had "an awful nice colt." A grandson of Northern Dancer, a half-brother to Triple Crown winner Seattle Slew and the son of Nijinsky II, a European horse of the year, 215 was, on paper, as good as they get. Sales, Jones knew, were down at Keeneland that year. The average price for the 130 yearlings led into the circle on opening day was $454,153 as compared to $605,319 in 1984. The record — $10.2-million, paid in 1983 by Sheik Maktoum for a son of Northern Dancer — had not even been approached, but two horses, one of which Jones had owned himself, had already sold for $2.6-

million each. More interesting than anything, perhaps, the biggest buyer on opening day had been not the Arab or the British interests but a relative unknown, the American trainer, Wayne Lukas. And Lukas, Jones knew, had looked very carefully at 215.

Lukas, who represented a three-man consortium of Texas, Oklahoma, and California money, began as a quarter-horse trainer, and manages to find the continuing references to his unpropitious beginnings amusing. "Some day I'm going to win the Arc de Triomphe," he said, "and someone in France will come up to me and say, 'You are noth-*eeng* but a quarter-horse train-*aire*.'" Lukas was representing people who were serious about horses, and there was one remarkable fact about the horse world that Lukas made sure his clients understood: not since 1975 had a sales-topper stayed to race in North America. The blood had all been going overseas, and if his people wanted a horse like 215 they had to be ready for a fight.

For about ten years it has been the Arabs and the British who, in bidding against each other, fighting primarily for Northern Dancer blood in order to establish their own empires, have been driving through the roof the prices of American-bred horses at Keeneland. Since the end of the Second World War, North American breeders have dominated the bloodlines of the thoroughbreds. The postwar boom of the American economy coincided with advances in air travel that simplified the logistics of international breeding. Nowadays, English royalty comes to America to inspect stock. Kentucky, and not Ireland, has become the home of the best horses in the world and, a century after the Duke of Portland's St. Simon won at Ascot, the most interesting horse at Keeneland in 1985, the yearling that wore number 215 on his hip, was bred by an American commoner named Jones.

Northern Dancer was born on May 27, 1961, at Windfields Farm in Oshawa. His parents had bred late in the season and, as a result, he seemed even smaller than he was; for purposes of registration, a horse born in January and a horse born in May of the same year are both one year old the following January. A five-month disadvantage in size and strength as a yearling, in training and experience as a race horse, isn't easy to overcome. By September, 1962, Northern Dancer was still just a runt out of a mare with good pedigree but bad racing luck. His father was still unproved as a sire. E.P. Taylor was optimistic, as horsemen often are, but in 1962 he put the little stallion up for sale.

By 1954, the year after Lady Angela was shipped from England to Canada, Taylor realized that he was breeding more horses than Windfields could race, and he devised a scheme for maintaining the delicate balance between his breeding and racing operations. Each September, Windfields invited serious buyers, mostly Canadians, to the farm. Every yearling was for sale, each with a fixed price. The buyers sat in rows of directors' chairs, in the crisp September sun, as Taylor's crop paraded before them. As the owner of the pre-eminent stable in the country, Taylor knew that he would be accused of keeping the best horses for himself if he selected what horses to sell. Therefore, everything was for sale, and Taylor kept only what was left when 50 per cent of the yearlings had been taken.

At the 1962 sale, nine colts and six fillies were sold. The buyers, as usual, were astute horsemen, but at the end of the day everyone had passed up on the short bay colt with the white blaze on his nose. He looked good on paper, and was obviously spirited enough, but he seemed far too small for the price Taylor had put on him. In 1962, $25,000 was a lot of money. E.P. Taylor was forced to keep his little horse.

Northern Dancer was fiery and difficult and, in spite of his size, more than a handful for his riders. The next summer, in his maiden race at Fort Erie, he finished first, six lengths ahead of the rest of the field. Trent Frayne the sportswriter, said he had the look of "a middleweight fighter." Despite his height, his 73-inch girth was no smaller than many taller horses' — he had a good heart and lung room, horse people said. His stride, as Charles Hatton wrote in the *Daily Racing Form*, seemed "two sizes too big for him, but it is precisely controlled, like something they do at the Bolshoi Ballet." Within a year the stride was famous. On May 2, 1964, under Bill Hartack's whip, Northern Dancer set a track record at Churchill Downs and became the first Canadian-bred winner of the Kentucky Derby. At the Preakness, he finished two and a quarter lengths in front of the field. Then, at the Belmont, he came third, apparently confused by an unpredictably slow pace. Back in Canada, he won the Queen's Plate by seven and a half lengths. Ten days later, a bowed tendon in his left foreleg ended his racing career and began his career as a stud, a career that would change forever the thoroughbred world.

Traditionally, the value of a horse was gauged by its potential for winning on the course. St. Simon, for instance, was purchased for 1,600 guineas, a sum the Duke of Portland could easily recoup on the track. In 1925, a filly by Man o' War, the fiery chestnut stallion who had been beaten only once in his career, sold for what was regarded as the staggering price of $50,500. Over the next 50 years, yearling prices edged upward, sliding past $100,000 in 1961. By the early 1970s, the best yearlings were routinely selling in the six figures. But even this was not wildly out of line with the purses they might win. Then, in 1976, the million-dollar mark was broken at Keeneland by a consortium of Canadians. Secretariat, the 1973 Triple Crown winner, was a horse of irresistible distinction to breeders, so the consortium paid $1.5-million for a colt from Secretariat's first foal crop.

It had always been understood, of course, that a stallion, following his days on the track, could earn substantial profit as a stud, but this had been perceived as secondary to the glories of racing; the term "retire to stud" was not idly chosen. But in the economic climate of the 1970s, the uncertain days of recession and recovery, the notion of horses as international currency was beginning to take hold. And the horse at the centre of this thinking was Northern Dancer.

Protected by agricultural tax laws designed to assist debt-ridden farmers, and based on a bona fide aristocratic tradition that could be, and frequently was, traced back 300 years to three stallions, the Godolphin Arabian, the Darley Arabian, and the Byerley Turk, the thoroughbred was becoming a commodity and a shelter as much as an athlete. Unlike many earlier sportsmen, the Canadian consortium was betting as much, if not more, on the stud's potential as on its racing future. A good stallion could easily cover 800 mares during his stud career, and there were more than a few stallions who earned half a million dollars for each live foal they sired. Canadian Bound, the stallion the consortium purchased, was a bust in both the racing and breeding departments, but the thinking was correct. And it was precisely this thinking that both Robert Sangster and Wayne Lukas were doing when 215 was led into the auction arena.

The game still had its surprises; there were dark horses. Seattle Slew was purchased for $17,500 in 1975, and two years later was in the winner's circle at Belmont Park, Pimlico, and Churchill Downs; by 1985, standing at Kentucky's Spendthrift Farm, he was insured for $140-million. But increasingly, the equation of price and winnings was being ignored in favour of an investment that addressed itself directly to futures in bloodlines. Only in the breeding shed could a horse that cost several million dollars as an unproved yearling become meaningful tender. Snaafi Dancer, the Northern Dancer colt that blew the lid off Keeneland in 1983 when Sheik Maktoum calmly nodded his way to $10.2-million, never entered a gate. It was almost as if racing no longer mattered.

Almost, but not quite. It was apparent by the mid-1970s that Arab and British interests were intent on regaining control of the source of thoroughbred excellence — and that, no one doubted, was the Northern Dancer bloodline. Clearly, it was no use investing in a form of currency if someone else was the proprietor of the mint. There were consignors who believed that, once the control was established, the blazing duels at Keeneland

would die down and the market would return to something approaching calm. But for people such as Robert
Sangster and the Maktoum family, there was a wrench in
their works, and the wrench, ironically enough, was racing. Even if owners no longer bred to race but rather raced
to prove their breeding, there was still a track to get
around, and in Europe the tracks are grass, in North
America dirt. In Europe horses run both clockwise and
counter-clockwise, in North America they run only
against the time. It had long been accepted that horses
bred in North America had trouble on European courses.
In popular imagination, American horses were thought
to be precocious sprinters, faster out of the gate than
their European cousins but disasters on the extra quarter
mile that distinguishes the Derby and the Prix de l'Arc
de Triomphe from such arriviste tracks as the one August
Belmont II established in New York in 1905. In the 12
years after the Second World War, only two American
horses posted victories in Europe.

This, for the people involved in the process of returning the source of the best bloodstock in the world from
Kentucky bluegrass to the green fields of Ireland, was a
bit of a problem. The bidding wars of Sangster and the
Maktoums, and the subsequent revolution of the economics of thoroughbred breeding and racing, might never have
occurred had not Sangster joined forces with an Irish
trainer named Vincent O'Brien. It was O'Brien who proved
that North American horses could run, almost anywhere.

Considered by many to be the most astute horseman
on either side of the Atlantic, O'Brien was constantly at
Sangster's side at Keeneland and, once the purchases were
made, he took Sangster's North American bred yearlings
and trained them to run against prevailing European wisdom. It was O'Brien who proved the true value of Northern
Dancer offspring. In 1970, Nijinsky II became the first
horse in 35 years to win the British Triple Crown and, in
1977, The Minstrel, another Northern Dancer son, won
the Derby, and became British horse of the year.

If any doubts about North American bred horses

remained, they were dispelled at the Epsom Derby on
June 6, 1984, when Secreto and El Gran Senor finished
one and two, only a short head apart. Both horses were
sons of Northern Dancer. A half interest in Secreto, a colt
purchased for $340,000 — at Keeneland in 1982 from
Windfields Farm — was later sold by his Venezuelan
owner for $20-million.

Of course, by this time, neither Sangster nor O'Brien
nor the Maktoums needed any convincing. A decade of
dizzying prices lay behind them and, as it became more
and more apparent what the focus of their spending was,
there was little doubt that the highest prices at Keeneland
would remain very high indeed. The thoroughbred market is carefully protected by the numerical limitations of
natural breeding, and by the 1980s the upper reaches of
the horse world were becoming an auctioneer's dream:
something was for sale that was very expensive — the
Northern Dancer bloodline — and there were a few people
who would pay almost anything to get it.

For Wayne Lukas, the American trainer who represented American money, there was a lot at stake as well.
He had already made up his mind about 215. He understood that American interests could either stay in the game
— for a price — or pay an even more unconscionable price
to get back in a few years down the road.

These were the dice being rolled when 215 was led
into the bidding ring on July 23. "It's a recent phenomenon for Americans to show the financial endurance that
has netted foreigners the top-price yearlings in recent
years," noted Maryjean Wall, the racing columnist for
the *Lexington Herald-Leader*. "Yet Lukas and his partners
fired their bankroll with a vengeance in the dramatic
shoot-out that took place at the Keeneland corral."

It was for this that the Lears and the private 727s were
lined up like limos on the sun-cracked tarmac of the
Lexington airport. (It was the jets the consignors kept
their eye on, knowing there was still money in the game
if the airport was still full; in 1984, when the fifth horse
up at the Monday evening sale, a son of Northern Dancer,

was bought for $8.25-million for Windfields Farm, the other consignors, arriving for business Tuesday morning, drove past an empty airport and knew their profits had left with the 727s on their way back to Dubai.) For days, in the Hyatt and the Radisson, in what is usually a sleepy southern college town, well-dressed hookers cruised the lobbies. In the bars, Oxbridge accents called for another round of St. Pauli Girls, and in the corners, dark-skinned young men in open-necked silk shirts and gold necklaces leaned over their drinks, talking intently with Irish rogues in tattersall shirts and practical shoes. And it was this, this confluence of investment and imagination, money and the meaning it gives to things, that sent a buzz of anticipation through the Keeneland hall when number 215 was led into the auction circle. The horse people, glancing at the closed-circuit TV in the bar, stubbed out their cigarettes, finished their Dubonnets, and hurried to their seats. Nobody here was fooling around. The bidding *opened* at $1.25-million.

For nearly 20 years, Windfields Farm in Maryland has been the home of Northern Dancer. It has acres of pristine white fences and carefully tended stables. Principally, the farm's colours seem to be green, blue, and brown — the green of the rolling hills and the richer green of the windbreaks of trees, the soft expanse of spring blue sky, and the brown, like burnished wood, of peaceful grazing horses. But the farm's official colours are not nearly so quiet or harmonious. Turquoise and gold are the colours of Windfields, a racing stable established by E.P. Taylor on the outskirts of Toronto just after the Second World War. Now, they are the colours of a multimillion-dollar business — a business with assets that far exceed the portfolio that began E.P. Taylor's company, Argus.

In 1963, the year of Northern Dancer's maiden race and the year E.P. Taylor became the first Canadian breeder whose horses earned more than $1-million in a season, Taylor purchased 700 acres near Chesapeake City. It was an easy vanning distance from the New York and

New Jersey tracks, and it was originally intended as a training stable for his racehorses. As early as 1968, however, things had begun to shift. Taylor sold the Toronto farm, leaving two bases of operation, Oshawa and Maryland. In 1968, Northern Dancer left Canada. "It was a difficult decision," Taylor said. "He's a Canadian hero and has done well here, but in justice to his promising future I think we must make him more accessible to the finest mares in North America."

E.P. Taylor, 86 years old, now passes his days in the Bahamas; Windfields is run by his son, Charles. A journalist, he once seemed very different from his father. By his own admission, he was "not a lover of horseflesh." Neither did he seem particularly interested in business. And yet now it is the business of horses that holds his imagination.

He oversees an enterprise that allots to racing the secondary role his father once allotted to breeding. This is not entirely a matter of preference. Charles Taylor is not so much a fan of racing as a man who understands that sport remains the foundation of breeding, and that if the sport continues its decline the industry will eventually follow. He has taken a prominent role in establishing the Breeders' Cup as a high profile conclusion to the North American racing season; with its extravagant purses and its emphasis on television coverage, the Breeders' is a sort of racing Super Bowl, and an attempt to redress the disparity between the money that can be made racing and the profits that are earned in breeding. Taylor is active in the Ontario Jockey Club, and by no means approves of the rush for the breeding shed that has shortened the racing careers of horses the public now scarcely gets to know. "The horses have become too valuable," Taylor said in 1985. "That's the problem. It's not healthy, and I don't like it. But I can't be too critical. This is what fuels Windfields." But he's a businessman who listens closely and deferentially to the experts his father hired. It is no accident that in 1986 Windfields stable, once the pre-eminent racing stable in Canada, failed to win a stakes race in Ontario.

The shift in priorities was simply a matter of economics.

The paddocks at Windfields in Maryland are divided by flat white fences and lanes of graceful oak trees. Northern Dancer's running area is next to that of his son, The Minstrel, and only a short walk from the main doors of the stallion stable. The stable contains eight stalls, each with polished wooden doors and a brass nameplate. Across the road from the stallion stable is the heart of the operation, the breeding shed. This — stable to breeding shed, breeding shed to stable, stable to paddock and back — was Northern Dancer's universe from 1968 until his retirement 19 years later.

Essentially Windfields does two things: it services clients' mares for fees that range from $15,000 to $250,000 and, in providing its own brood mares to the resident stallions, produces the foals that become the farm's product at the yearling sales. A stallion can service over 40 mares a season, visiting the breeding shed twice each day, in the mornings and the afternoons. The shed itself is barren-looking. The sound of horses' hooves echoes on the floor as the male is led to the female. The mare's upper lip is held by an attendant in the noose of a tightly-pulled twitch, her left foreleg is tied to prevent her kicking her multimillion-dollar sire, her backside has been carefully washed down with water and antiseptic. The snorts of the stallion, reverberating off the walls, are loud and violent. The stallion, forelegs thudding on the mare's shuddering sides, is guided into the mare by one of the five attendants. In a matter of seconds it is all over, and the horses leave the shed by separate doors. They have never actually seen one another, head to head. "Basically," one attendant says, "this is organized rape."

At just over 15 hands, Northern Dancer is short. A man of six feet has to bend slightly at the knee to be at eye level with the most distinguished stallion in the world. During his years as a stud, he used a low ramp to give him the height he needed in the breeding shed. Businesslike and eager, he was known to walk on his hind legs from the stallion barn to the breeding shed.

In 1980, when Northern Dancer was an already elderly 20-year-old, his syndicate *turned down* a purchase offer of $40-million from a group of French businessmen — this for a horse that could have dropped dead the day after the deal was signed. In 1983, Windfields was offered $450,000 for a spot in Northern Dancer's 1984 season, cash to be paid whether or not the horse even managed to live to 1984.

In the last years of his stud career, in deference to his age, Northern Dancer was bred only in the mornings. Even so, the old routine of two assignations a day was hard to give up. On afternoons during the breeding season, when the other stallions — some of them his sons — were led through the wide screen doors to their afternoon appointments, Northern Dancer stood motionless in his stall, an indignant look in his still imperious eye, an erection between his legs.

Charlie sits at the counter of Brookings restaurant, in his green Keeneland blazer, perusing the menu. It was Charlie who, earlier that day, signalled to Tom Caldwell, the head auctioneer, each time Wayne Lukas upped his bid.

In the Keeneland auditorium, Warner Jones Jr., the owner of 215, watched the numbers climb. Not far away, Wayne Lukas signalled his bids to Charlie, knowing now, because the counterbids were coming from behind the pavilion, that Robert Sangster's British Bloodstock was in competition. Sangster liked to stand behind the auctioneer's podium, back where you can smell the horses and where buyers gather for one last look before the yearlings are led into the ring. Sangster's bidding was determined, fast, and ruthless enough to shake off all but the most serious contenders. Before most people had reached their seats, the auctioneer was looking beyond $3.5-million. By then it was clear that the numbers were not climbing any more, but leaping, $500,000 a jump.

Lukas and Sangster found themselves at the still point of a turning world that afternoon. Three hundred years of bloodlines and a century of economics had set the two men against one another — and yet, there was someone else at Keeneland that day who was as much at the centre of the whirlpool as anyone. A casual observer would never have picked him out as a pivotal figure in the battle being fought. He seemed too calm. In one of the five seats reserved for Windfields Farm, Charles Taylor sat watching the bidding, impassive and, so it seemed, detached from the proceedings. But Taylor understood, as did everyone in the room, that number 215 had many superlative qualities — faultless conformation, a clear and intelligent eye, an obvious spirit, a graceful fluid gait, and, above all, his blood.

Hip 215 had a lineage that could be traced back to St. Simon and further, but the horse people gathered at Keeneland that day knew it was 215's more recent ancestry that was pushing his price up. A son of Nijinsky II, a grandson of Northern Dancer, he would eventually — unraced as a two-year-old, promising as a three-year-old — carry part of his grandsire's name. His owner would call him Seattle Dancer.

At Keeneland, the crowd had rushed to their seats as the price passed $3.5-million. The yearling stood in the ring, his halter held gingerly by an attendant, and, as the bidding climbed toward $9-million, it became apparent that neither Lukas nor Sangster was going to back off easily. At $9.8-million the bidding briefly stalled, and then, abruptly, passed the previous record of $10.3-million. From $11.2-million it inched up, $100,000 a bid, until, at $12.5-million, Tom Caldwell smiled and said, "How about 13 and let's just stop all this."

At Brookings, Charlene returns with another Michelob.

"So the Englishman got it," she says.

"Yes ma'am," Charlie replies.

"What was it they ended up at?"

"Thirteen point one," Charlie said. "Million."

"Isn't that something," says Charlene. "For a horse."

"It's something all right," says Charlie. "I'll tell you what it is, Charlene. It's one hell of a lot of chili dogs. That's what it is."

(First appeared in *Saturday Night*)

WHAT HOCKEY IS ALL ABOUT

Robin Short

You gingerly lay your skates to one side so as not to dull the freshly-sharpened blades.

Piece by piece, you remove the paraphernalia from the oversized equipment bag, ensuring everything is intact and present.

The drop of the puck is still some 24 hours away, but already the preparation has begun.

Glove, check. Elbow pads, check. Jock, check. Plenty of tape, check.

Hockey, these days, invokes thoughts of strikes, lock-outs and big-money players and owners crying poor mouth. But in reality, the game belongs to the hundreds of thousands of children and adults who play in every nook and cranny from coast to coast.

It's a game that is as much a part of the Canadian fabric as the potato fields of P.E.I., the Saskatchewan wheat fields, ice and snow of the Northwest Territories and the B.C. Rockies.

Hockey does not begin and end with the professionals. Yes, we watch and marvel at their skill and we religiously follow our favourite player's every move.

But what it boils down to is it's there for our own personal enjoyment.

It's as much a game for the kids as the adults who try and rediscover weekly the childlike innocence in each of us.

Why else do we, overweight and out-of-shape has-beens (or wannabes), punish ourselves each week, desperately trying to recapture the moves you made as an 18-year-old, struggling to find the legs you never thought would leave, wishing you had a new set of lungs?

Why? Because we love the game.

We love getting the new stick, cutting and filing it down to exact specifications, knowing deep down that no matter how much attention we pay to the treatment of it, the stick won't add to our quota of three goals a year.

We love making the rink-length dashes, believing we're travelling faster than we really are. We love the tic-tac-toe plays — when they work — and beating the goaltender high to the glove side, forgetting the fact the goalie's only real weakness is indeed stopping shots.

We love the dressing room, the sacred place where boys can be boys, a place where the discussion centres somewhere between Doug Gilmour and beer.

No talk of the big sale at WalMart here.

We love the dressing room banter, the abuse we (must) learn to give and take. We love taking the first stride on the ice and the sound of the final buzzer after a gruelling one-hour game.

And, of course, we hate it when only one goalie shows.

So screw the pro hockey players who have robbed us of our Saturday night "Hockey Night in Canada" ritual. Go out and enjoy the game the way it's meant to be enjoyed.

After all, there are no big contracts here, no jealousy. No talks of strikes or lockouts.

Just a passion for the game shared by all.

It's what hockey is really all about.

(First appeared in *The Evening Telegram*, St. John's)

LOCAL HERO

Michael Posner

Like supplicants at Lourdes, their hands outstretched, the crowd strains against the chain link barrier. "Duane! Pat! John!" they call, their faces pink with Florida sun and the stupid, worshipful grin of idolatry. "Juan! Dave! C'mon!" From the frozen north they have made this pilgrimage; from Corner Brook and Kamloops, Orangeville and Oshawa, they have come to pray at this unlikely shrine, to stand patiently behind this modest fence at the Cecil P. Englebert Recreation Complex in Dunedin, winter home of the Toronto Blue Jays, 1992 World Series champions — come to see the miracle of signs and recognition, some validation of their enduring faith.

And now, while the dew rises, and the long rakes rub against the red earth, and the wind whips and whistles in the flags, they thrust forth relics — balls, bats, shirts, scraps of paper — and cry out, "Devo! Devo! Over here! Please! For my grandson!" And Devo — centre fielder Devon White — loping toward the daily ritual of calisthenics, raises his arm and shouts, "Gotta do this first. Get you later!"

It is the first official day of that annual religious ceremony known as spring training, and the cool morning air fairly hums with song and purpose — the scrape of cleat on concrete, the clean crack of bat meeting ball, and the easy laugh of these graceful, well-paid young men, whose lives are lived on the other side of the chain link barricade, playing catch.

Of course, it would be a simple matter for the faithful to breach the divide, to push the gate aside and enter the sanctuary reserved for players, coaches and temple scribes, the media. But the crowd, Canadians all, instinctively knows its place. To mix would be a violation of the unwritten code, and they do not need to mix; they need only to be acknowledged — "Jack! Jack! Think you'll win 20?" — and given evidence, written or photographic, that a contract has been made, confirmation that in an age of spiritual decay and social disintegration, those who pass for gods are still signing autographs.

Now, in the distance, the players are arrayed on the green grass, stretching ligaments. Pitcher Mike Timlin hoists his long legs into the air, spread-eagled. "Oh, do me, do me," he squeals. "Jesus," gasps Todd Stottlemyre, rolling on his back and bringing his legs overhead. "Haven't done this since October." Nearby, Devon White is discussing a new Mercedes. "Twelve cylinders, man," he says to shortstop Alfredo Griffin.

"Twelve?" says Griffin.

"Yeah. Like two complete systems. If one breaks down, the other takes over."

Outfielder Derek Bell twists his body into a hurdle exercise. "Hey," he says to Roberto Alomar, "where you stayin' at?"

"The beach," Alomar says, referring to his luxury, two-bedroom condo on pricey Sand Key, in nearby Clearwater.

"The beach?"

"Yeah ... you should stay at the beach, man," Alomar says. He pauses a beat and smiles. "You just need money."

Afterward, carrying his black-topped bat, Alomar strolls toward the batting cage, and the crowd stirs. In the pantheon of Blue Jay deities, he stands at the very pinnacle. Like Mantle and Mays, Alomar is no longer just a gifted athlete; he's an icon, a genuine celebrity. This status is the result of his God-given talents; his never-quit hustle; his cherubic, bright-eyed, Kodak smile (outfielder Joe Carter calls him "baby"); and his sheer, undiluted rock star sex appeal. If he played for the Yankees, he'd be hosting "Saturday Night Live."

In Puerto Rico, the Alomar name now has an aura normally accorded to patron saints. Toronto is no less enthusiastic. In bars and restaurants, he is routinely mobbed. Last year, he had to be escorted out a back exit at Maple Leaf Gardens after the crowd refused to leave him alone. One night, he and a few friends went for Chinese food at the Pearl Court, a favourite haunt. As soon as he walked in, the Chinese waiter rushed out and came back with a bat to be autographed. Another night, at Splendido, Donny Osmond came over to ask for an autograph. ("Who *was* that guy?" Alomar asked afterward.)

In Dunedin, where fresh boxes of fan mail are deposited daily by his locker, he's allowed to park his rented Chevrolet Lumina in a space reserved for management; it would otherwise take him hours to satisfy autograph seekers — mostly women — prowling the main lot. All professional athletes are familiar with adolescent groupies, but Alomar's appeal seems to span the age spectrum. As baseball mystery novelist Alison Gordon once quipped: "Half the women in Canada want to mother him; the other half have different ideas."

Still, many seem content simply to step for a moment within his magnetic field — as happened when Alomar flew to Toronto to promote a board game, Baseball Mania, at an industry-only trade show. Long before he arrived, the crowd started to gather; by the time he turned up the other exhibits were deserted. For the next two hours, buyers, sellers and models came by to have Polaroid pictures taken with Alomar, immaculately dressed in his multi-coloured leather World Champion Jays jacket, pressed blue jeans and black cowboy boots. The men shook his hand warmly and moved quickly on. The women lingered, draping an arm around his waist, sitting nervously on his lap, making small talk. "It's getting warm in here." Alomar joked, as one young model in a skimpy outfit settled on his knee. "Get me some water, please." Two teenage girls who had invoked family connections to gain admission stood frozen in a sort of catatonic rapture, then rushed off to call friends. "I'm not kidding," one hissed into the phone. "It's him. Yes! *Roberto Alomar!*"

The charisma is magnified by style. On this Florida morning, he wears a sleeveless blue satin pullover atop a long-sleeve turtleneck sweater, fluorescent blue-and-green batting gloves, Oakley sports sunglasses and a brilliant white bandanna. The sweater has his name on the collar; the bat carries his signature. For Alomar, everything — bats, batting and fielding gloves, shoes — is custom-made to exacting specifications. Last season, he went through 178 bats, the most of any player in the majors. "Robbie's high maintenance," concedes Dave Peets, the Puma Canada promotions and advertising manager. "*Fun* high maintenance. He knows precisely what he wants." Last fall, he signed a two-year contract with Puma, worth about $100,000, to help design and promote a new line of sports clothing. Alomar has also endorsed bats, batting and fielding gloves (Cooper Canada); a line of men's casual wear (Zubaz); and a formal rental chain (Tuxedo Junction). New offers continue to pour in, fielded by his San Diego-based marketing agent, John Boggs. (Alomar's contract negotiations are handled by another agent, Chicago's Jaime Torres.)

"Hey, Robbie!" Cameras poised, the crowd moves with him. Several women edge along the fence for a better view. Politicians would kill for this attention, but few politicians can leap, catch the ball, pivot and throw — and in one motion — and still nab the runner at first. "Robbie! Over here," a woman shouts. He turns to acknowledge her, flashing the big-eyed smile, awaiting his turn at the plate.

He is 25 years old, already a multimillionaire. His four-year Blue Jays contract, now in its second year, pays him $4.5 million (U.S.) a season. He likes the money, likes the adulation — what's not to like? But it is an important aspect of Alomar's character that the accolades have not dimmed his understanding of what brought him to this place — his passion for the game. "Robbie's work ethic," says Jays batting coach Larry Hisle, "is second to none." One night last season, after a rare 0-for-5 performance at the plate, Alomar set up the pitching machine and was still taking batting practice at 1 a.m. He is said to spend hours in hotel rooms watching video tapes of opposing pitchers, studying their motions and their pick-off moves. Defensively, he analyzes other batters, noting where they tend to hit ground balls; this, suggests TSN broadcaster and former Jays catcher Buck Martinez, is the single aspect of Alomar's play that could still stand improvement. "He's a student of the game," says Alfredo Griffin, reaching for cliché — the mother tongue of all baseball players. "You've got to work at it. Talent only takes you so far."

There is something more than discipline involved here. The universe he inhabits is a chimera, an artificial bubble that time will one day burst. Alomar knows it. "If I'm lucky and stay healthy, maybe I can play 12, 13 more years. Baseball doesn't last forever." He acts accordingly, living well below his means, as prudent as any Pensacola pensioner. And while he spends liberally on clothes, most of his pay cheque is invested in tax-free U.S. municipal bonds, secure, government-backed mortgages and money-market funds.

"I could live like a millionaire," Alomar acknowledges. "But it's not worth it. I could retire and live on the interest, and I'd be OK. But why is that? Because I'm saving. Saving, saving, saving. I don't want to spend my money on cars and material things where the value just goes down. Then I could be hurt. But I will have my car, whenever I decide it's time to enjoy the money. And I'll have a big house — the one I want, the way I want it." In fact, until recently, Alomar owned two magnificent homes near San Diego. One has been sold; the other, overlooking the beach at Del Mar, is now for sale. Asking price: $1.2 million (U.S.). During the baseball season, he leases a suite at the SkyDome Hotel. He spends the rest of the year shuttling between his home town of Salinas, Puerto Rico, and his Clearwater condo.

"Some guys," observes Tom Reich, "suffer from the

Peggy Lee syndrome — Is that all there is?" Reich, an agent and 23 years a baseball fan, has dropped by this morning to see his client, Duane Ward. "Some guys have everything and they're still not happy. Robbie's drinking in the whole experience. He's smart enough to realize that while you're here, you've got to enjoy it. He keeps it all in perspective."

Alomar's Phoenix-based financial advisor, Scott Merrill, to whom he talks several times a week, describes his client as "ultraconservative. The average big-league career is five years," Merrill notes. "My goal is to allow my clients to enjoy the same lifestyle after they leave the game. With Roberto, we're working on a ten-year business plan, monitored on a daily basis. There's no room for any risk. He's very good with his money, light years ahead of other players."

It is his baseball skills, however, that inspire the real economia. Other players hit more home runs, steal more bases, get more hits. But Alomar excels at every aspect. At second base, he's a Gold Glove fielder. At the plate, he's a solid .300 switch hitter (.310 in 1992, seventh in the American League). Last year, he had the sixth highest on-base average (.401) in the league. "How do you pitch him?" laughs Toronto reliever Mark Eichhorn. "Four balls in the dirt and let him take first." But if you give him first, he might take second and third. He's a superb base runner (forty-nine steals in '92, fifth in the American League), blessed with an uncanny ability to read pitchers. "I'll tell ya, it's scary," says Joe Carter, "because you don't know how much better he can get."

Indeed, among cognoscenti, there is a gathering consensus that Alomar ranks with the best players in baseball. Says Tom Reich: "Robbie's a certain Hall of Famer, with a Hall of Fame state of mind." It's not just the talent Reich respects; it's the attitude. Too many players have been corrupted by the money. They still play well enough, but something fundamental, their commitment to baseball itself, has been lost or tarnished. Not with Alomar. Adds Reich: "He's the essence of what the game should be for the breed of the affluent player."

And the great, it seems, can recognize the great. In 1990, the revered baseball writer Bill James had this piece of advice for North America's millions of card collectors and rotisserie league managers. "This is my number one tip," James wrote. "GET ROBERTO ALOMAR." James predicted that Alomar, then just 22, starting only his third season in the majors, would one day be talked about in the same breath as the legendary second basemen Frankie Frisch and Rogers Hornsby. And he added presciently: "His support network" — father Sandy Alomar, a minor league coach, and brother, Sandy Jr., a Cleveland Indian catcher — "will be able to help him deal with the problems of growth better than might be the case otherwise."

As James suggested, the family is very close. Not many married women choose to live next door to their mother; Alomar's sister, Sandia, did. Family reunions often begin with the release of joyous tears. And Alomar continues to rely on his father for help with his game. "The only people you can trust in all the world is your family," he says. "Everybody can say this to you and that to you. But if you go to your dad and he starts giving you advice, that's the one to listen to."

His turn at last, Alomar steps in to face the veteran Jack Morris. "Seven swings, Robbie," says Larry Hisle, softly. "If I were teaching someone who's never played the game, I'd have them mimic Robbie's style," Hisle says. "There's very little wasted movement." Hitting .300 in the major leagues, however, is more than a matter of good mechanics. "Watch his eyes," Hisle says, as Alomar lifts a Morris fastball into left field. The concentration is intense. At this level, the difference between the good and the great is that degree of concentration.

It was clear early on that Roberto Velazquez Alomar had a natural affinity for baseball. The youngest child of Maria and Sandy Alomar, he grew up in Salinas, a small town (pop. 28,000) about a 45-minute drive from San Juan. For a time, the family lived well, thanks largely to his father's

15-year career with six major league teams. In his final season, 1978, Alomar Sr. earned $65,000, good money in those days. After that, the family finances grew more uncertain — the source, perhaps, of Alomar's thrift-oriented philosophy.

As a child, his ambition was to be a better second baseman than his father. "He was always following me," says Sandy Sr. "I couldn't go to my games until he got out of school." From the age of five, Alomar would watch his father play, then pepper him with questions. In baseball terms, he was both physically and intellectually precocious. He attended private Catholic schools, was a good student (all As and Bs), and played intramural volleyball and basketball. But in his own mind, there was never the slightest doubt about what he would do with his life. "God gave me that ability," Alomar says. "He didn't give me other abilities. A lot of people have abilities and they don't use them, don't go the right way. I wanted to go the right way."

When Alomar turned seven, his older brother, Sandy Jr., invited him to attend one of his Little League practices.

"Who's the kid?" the coach asked.

"My younger brother," Sandy explained.

"Well, sign him up."

So at seven, Alomar not only played against boys aged nine to 12, he was the all-star shortstop. According to his mother, "Sandy Jr. liked motorcycles, karate, flying planes. Robbie ate, he slept, he played baseball, he went to church on Sundays." (Not much has changed since, although women have been added to the menu, and he now prays principally in the Jays' clubhouse). Alomar's only problem, says his father, was his temper. "Robbie hated to lose. He still does. He'll do anything not to lose. It doesn't matter what it is — dominoes, backgammon, baseball. He'll cheat in order to win. When he would lose his temper in Little League, I told the coaches, 'Take him out of the game.' He had to learn to control his temper."

By the time he turned 15, Alomar had caught the attention of scouts. San Diego showed particular interest.

Ironically, the Jays had also noticed him — and offered "a lot more money" to sign. But Sandy Sr. "had already given my word to the Padres. That's the biggest thing you have, your word. So it didn't matter how much Toronto was offering."

At 17, Alomar joined San Diego's farm team in Charleston, South Carolina, earning $700 a month and $10-a-day meal money. After three all-star seasons, he expected to make the jump to San Diego, especially after leading the league in batting during spring training. When the Padres sent him down to Las Vegas, Alomar wept. Then, only nine games into the 1988 season, he arrived at the ballpark to discover he'd been scratched from the lineup. "What's going on?" he asked. "I'm leading the league in RBIs."

"You're going to San Diego," he was told.

Two days later, Alomar recorded his first major league hit, a single off the great pitcher Nolan Ryan.

The trade that brought Alomar to Toronto in 1991 was engineered by Blue Jay general manager Pat Gillick. In search of some right-handed power, Gillick told San Diego general manager Joe McIlvaine in November 1990 that he was interested in acquiring Joe Carter, then patrolling centre field for the Padres. McIlvaine said he would only consider the deal if the Jays, in return, were prepared to give up first baseman Fred McGriff. Gillick's eyes narrowed. "That's interesting," he said. "If we put [shortstop Tony] Fernandez in the deal, would you talk about Alomar?"

It was an inspired suggestion. Fernandez, though extremely talented, was a glum and sour presence in the dugout. No less gifted, Alomar was just the opposite. The Padres were already thinking of moving Alomar to shortstop — against his wishes. They had two other young second basemen. And without much notice, they had fired Alomar's father from the coaching staff, a decision that inevitably stirred familial resentment.

The final deal — Fernandez and McGriff for Alomar and Carter — was ratified a month later. Carter heard the news from his caddie during a golf tournament. "I was surprised for myself. But I was shocked they traded Robbie. He was the future of the Padres, the guy you could build the team around."

Now, Alomar is anchoring the Jays — never more dramatically than during the fourth game of last fall's playoff series against Oakland. Trailing 6-1, the Jays rallied, sparked by Alomar's two-run homer off baseball's best relief pitcher, Dennis Eckersley. "I wasn't trying to get a home run," Alomar says. "I was just trying to get a hit … It was my best game in baseball."

So what sort of life does a 25-year-old millionaire idol lead? A damn good one, dominated of course by baseball. "He's completely literate at one thing," says Stephen Brunt, author of an upcoming Alomar biography. "He can tell you absolutely everything about how the game works, decode it all in minute detail. In baseball terms, he's a genius."

Outside of baseball, Alomar claims to be just "a normal 25-year-old guy." He usually sleeps late, does 100 push-ups and 200 sit-ups a day, rides an exercise bicycle, plays pool, backgammon and mini-golf, watches movies (Steven Seagal-style action films), has been known to sing (not well) in karaoke bars, loves lobster and Japanese food, shuns red meat and hard liquor (but will drink wine with dinner), and devotes time to charity (the Hugh MacMillan Rehabilitation Centre).

Alomar's best Toronto friend is Jim Tipton, 33, a former Argo equipment manager, now president of his own marketing and manufacturing companies. After Blue Jays home games, the two men can be found dining at Alice Fazooli's or the Loose Moose, or playing pool at the airport O'Toole's. "Robbie's a great pool player," Tipton laughs. "Hand-eye co-ordination. But you have to watch him. He hates to lose, so he cheats." More seriously, it is Tipton's view that Alomar's intelligence is underrated. Because English is not his first language, and because he speaks it with a Spanish accent, and because his vocabulary is limited, people assume "Robbie's not smart" — a problem that confronts other Latin Americans. "Well, believe me," says Tipton, "he's sharp. He doesn't miss a trick."

There are, Alomar claims, no steady girlfriends, but there are women — not including those who knock on every room door at the Skydome Hotel in attempts to find him. "I'm 25 and I'm single," he says, smiling. "I'm a man and I like girls." He is also anxious to dispel any suggestion that he's a rampaging Romeo. "I try to be friendly, but sometimes people take it the wrong way. Make assumptions that are wrong." He is not, he firmly insists, trying to break Wilt Chamberlain's unofficial record for most women slept with by a pro athlete (20,000). And he is acutely conscious of risks, sexual and otherwise. "You have to be careful, man," he says. "I have money. They can take your money away."

Still, women pursue him and are often pursued, not always successfully. Standing at second base during a game last July at the Skydome, Alomar noticed an attractive blonde near the Jays dugout — evidence that his powers of concentration are not directed solely at events on the field. Later, using a press photographer as an intermediary, he sent over a note, inviting her to join him later for drinks on Queen's Quay. Flattered, the woman accepted. During the next two weeks, they had three or four dates. "I guess I'd call him an introvert. He doesn't really like to go out. We played pool once," she recalls. "He talked a lot about his family. I visited his suite once at the hotel. The phone rang every five minutes. Friends, lawyer, accountant. He took the calls and left me sitting there."

Indeed, the entire encounter seems to have left her with a distinctly sour taste. "He's not the angel everyone thinks he is. I kept hearing of other women, maybe ten of them, all of whom had met Roberto Alomar in much the same way. He is only interested in one thing, and when he didn't get it, that was it. He moved on. I felt he was taking advantage of who he was. But he was quite open about it. He said he wasn't interested in having a girlfriend." Later, after they had stopped seeing each other, the woman bumped into Alomar at SkyDome. "He was rude. He didn't even acknowledge me."

The day's practice done, Alomar turns at last to his fans, some of whom now have been standing for four hours. He flips a baseball over the fence to a young boy, poses with someone's baby for a photograph, makes small talk. This is what they've come for, and now that moment has arrived; now that Alomar himself is physically before them, the wave of gratitude is almost palpable. "Touch me," one woman sighs. "Roberto, I love you," says another, as he hands her his autograph. Alomar shakes his head and blushes. He moves slowly down the fence, signing his name and his number 12 on baseball cards, hats, other paraphernalia. For every signature, there is a thank you. "I'm sorry," he jokes. "I can't say 'you're welcome' to everyone." Finally a Jays official rescues him from incipient writer's cramp; he must tape a few lines for an upcoming TV awards ceremony. The crowd groans as he steps away.

"Are you going to be here tomorrow?" someone asks him. Alomar does a double take. "Jesus," he says to the spectator. "What a question."

(First appeared in *Saturday Night*)

SAM

Red Fisher

The hard, white light played on the round face, catching the blush in his cheeks and the thin line of wetness above his upper lip. Sam Pollock dabbed at his forehead even as a few individuals at the sports celebrity dinner rose to their feet. Then, as if by lemming-like instinct, more and more followed, and soon there was no longer applause from the thousand guests sweeping through the grand ballroom of the hotel in downtown Montreal, but a noise engulfing it.

The Canadiens' general manager stood there, blinking into the lights. Just a few months earlier, in September 1978, he'd been admitted as a "builder" to the Hockey Hall of Fame. His knuckles whitened where he gripped the back of his chair. A small, embarrassed smile started to form at the corners of his mouth.

"Thank you," he whispered. "Thank you ... please ..."

The Canadiens' organization has always been blessed with high-quality general managers, but none was as successful as Sam Patterson Smyth Pollock. Frank Selke was starting his tenth year in the post when I started to cover the Canadiens for the *Montreal Star*. Pollock replaced him at the start of the 1964-65 season and watched his teams win nine Stanley Cups during the 14 seasons of leadership. Irving Grundman replaced Pollock after the 1977-78 season, and promptly won a Stanley Cup with the team he inherited. Serge Savard has filled the chair since 1983-84, and won Cups in 1986 and 1993. Pollock was special, though. Even today, more than 16 years after leaving hockey for the corporate world (he's now chairman of John Labatt Limited), his name still has a special ring in hockey circles.

"When great general managers are mentioned," the late Clarence Campbell once said, "you think of names such as Jack Adams, Lester Patrick, Art Ross, Frank Selke — and Pollock. And except for Selke, Pollock didn't have the advantage of others I mentioned. Adams, Patrick and Ross were major-league players themselves. They were coaches in the National Hockey League. Pollock wasn't.

"What Sam had going for him, though," said Campbell, "is that he knew what was needed to win. He was as shrewd as anyone in the judgement of players and I don't know of anyone who was more knowlegeable as to the workings of the bylaws.

"There was an element of suspicion in Sam all the time, but despite the enormous input he had into the creation of what were deemed to be improvements, I'm not aware of a single situation where he designed it for his own benefit. He was very resourceful in the ways he went about some of the things, but none was off-colour, nor could you say they were the product of a scheme."

What Campbell meant was that Pollock didn't allow his personal feelings to affect the way he handled his job. He was, for example, deeply disturbed when a number of his players defected to the World Hockey Association in 1972 and '73, among them Marc Tarif and Rejean Houle. He was irate when Ken Dryden decided to retire only a few days before training camp opened in 1973 after Pollock had declined Dryden's request to renegotiate his contract. However, when the opportunity arose to get Dryden back into the fold, Pollock didn't hesitate. It was the same with Houle.

"Exactly one minute ago," Pollock told me on the telephone one day in 1976, "I signed Rejean Houle to a contract."

"You what? Is that the same guy that had you screaming when he jumped to the Quebec Nordiques? What made you change your mind?"

"He can help our team," said Pollock. "Is that a good enough reason?"

That's what made Pollock so good at what he did: he always seemed to have the right answers. He was a private person who made a career out of keeping things to himself. He did, however, have all the answers. Even his opponents knew that.

When, in 1971, the late Stafford Smythe, who owned the Toronto Maple Leafs in partnership with Harold Ballard, was facing a prison sentence on charges of defrauding Maple Leaf Gardens of hundreds of thousands of dollars, he told me he'd have "a lot of time to think" behind bars.

"So?" I said.

"Well, when I come out," observed Smythe, "I'll have all the answers. Pollock won't be able to put over a thing on me."

Smythe died before he went to jail, in October 1971, but the reality is that nobody in hockey ever truly had as many answers as Pollock. If he didn't, he pursued them relentlessly and, somehow, always found them.

The Dryden situation, for example, dismayed him — if only because it was unlike any he had ever encountered. In Pollock's time, players didn't challenge constituted authority. If a general manager instructed a player to jump, the only acceptable response was: "How high?" That's the way it had worked for years, and that's the way it was supposed to work forever.

"Why don't you talk to Dryden?" Pollock was asked one day. "How are you supposed to settle this thing if you don't talk?"

"He's got a contract," said Pollock. "He hasn't honoured the contract, so we may go to court. If he wants to talk to me, he knows where I am. If I approach him, I could damage our case. I can't do that."

The temptation to write Dryden off was great, even though Dryden had led the Canadiens to a Stanley Cup in 1972-73 against Chicago. However, Pollock was a businessman. As the 1973-74 season wore on, it was clear that there was a weakness in the nets, which is why the Canadiens were eliminated in the first round of the play-offs. At the same time, Pollock knew that Dryden had kept in touch with developments within the organization through regular telephone calls to me. Similarly, Pollock delivered several "unofficial" messages to Dryden through me. In other words, each knew exactly where the other stood. However, what Pollock and Dryden needed was a reason to get together. This finally happened several weeks before the start of the 1974-75 training camp.

"You know, I've never given Dryden his miniature Stanley Cup for '73," Pollock said to me one day in his office in the Forum.

"So?"

"He was on the team. He's entitled to get it."

"Do you want me to deliver it the next time I'm in Toronto?"

"Uh ... no, I think that's something I should do myself."

"What about your court case? What if it comes out that you met with Dryden? Remember, you told me you might take him to court and meeting him could damage your case."

"All I want to do is give him the cup. That's all. We're not going to talk about anything else."

"Sure, Sam."

Well, they did meet. They did settle their differences. Dryden would return for the 1974-75 season. Admittedly, Dryden and Pollock would have resolved their differences even without the small role I played in getting them together. However, I had earned first rights to the story, hadn't I, because friends is friends and business is business.

"Have you talked to Dryden lately?" a friend asked.

"Not for a while."

"Give him a call."

Dryden wasn't home. He telephoned me about 11:00 that night. "I've been trying to think of a number of reasons why I shouldn't return your call," he sighed, "but I had to do it."

"You're coming back, aren't you?"

"The Forum will announce it at a press conference tomorrow. I'll be in Pollock's office at 10:30."

The story was in the *Montreal Star*'s morning edition, which landed on the streets at a little after 10:00. I was in Pollock's office at 9:30, so he had no idea the story was in the paper.

"When is the big guy coming in?" Pollock was asked.

"When is *who* coming in?" he asked.

"Dryden," I said. "Ken Dryden."

Pollock stared wordlessly at the ceiling.

I left.

Pollock was different, starting with the element of suspicion that he carried with him. He never trusted anyone completely. That quality irritated a lot of people in his employ, but it and they served him well. He was in control, and one of the reasons was that he had to know about everything that was going on.

Pollock, who was born on December 15, 1925, was always several steps ahead of everybody. He always had to get the last word. I knew him when he was a teenager, and even then he was developing a mystique for winning. He was only 17, for example, when he managed a fastball team comprised largely of Canadiens players. Goaltender Bill Durnan was his pitcher, the best in Canada. Doug Harvey was his third baseman. Toe Blake and Elmer Lach were on the team, as well as Ken Reardon. They were among hockey's grandest, no-guff names, but Pollock was in charge. He put the pieces together and, more important, held them together, as he was to do with his teams when he succeeded Frank Selke in 1964.

Unlike most general managers, he didn't travel as much as he would have liked because a fear of flying stayed with him for most of his 14 years in the general manager's chair. But woe to the coach who wasn't on the telephone to Pollock within minutes after a road game.

He had to be told everything: who played well, who played badly, why wasn't this or that done — everything.

"Sam! Sam! You've got to come out here," coach Claude Ruel would yell into the telephone near the Canadiens' dressing room after a road game. "You've got to talk to the players, Sam. They're not listening to me, Sam!"

Nobody ever knew what Pollock was really thinking. Not completely, at any rate. It was business, and Pollock's business was nobody else's business. His need to win was more important than anything else. Nothing else mattered. Nothing else was acceptable. Was Sam Pollock smarter than any of his peers? Probably. Did he work harder at his job? Definitely.

"I'm heading out your way," he said one day. "Need a lift?"

"That would be nice."

At the time, Pollock's Canadiens were well on their way to another season rooted in excellence. Pollock was feeling good about a lot of things.

"Your team's playing well these days," he was told.

"Yeah, pretty well," he said. "We could use a little help in a couple of positions, but we'll be all right."

"Everybody says you're by far the best general manager in the game, and there's no question you are, Sam, but I've got news for you ..."

"What's that?" he grunted.

"You're the best, but some of the other general managers in the league are making you look better than you are," I said. "You're surrounded by a pack of dummies."

Pollock coloured slightly, but stared straight ahead.

Ten minutes later, after he had dropped me off, the telephone rang in my home. It was Sam. "What you said to me in the car ... about the other general managers making me look good."

"Oh, that. I was only pulling your leg, Sam. Tryin' to be funny, Sam. I hope you didn't take me seriously."

"What about you in the newspaper business?" he snapped.

"That's exactly what I mean, Sam!"

Click!

His teams won Stanley Cups in his first two years, and they were to win seven more in the next 12 seasons. Pollock, of course, had many memorable seasons with the Canadiens, but none, he once said, was as gratifying as 1970-71.

"It came after the year we missed the playoffs, which was a very big disappointment for all of us who were connected with the club at that time. We had won the Cup in 1968-69 [Claude Ruel had succeeded Toe Blake as coach] and the second-to-last day of the season we were in third place [in the Eastern Division], but we lost out on goals on the last day of the year to finish fifth behind the Rangers.

"The next year, nobody gave us much of a chance against the Boston Bruins in the first round. The Bruins had finished first. We had finished third. They had 121 points. We had 97. They had Bobby Orr and Phil Esposito at their best. Hell, they had won the Stanley Cup the year before, and it seemed that nobody would be able to beat them."

Everybody was right to think that way. They were the Big Bad Bruins in every sense of the word. Besides Orr and Esposito, they had Gerry Cheevers, one of hockey's best money goalies, Ken Hodge, Wayne Cashman, Johnny Bycyk, Derek Sanderson, Ed Westfall, and John McKenzie. They were, in short, a fun-loving, intimidating, and immensely talented team, the best of its time. The Canadiens weren't given even a remote chance of beating the Bruins, particularly since an unknown goaltender named Ken Dryden had drawn the starting assignment over Rogatien Vachon. Dryden had played in only six games after joining the team for the last few weeks of the season.

The Bruins won the first game, 3-1, but only after goaltender Cheevers had played splendidly. The second game also was in Boston.

When Bruins coach Tom Johnson told me he would be playing Eddie Johnston in the nets for that game, I was aghast. "Are you nuts? Didn't you see last night's game?

Cheevers had to stand on his head to make the saves he did."

"I promised Eddie I'd use him in he second game," insisted Johnson. "If I don't, I'll lose him for the rest of the playoffs."

"Screw him," Johnson was told. "You've got to use your best and, last night, Cheevers was the best player on the ice."

Johnson shrugged.

The next night, with Johnson in the nets, the Bruins toyed with the Canadiens for the first half of the game. Yvan Cournoyer had opened the scoring in the first period for the Canadiens, but Orr and Ted Green scored before the period was over. McKenzie, Cashman, and Sanderson ripped shots past Dryden in the second period before Henri Richard scored. Behind the Boston bench, coach Johnson barely arched an eyebrow. After all, with a little more than one period to go the score was 5-2. No sweat.

That third period, Jean Beliveau scored one goal, then another. Jacques Lemaire tied the game. Then, John Ferguson who, along with Beliveau, was to retire at the season's end, scored. Frank Mahovlich also scored. Montreal 7, Boston 5.

The Canadiens went on to take the series in seven games. They won the next series on the road in Minnesota, and headed to Chicago for the finals.

Al MacNeil was the Canadiens' coach at this time, having taken over from Claude Ruel behind the bench 23 games into the regular season. From there, the Canadiens enjoyed a 31-15-9 record. Then came the startling upset over Boston and the hard-fought series victory over Minnesota. Against Chicago, they lost the first two games, but won the next two in Montreal. Game five saw the Canadiens lose a game in which Henri Richard spent a lot of time on the bench. Richard sat there and burned. After the game, the Pocket Rocket went ballistic: "He's the worst coach I've ever played for," he fumed. "He's incompetent."

Asked for reaction on the charter flight to Montreal, MacNeil snapped: "I guess I must have been a pretty good coach when we won our two games in Montreal."

Meanwhile, back in Montreal, Pollock stayed cool. "If I know Richard as well as I think I do, he'll probably score a big goal before this series is over," he said. For once, Pollock was wrong. Richard scored two big goals. The Canadiens won the next game in Montreal and returned to Chicago for game seven. They fell behind 2-0, but midway through the game, Jacques Lemaire scored with a shot from beyond centre-ice that sliced through Tony Esposito's legs. Richard, by now playing a regular shift, scored the tying goal and the winner.

Pollock was successful before the NHL expanded to 12 teams from six in 1967. He was even more successful beyond it. He has nine Stanley Cup rings because the teams he put together mirrored the quality of their general manager. Nine rings ...

One day in the mid-1970s I informed Pollock that, having covered his team through 20 seasons and 12 Stanley Cups, I had "nothing to show for it. No rings. Nothing."

Pollock made no response. A few days later, he was on the telephone. "Who was coaching the team when you started covering the Canadiens," he asked. "Dick Irvin or Toe?"

"Actually, I joined the paper late in Dick's last year, but I didn't really start covering the team until Toe came along. Why do you ask?"

"It's got something to do with a memento I'm having made up for you," he said.

"Aw, c'mon, Sam, I hope you didn't take me seriously the other day. I was only kidding."

"No, no, I insist," he said.

"Look, Sam ..."

"I insist," he said.

"You really don't have to do it, Sam, but thanks. It's very nice of you."

That was 20 years ago.

Maybe it got lost in the mail.

(From *Hockey, Heroes, and Me* by Red Fisher. Used by permission of the Canadian publishers, McClelland & Stewart)

FALL GUY

James Christie

It's called Winstrol. It's called Stanozolol. It's called betrayal.

Ben Johnson is one individual taking a fall from great heights. But what may be at fault is an entire drug-monitoring system in Canada that is so full of holes that even someone with 50-inch shoulders and 24-inch thighs can fall through the cracks.

Here in Seoul a packed and often sympathetic news conference heard that Johnson's doping samples contained evidence of an illegal anabolic steroid preparation. Dr. Robert Dugal, Canada's member of the International Olympic Committee's medical commission, said the computerized steroid profile examined after the test indicated that Johnson had been on the stuff "for some time. Multiple administrations." The doctor's evidence told him that no one slipped anything into his juice at the last moment.

Then why didn't the Canadian Track and Field Association or the Sport Medicine Council of Canada or the Canadian Olympic Association know anything about it?

Paul Dupre, president of the CTFA, said Canada's best-known track star was previously tested in Canada in February of this year, and that the last solid record of his being tested at an international meet was at the world championships in Rome in August 1987.

Does it make sense that with an athlete of such high profile, with an equal potential to bring the country great glory or great embarrassment, that he should not be tested before the Olympic Games?

When the Canadian track and field championships were held in Ottawa in August the CTFA proudly said that drug testing was in effect. But it was done by lot. Two of the first three finishers in each event were handed specimen bottles. For the 100 metre men's final, which Johnson won in 9.9 seconds, the lottery said the second- and third-place finishers would get the test.

Much of the Canadian team was also tested during staging operations for the Canadian team in Vancouver before departure for pre-Olympic training camps. Three weightlifters were left at home and a fourth was sent back from Seoul before the competition began. But, again, Johnson was not tested. The CFTA didn't have proof of a single Johnson test for nine months.

Perhaps Canadian sport officials and sport-medicine officials figured there was no reason to test Johnson. Both he and coach Charlie Francis always denied drug use in the development of Johnson's phenomenal physique. From February 1987 to the Olympics in September 1988 he did have eight clean tests. But why risk scandal with such a high-profile athlete?

It is clear now that if Canada wants to flout its get-tough policy on steroids before the world, drug testing cannot be a hit-and-miss affair. The *threat* of a drug test is not enough.

Tom Tellez, coach of the American sprinter Carl Lewis, who will receive the gold medal Johnson cherished, went quickly on the attack — but not against the condemned athlete: "It's just dumb luck that somebody, his coach or doctor, made a mistake in telling him about when to take drugs and that he got caught. It's not just coming from Johnson. There's a group who know. His coach knows and Canadian officials know."

Lewis, Johnson's rival for eight years, would rather have won his medal by finishing first in a fair race: "I'm deeply sorry," he said.

One is reminded that the head of the Korean Olympic

Association resigned in disgrace a few days ago over an unseemly brawl in the boxing ring. Heads ought to be rolling in the halls of Ottawa's $60-million-a-year sport bureaucracy for allowing the country to be shamed.

Whither Ben Johnson? The IOC banned him from the Games. The COA sent him packing with his mother and sister on the third morning after he ruled the world. Sport Canada will cut off his $659-a-month supplement for life. His sponsors are under no obligation to honour contacts, which might have brought him some $10 to $15-million between this Olympics and the next, in the reckoning of his agent Larry Heidebrecht.

Big Ben is no more and it's a national heartbreak. The country thrilled to his performance last year when he set the record at 9.83 seconds and tested clean. A few days ago, he redefined the limited of human mobility and was a hero to the world. Today the simple kid who used to run street races for pennies is crucified. He shouldn't be alone.

(Reprinted with permission from *The Globe and Mail*)

THE ALCHEMY OF SAILING

Harry Bruce

All the dark winter she's in our driveway, up on her trailer, dead as a boulder on the ocean floor, a pathetic reproof of the terrible season that keeps her there. We tore up an old yellow tent in November and lashed it around her but it didn't work. The blizzards off the ocean came screaming up the bay in a way you'd have to feel to believe, and they rip the tent and yank it around as though they had hands, and then they dump the wild snow in her, and it melts, and turns to ice in her fibreglass belly.

By March, the bay that lies for miles below our eastern windows begins to break up and turn from white to blue, and move again, and the days lengthen and the sun comes at us from a better height, and I remember that she's not really as dead as a boulder, she's no more dead than the sleeping trees, or a winter bear. She's waiting, and so am I.

I begin to fiddle in the basement. I dust off her two small masts, touch up things with Pratt and Lambert Spar Varnish (Quick Drying), take her rust-brown mainsail downtown to get a tiny hole patched. I blow some bucks on *Yachting* magazine, I go out to the driveway and run my hands along her teak gunwales, inspect her rose bottom, her white boot top, her sea-green topsides, her eager bow. I love her plump conformation for the 700th time and I know that, together, we'll storm the glittering ocean, and I'll be *alive* again in a way I've not known at any time since winter laid her low.

I'll not be alone in this resurrection.

City people are increasingly desperate for evidence that they can be alive in a natural world, and there's a connection in yearnings between the back-to-the-land movement we hear so much about these days and a back-to-the-water movement in sailing craft. Back to Nature. Back to something clean and simple. Back to a life in which the main worries are not other people and what they do to themselves and to us but, rather, the right time to sow and the right time to reap, the proper construction of a root cellar, rounding up a lost animal, how to sink a well ...

Or the shape of the thunderheads over an empty horizon, how soon to run for the harbour, whether you can lay the marker buoy on the tack you're on now, whether or not to reef the main, the fog off the starboard bow, the mysterious breakers off the port bow, the biting flies under the hot sun of a sweaty calm, finding a safe anchorage, what the wind does as the sun dies, and the weather the morning may bring. Sailing reminds millions of men and women that they are alive, and during our moments afloat, a small part of each one of us becomes a Captain Joshua Slocum.

Lovers of literature about seafarers will know that on November 14, 1909, the great Joshua Slocum, Nova Scotia-born, aged 65, left the New England port of Vineyard Haven in his famous and beloved little sloop, the *Spray*, outward bound for what he'd told a friend were "some faraway places," and that no one ever again saw either the captain or a trace of his vessel. Eleven sad years had passed since he and the *Spray*, all by themselves, had made their immortal voyage around the world, and by 1909 they were both in tatters. No one will ever know exactly what was on his mind that morning.

Perhaps, somewhere in the williwaws of this strange man's head, there was an obsession blowing and it said the time had come for him to die at sea in the vessel he had come to know as well as any man had ever known anything. Perhaps not. But the thing that is clear — from his classic *Sailing Alone Around the World* — is that, through-out his middle age and maybe his whole life, he never experienced such fear and glory, such peace and high ecstasy, such visions and grace, such communion with the wild creatures of the seas of the spinning world or so deep and mystical an awareness of the fact of his *being*, as he did during the days and nights of his time alone with the *Spray*.

He loved her, and the meaning of his love is that sail-ing is not merely a sport; Slocum was not comparable to a Sunday golfer or a lunchtime handball nut; and sailing craft are never just sports paraphernalia. They do not belong to a family of baseball bats, lacrosse sticks, skates, shuttlecocks, Olympic pools and jockstraps.

Sailing is as old as riding horses. Men have been going down to the sea in ships to do business in great waters for as long as they've been building roads, raising cattle or writing words; but, despite thousands of years of accu-mulated sailing lore, no one will ever know all that we need to know about the relationships among sails and seas and winds and the powers of the sun and moon above. No, sailing is not a sport. It's a life.

Sailing is active worship, a sacrifice of what we usually are to the children of God we might once have been, a reunion with blowing forces and unknowable chemistries and whirling planetary laws that must surely have some-thing to do with the beginning of everything. Asleep in the black heart of February nights, I have dreams in which I am aboard gargantuan sailboats of unearthly beauty and unspeakable power, and they rush me over massive cush-ions of green ocean toward destinations I never discover.

Slocum, says his biographer Walter Teller, was "a kind of prophet of the value of insecurity," and although yachting experts have described the *Spray* as an unsea-worthy old tub, Slocum himself knew she was beautiful beyond words, and on the day he launched her he wrote simply, "She sat on the water like a swan." We can't all sail around the world. We can't all own *Sprays*. On the days we choose to sail, however, we can smell for a while just a breath of the value of insecurity. We can see the cat's-paw of change move toward us over the water and we can discover for ourselves, again and again, that no well-designed and usefully loved sailboat, no matter how small she may be, ever fails to sit on the water like a swan. (Except when the things none of us can control conspire against her.)

An eight-year-old girl, at the helm of a sawed-off seven-foot plywood pram with a pink sail that's smaller than her bedsheets, glides over a brown pond under city trees, through the shimmering reflections of skyscrapers, and across the park and down a long hot summer afternoon of her life. She is messing about with the same principles of propulsion that, each winter, drive tens of millions of dollars' worth of gleaming yachts crashing and sliding their way through hundreds of miles of tumbling seas in the Southern Ocean Racing Conference.

The yachts have dazzling equipment, towering grace, great white cloud after cloud of swinging, billowing, thundering sails. But they are all sisters to the little girl's pram, and the little girl is sister to the hard-drinking rich men who battle one another in the SORC because all winds are variations of an eternal wind, and those men would have to sail the pram pretty much the way she sails it.

It's this same wind that brings to life hundreds of thousands of other sailboats, out of thousands of ports and clubs, sailing in hundreds of racing classes, in more regattas than any yachting magazine had ever been able to list, over putrid canals, lifeless reservoirs, greasy harbours, a world of lakes, and among utterly trustworthy tides, currents of treachery, icebergs moving south, buoys, bells, lightships, horns, whistles, flags, markers, hail, warm plopping rain, and out, too, among the strange birds, flying fish, hallucinations and the long swells of the Pacific Ocean at the equator's line.

When the little girl hoists her sail, cleats her halyard, drops her centreboard, takes the mainsheet in one hand and the tiller in the other and starts across the park, she is not only joining a fraternity of experience that included

Captain Slocum and everyone else who has ever sailed a boat, she is not only offering herself to an infinity of possible adventures, she is also accepting the power of whatever laws govern the relationships between people, sails and hulls on the one hand and, on the other, moving water, the location of the stars, and the sun-driven wind. She will watch what she's doing this afternoon. She will consider the influences on the pond because, at the moment, the pond is exactly where she is alive.

Sailing restores your ability to hear things one at a time. The city may have wrecked for a while your ear's readiness to discriminate. There is a sound I'll know in my head even when I've lost all true hearing, and it is the gentle, ringing clap-clang of steel halyards slapping aluminum masts aboard boats at their moorings. If you're trying to sleep on one of those boats it can be maddening, but this sound of insomnia is also the sound of evening peace in a perfect world, like cowbells in the pastures of your childhood; and it is the sound, too, of a dew-wet sunny dawn in the fragrance of a port you've just awakened to see by daylight for the first time. It summons you to coffee you can count on tasting better than coffee has ever tasted before.

The halyards are a sound of port, like the clunk of ice cubes in plastic tumblers, the creak of rowlocks, or a greeting called across quiet water under the voluminous trees of a friendly shore. The seagoing sounds are more violent: the explosive thwack of a balloon spinnaker catching all the wind it can hold in a fantastic split second; the fluttering thunder of a luffing mainsail; the metallic rattle, the smooth, hard, ratcheting click of a job-sheet winch. There is the sound, in our own boat, of the heavy centreboard vibrating in its trunk — a kind of dull, chattering, humming complaint against the pressures of the sea.

Every boat has her unique creaks, groans, rattles and noisemaking partnerships of things; and always, in addition to the wind's whistling affair with the standing rigging, there is the sound of the water rushing against the thin, curvaceous skin of the hull that separates you from the depths. If I were to go blind, I'd want people to take me sailing.

The sounds are a part of being at the very centre of something important, and aboard a powerboat you do not hear them. You do not glide. You *shake* your way through the water and things that are alive would rather not have much to do with you. "Porpoises," Slocum observed, "always prefer sailing ships." And today, whale researchers out of Halifax track the great beasts of the sea by schooner.

Then there are the things you see. They are part of a great distance, all of them swing with the motion of your craft, which obeys the motion of the water, and you can see all of the sky, a *complete* horizon, the dome above, the moving ceaseless plain below. Slocum knew.

Slocum was well off Nova Scotia, on the first leg of his circumnavigation of the globe, when he discovered the *Spray*'s amazing ability to hold a course on her own, and on the night of July 5, 1895, she was making eight knots, and he was feeling just fine: "The fog lifting before night, I was afforded a look at the sun just as it was touching the sea. I watched it go down and out of sight. Then I turned my face eastward, and there, apparently at the very end of the bowsprit, was the smiling full moon rising out of the sea, Neptune himself coming over the bows could not have startled me more. 'Good morning, sir,' I cried. 'I'm glad to see you.'"

It pleases me to live in the province where Slocum was born. Our current boat — the one in the driveway — is a chunky, open 18-footer with three loose-footed sails, lots of freeboard and for her size, marvelous abilities in heavy weather. She must be one of the world's smallest yawls, and though she looks like a converted fishing dory, she sails as an antelope runs.

We moor her a few hundred yards from our house, and since the wind usually comes up the bay, she tugs at her float with her nose raised toward the open sea and, all day, she mutely begs us to let her set us free. We buck out to the ocean, tacking between the slowly widening shores of scrubby spruce and bright, bald, salt-scoured rock, and we're still close-hauled as we pass the ever-barer islands and the midstream rocks that are deathtraps for vessels and heaven for the cormorants … and then, beyond the farther islands on the long wave-corrugated skyline, we can see it all, blazing and gleaming under the summer sun, the whole, great, bounding, marching, magnificent mess — the Atlantic Ocean — and just about then, the boat seems to slip up over one of the more gentle slopes on a roller coaster and we can feel the ride in our stomachs. Then she does it again. She slips up and over the ocean swell and moves on to the open sea, and the feeling is not quite like anything we ever knew in all the hours of happy sailing we spent during the years on Lake Ontario.

We reach back and forth along the coast, shuddering at the awful weight of ocean water on rock, watching it blam skyward like the cold bursts of white firecrackers, and considering uneasily the terrible suck of it as it slides home again. We find secret islands, anchorages in calm backwaters of such Caribbean clarity we can see fish moving ten or 12 feet below, and we unpack mountains of sandwiches, grapes, oranges, soft cheese, and drinks that are exquisite under our own sun. Hawks sail, seagulls wheel and squawk, the ocean roars on the windward shore of the island, and we lie down on the hot sand here on the lee side, and watch our little vessel as she rides at anchor and sits on the water like a swan. Before dark we run up the bay and home to supper.

Usually, we take our three kids on these southbound dashes to the ocean, and once we all saw two slick black porpoises gamboling and arching and dancing through the cold rollers as though they were lovers in a field of grass, and the sight of them — the big, precious, utterly wild creatures out there exactly where they belonged — shocked us so that the memory is with us now, and for a long time.

There was a day, too, my wife and I left the kids at home because the wind was gusting beyond 40, and we got out there a few hundred yards off the real shore, the outer shore, and we saw a sumptuous 40-foot cruising sloop reaching inshore through the long beams of the late sun, heading for quieter water, and the whole ocean sparkled crazily and threw up such a commotion that this big, prudent deep-sea racer flew only her jib.

All three of our little sails were drawing beautifully and our boat charged up one side of the waves and shot down the other with a zest and courage that I was sure could not help but astound the sloop's skipper. (How could he know we were too scared to lose way long enough to reef our main or, indeed, that for a while we were too scared even to try going about so we could go home?)

But enough. You get a sailboat-lover reminiscing, and he'll go on all night. The point is only this: you learn from sailing that, although you must forever deal with forces of wind and weather that predate all memory and still defy our understanding, no two days of sailing are ever the same. If we were capable of measuring the changes, we'd find that no two *seconds* of sailing are ever the same either. Sailing is as infinitely various as the changing face of the sky, and once you begin to feel this you will be able to say with Captain Slocum, "The days passed happily with me wherever my ship sailed."

(First appeared in *Saturday Night*)

TOUGH GUY TO FORGET

Allan Maki

If nothing else, John Mandarich will be remembered as the only Canadian Football League defensive tackle wearing earrings, a bad haircut and the words "Heavy Metal" scrawled on his shoes to be carried off the field by hysterical fans.

That scene, after Edmonton Eskimos' win in the 1986 Western final, was so spontaneous, so bizarre it could only be described as pure Mandarich. Humorous. Frenetic. Wildly out of control. The Juice was all those things. But he was also sensitive and calculating, a passionate man driven by his willingness to do whatever it took to be the best player in shoulder pads.

Like that one shining moment in 1986, Mandarich's life ended much too soon. He died Monday night in the arms of Glen Kulka, a former teammate. He was 31. A cancerous melanoma that had claimed his ring finger on his right hand had spread so quickly through his once rock-hard body that his friends could only nod politely when Mandarich told them how he was going to "kick cancer's butt."

"A few months ago when the Rough Riders were in town I asked Glen Kulka how John was doing," said Scott Flagel, who had played in Ottawa with Mandarich. "He said, 'Not good.' I told Glen to give Johnny my best. What else could I say? I mean, I'm 31. I can't picture that being the end."

John Mandarich lived in contradiction. He wasn't as

self-destructive as John Kordic, the hockey player who died in a haze of drug and steroid abuse. He wasn't a felony looking for an alarm to trip. But there was something short term about Mandarich. He looked like a candidate for a burn-out. He craved attention and he lived for football. Everything he did was justifiable as long as it made him a better player. That was the Mandarich credo.

"Football was his identity. He put everything into it," said former Ottawa general manager Jo-Anne Polak. "He was scared about life without it. After we released him he came into my office and said he'd even play offensive lineman."

Most people won't talk about Mandarich's steroid usage. He did his share, which led to his not-so-subtle nickname, Juice.

When asked about it once he smirked, looking off in the distance and replied, "You guys trying to get me in trouble?" He knew the CFL would address any steroid admission with a fine or a suspension.

"When people asked him about his nickname he was smart enough to joke about it," said Flagel. "He wasn't going to cut his own throat. And people would leave it alone. Everybody liked him."

Mandarich passed all his medicals and never once tested positive for steroids. And having said that, there is no proof steroids were a factor in his death. Even when Lyle Alzada died of what he claimed was steroid-induced brain cancer, not every doctor agreed.

"My father is a pathologist," said Jo-Anne Polak. "I talked to him Monday night and what John had was a malignant melanoma, the most serious skin cancer. It was in the fibrous tissue of the skin. Then it got into the lymph channel and then into the lymph nodes. The speed in which it spread is common. This was not a freak thing. I think doctors would have a hard time speculating [if Mandarich's steroid use contributed to his death]."

Still, Mandarich fulfilled all suspicions by dying young. Somehow, we knew. Sadly, it was only in the past few months that Mandarich was able to come to terms with a life without football. He was able to put all the light-ning-bolt haircuts and media scrums behind him and move on. Cancer had given him a new perspective, a challenge. The big C was going to get sacked by the big M. It was another act. He talked the big talk knowing his time was running out.

That was his way.

That's how we'll remember him. This is what Polak will remember:

"I took my five-year-old nephew on a team flight from Ottawa to Vancouver to see his dad for the first time in a year. And when we met at the airport everyone was crying. I looked over at John and he was bawling too. He was passionate about everything. There was no halfway for John."

(First appeared in the *Calgary Herald*)

YEAR OF THE HORSE

Barry Callaghan

It all began in the South China Sea, in Macao, where I'd gone to play the casinos, crowding into the gaming rooms with Chinese who stood sleepless for hours waiting for someone to surrender a chair at the tables, and then holding onto the chair with a squatter's right for ten hours, a day, two ... stamina and a little luck, stamina and the clatter of the steel ball in the wheel as the hours slipped away, lost, all sense of time lost, playing fantan and roulette until I went out, suddenly bored by the ache in my shoulders, satisfied that I had the price of pearls in my pocket, and there, only a few feet from the door, the ocean slapped against the breakwall, and so I went for a walk along the ocean road, calmed by that curious watery milk-light before dawn, everything so fresh, cleansed: but there were no birds crying along the shore, and the air seemed empty, empty and still.

Macao did not seem right for me, so I went to a temple and had tea with an old monk under a huge tree that was three trees twined together and had him toss the fortune sticks, and then went back to Hong Kong on one of the jetfoil boats, passing between islands that are stone humps in the sea, arriving at last at the Peninsula Hotel, a place of grace that caters to dreams, surrounded by the rich and reputable, producers and perhaps a gunrunner, exquisite women and the odd warphead. I strode between

Silver Clouds, the white stone lions at the door, and little boys in white suits wearing white pillbox hats, and found my friend George Yemec — lean and aloof and greying at the temples — and he said, "Hello, can you get up at four in the morning? You should come with me and see the horses."

In the morning hours, in the cold dark hours overcast with no stars in the sky, I found myself hunched against the cold beside a racetrack, and there were great amber floodlights high in the morning mist, suspended flowers, but I couldn't see anything, not around the turn in the rail, but I heard the muffled sound of hoofs and suddenly a huge horse broke into the half-light, lunging past.

"Aw, she's a might slow this morning," said the small Cork trainer, clocking the horse and staring into the gloom, waiting. Others horses, appearing out of the dark, disappeared.

After half an hour, I shuffled down the slope, shivering, to sit alone in a steel shed that cut the wind, but I was so cold I crouched down and thought, "Jesus, goddamned horses in the gloom. What am I doing?"

As the sun rose and the sky cleared, I went down with Yemec to eat at a local market, sprawling stalls and narrow walkways covered with corrugated tin sheeting or corrugated coloured plastic, and the tables were piled high with fresh meats, fish, squid, eels, crabs, lobsters, melons, rice, fruits — and the gutters ran with water and blood. In the centre of this flesh and pulp, the hacking and chopping and slicing, women were sitting beside steaming chrome tanks sipping tea, eating delicacies. We sat down, warmed by steam from the tanks and tea, but in a near corner an old man huddled beside a large wicker basket, lifting live quails out of the basket, and with his long thumbnail he slit the breast and belly, peeling the skin off the still live bird.

"Yemec," I said, "the omens are all wrong."

"Omens mean nothing," he said.

"You believe that?"

"Omens are for when you're confused."

"I don't know what I'm doing here," I said. "I don't know anything about horses."

"I don't know anything about women."

"You mean I'll end up dreaming about horses?"

"I do all the time, wonderful dreams. I wish women were horses."

That afternoon, we were at Sha Tin racetrack north of the Kowloon foothills, an extraordinary racecourse on land reclaimed from the sea. We had our own air-conditioned box with a balcony, a small kitchen, a chef and serving boys. There were 35,000 people in the stands betting on geldings and a few odd mares (there are no pastures in Hong Kong, and therefore no breeding), and throughout the city another 500,000 people were crowded into off-track betting shops, wagering more than $26-million a day (the daily average at Woodbine is $1.5-million), and while soothed by escargots in pastry shells and white wine, I sensed something sensual in Yemec, a rush of energy, covert under his diffident graceful air, a channelling of all his attention while still making small talk. I grew fascinated watching him read the *Form*, constructing out of circled fractions and underlined times a conviction about the upcoming race. Even when surrounded by backslappers, he had a strange capacity for silence, sealing himself off so he could concentrate, and when we went down to the paddock to look at the horses he disappeared, melted into anonymity, so that I was left looking around, wondering where he was — and then he appeared again out of the crowd, casually elegant in his Continentally-cut jacket, saying quietly, "I'd box the 2-4-7," striding off to the windows as if we were all grown men who knew exactly what to do. We began to win a lot of money, betting three-horse boxes, key-wheeling, back-wheeling, catching quinellas ... it was all magical — and when the day was over, we had won several thousand dollars. It was like that for three days and I said, "Those quinellas are terrific, the payoffs are so big."

"You should try the triactors back home."

"What's that?"

"It's the last race, and you pick the first three horses, in order. I once hit for $23,000 with a $2 bet."

On the last night, we celebrated at Gaddi's, the finest European restaurant east of Suez, eating quail breast, prawn dumplings in a champagne sauce, and pigeon with truffles. We sat in the shadow of a Ch'ing Dynasty Coromandel screen depicting summer scenes with the emperor.

Back home, the weather was cold. It was the grey tail of winter, suspended time, the ice melting down to old stubble on the ground. Every now and then in the morning I looked at the race results, fascinated by the triactor — $350 one day, $4,000 the next — and then one night I had a dream. There were three birds in white wicker cages, the cages like cubes or dice. The next night I had the same dream, except the birds suddenly became numbers: 2, 3, 9. In the morning I phoned Yemec and told him to book a table at the track. It became a long meal. We lost race after race and I was almost tapped out, weary and saddened, but I held on until the ninth and made the bet: it won, 2, 3, 9, and paid $1,400. That was my first triactor. By the end of August, I'd won the triactor 71 times.

It was a curious summer, casual and yet intense. Each morning I sat at a window close to a ravine slope of ferns and tiger lilies and wrote poems of dread along the ice-locked canals of Leningrad where

love is like a silent prayer
sung for the living
by the dead.

At about 10, I went to the university and talked for two hours to students under a willow tree, about Robert Lowell and Hart Crane and John Berryman, poets "free-lancing out along the razor's edge," and then I had a light lunch at Cowan's Bottom Line, across the road from a firehall, the firemen regularly running their ladders into the air, practising, climbing high into nowhere. Toward 2, I began to feel a strange, almost sensual arousal, and so, eased by the sun and talk and laughter, I drove to the track, a late-afternoon outing. I carried with me a small notebook of poems I was translating from the Serbian, a little work for between races.

There were several men I saw every day: my friend Yemec — entrepreneur, publisher and sometimes poet — his aloofness a lure, yet he stands so alone he seems unapproachable; Shoebox Victor, in his blue suit and bow tie, a clipped moustache and pockets stuffed with sweet pink candies and computer print-outs — soil conditions and speed ratings, quarter-fractions and breeding, all visioned in his mind along the arc of quantum mathematics; Patrick Donohoe, a gentle-spoken Wexford man, whose love is the horse, whose contempt is for computers, quoting not fractions but a whimsical line from Yeats or Service; Fat Saul, Nelson the Bat, Gardos, Statistician Steve, and sometimes Michael Magee, astute horseman, inveterate horse player, the most acerbic satirist in Frumland, and aficionado of military bands, brass bands, pipe bands and drum corps. Behind us all, the benign silent presence of King Clancy, on in his years, a man who seems to know how to bide his time when there's so little time left to bide. It was always fine, casual and yet intense — making a small bet or two, sitting in the open stands with sea gulls far inland circling and swooping overhead ... until horses broke from the gate, striding beautifully, six or seven sprinters turning for home, to the wire ... all of us together on our feet at the finish, yet each of us alone, for betting is a lonely business. The best are at ease with aloneness, and the worst fill every space with complaint, chatter, confusion. Myself, I was waiting, translating a line or two

a curtain of smoke
descends:
an angel falling

but waiting for the last race, waiting until it was time to concentrate on the triactor, or as it is known, the Tri.

As Ezra Pound said, genius is ten per cent talent and 90 per cent character. What's true for the poet is true for the punter: the proof is in the pudding. Or, as Yemec says, "Show me winning tickets."

Though the track is the last refuge of ontological man, I do not believe in systems. Distrust all men, whether in politics, poetry, or punting, who have a system.

Each race presents a new and special situation. The task is to see the situation clearly. Clarity is the aim, confusion the game.

Beware all men, whether in politics, poetry or punting, who say they are pros. It is the first excuse and their last resort.

I am not a professional. I am not even a handicapper. I have simply tried to understand what's at stake in one kind of wager, the triactor.

I am an amateur who knows what he knows. To actually know what you know is not so simple as it sounds.

The rest is intuition.

So: what do I know?

Among other things, the track is a hive of opinions. Free advice, tips, tip sheets, doubts, touts, they're all about, beating on your brain. The horses constitute enough confusion without all this clatter and clutter. So, the secret is to stand alone in the whirlpool, singing silently to yourself. In that spirit — never listen to losers. Losers cheer each other up by beating each other down. And if you lose, forget the loss immediately. Celebrate when you win and celebrate when you lose. Never let losing become a habit of mind. The more experience you have with losing, the more ways you find to lose.

There is one exception to this rule. If you are lucky enough (for punting purposes) to have a friend who loses all the time, then seek out his top choice and immediately stroke it out, even if it is the odds-on favourite. This requires real strength, being the betrayal of a friend's best judgement.

Avoid the advice of players who never look at the

horses and only read the *Form*. They are like theologians who reduce God to checkpoints on a chalk board (I once had a professor at the Pontifical Institute of Medieval Studies, a humourless man to be sure, who drew the operation of God's "intellect" as a series of little doors opening and closing, at the gate, so to speak).

So, you must look at the horses as they saddle and parade. But look for what?

The smell of liniment, iodine stains on the fetlocks, fatness, a horse "washing out" (over-sweating), a tail bolt-out from the backside (the horse is hurting), front bandages, etc. ...

Haw: once you've seen what you think you see — then what?

Well, anything is possible, but unless a horse has a proved record of winning with front bandages, never bet on it.

A horse dripping wet is usually washed out. But not always.

Fat is fat. But not always.

You have to use your own judgement. Anything is possible.

And so you say to yourself: if only I knew someone in the backstretch — the vet, the trainer ...

Well, in a way, you do. As soon as the odds for the last race go up on the tote board, you should check the "win pool" — the amount of money already wagered, the "barn money." You will often find long shots heavily bet, favourites underbet. These distinctions begin to blur as the crowd begins to bet, but barn money, money bet by men who think they know something, is a factor.

And then there is that "gift" — the thing that fascinated me about Yemec at Sha Tin: the ability to simply "see" that a horse is ready. There is no way to explain this, but I have lately acquired it. The trap, however, is that you "try" to see, and then you believe you see what is in fact not there.

The same is true of hunches. You must trust your hunches (intuitions) but not seek them. The sought intuition is a sign of confusion. The true hunch comes to you clean, like grace. And like grace, it is preposterous.

There must, however, be some judgement you can trust. I trust two.

I trust Yemec, whose insights, as he studies the *Form*, are often uncanny. He sees relations that are electrical in their insight, and as art is seeing the relationship between things, Yemec is an artist.

I trust Michael Magee, who is tight-lipped, and seldom tips a horse because he is an honest man who does not want to mislead. An honest man, even more than a good man, is hard to find.

It is a sad story, but some people bet to lose. It is also a sad story that some people bet only to win. Eager for exhilaration, they play exactors (picking the first two horses in either order) all over the board, spending and spending, and though they often have a winner they always lose money. I bet to win money. Which means making a choice, a final decision rooted in discipline.

So: what else do I pay attention to?

The *Racing Form*: but never give too much attention to speed ratings. Track conditions and situations are too variable. This is as bad as relying on statistics.

The opening mutuel odds (or "morning line") of *each* horse in the program. This is the result, after all, of a considered judgement.

The horses carrying the five top jockeys: good jockeys tend to get good horses, or the sleeper that's ready. I've won Tri after Tri because a top jockey has nosed out, for third place, an inferior rider on a superior horse.

The percentage jockeys: the leading riders are not always the top jockeys in terms of percentage finishes in the first three positions, and this is a crucial triactor consideration.

A marked low weight advantage.

The top trainers.

And the three-minute money move: the movement of the horses in relation to the morning line, from seventh position to fourth, for example, as a betting favourite.

This calculation has to be done at the very last moment and factored into all the other information, judgements, intuitions, considerations.

All of this takes place in some 25 minutes, and most of it in the seven minutes before post time. And even as you stand alone, you are confronted by all your confusions and calculations. Obviously concentration is the key: concentration while surrounded by shuffling, mumbling crowds, concentration while standing in line at the wickets, concentration while friends interrupt to say hello, ask advice, give advice ... all of this as time, relentless time, clicks away. The secret is to lock your will, to focus on what you know, seeking the conviction that has the most clarity. When the moment comes — that still moment of lucidity — indecision ceases and you hear the sound of one hand clapping: a piercing, almost pure moment of perception. The immediate temptation is to suspect such clarity. The solution, you think, cannot be so simple, so you are tempted to go with a last hunch or a word whispered in the ear. This is unavoidable, and panic may set it, because even clarity of choice is not enough. You must know how to bet your choice.

I have a simple procedure: if, in a field of 14, my top choices are 3, 5, 8, 11, 12, I will bet a five-horse box as a security (in a box, the three horses can finish in any order).

Then I construct a series of bets that "press" those choices, so that when I go up to the window I have a card that might look like this:

3   5   8   11 12
5-horse $1 box, cost $60

5   8   11 12
4-horse $1 box, cost $24

8   11 12 6
4-horse box with long shot possible, $1 box, cost $24

8   11 12
3-horse $2 box, cost $12

11 12

12 11
2-horse bet on top, with the whole field for third, $1, cost
$12 each; total $24

11 - 3   5   6   8   12
key wheel, in which the 11 must win and the others finish in any combination, $1, cost $20

Total: $164

This is a minimum bet, and any individual move can be
increased, but if — in the above series — the first three
horses had finished 11, 12, 8, you would have had the Tri
six times. If the payoff had been $1,000 for a $2 bet, you
would have won $3,500.

This is not a system, this is a method totally depen-
dent on individual judgement, open to several variations
of the moment, and errors of all kinds. This is a method
that only an amateur could create, and only an amateur
can afford. This is not the world of the pro. As Patrick
Donohoe says, "Like the story of *The Song of Bernadette*,
for those who believe, no explanation is necessary; for
those who do not, no explanation is possible," but by the
end of the first week in August, I had won the triactor 66
times, and on two or three occasions, five days in a row.

Years ago when I was sitting for my PhD examinations,
trying to clear my mind and clarify endless information,
I complained angrily to the great Milton scholar, A.S.P.
Woodhouse — a grey puritan presence — that exams
proved nothing about intelligence. He looked at me sadly
and said, "But you miss the point. We take intelligence
for granted. It's a question of moral stamina, a question
of character." In August, as the summer meeting shifted
to Fort Erie and I went off to Saratoga, I understood the
great scholar's point. I had not only survived at the racetrack every day, but it had been a moral triumph of a
peculiarly puritan kind, a matter of some character.

I confess that as I set out for Saratoga Springs I felt like a questing knight in a medieval play. Saratoga, the loveliest track in America, is known as the Graveyard of Champions, a town of healing waters and a track with a long stretch run that saps frontrunners, and breaks the hearts of bettors.

The rhythm of the town revolves around the track: the *Racing Form* arrives the night before the race and Bronx plungers and balletic puffs sit on the balcony of the Rip Van Dam Hotel, hard at work in the half-light; there are afternoon parties on the lawns of graceful mansions, the very rich idling in town for the four-week meeting; lunch at Mrs. London's Bake Shop or Hattie's Chicken Shack is over by one o'clock, and the woman behind the desk at the Adelphi Hotel tells the hour in terms of how long 'til post time; after lunch, people hurry along the streets and through the park past the duck pond (where orthodox Jews who are in town only for the waters take the sun, prayerful men wrapped in their black coats, like black birds: "*'Prophet still, if bird or devil!/Whether Tempter sent, or whether tempest tossed thee here ashore,/ … is there balm in Gilead? — tell me — tell me, I implore'* Quoth the Raven, 'Nevermore.'") and the track — set among homes so that it seems nestled in the neighbourhood — is groomed beautifully: a grassy saddling area under tall maple trees with the horses within arm's length, a small string band and step dancers and two fiddlers among the crowd and restaurants that are open to the race course serving lobster, crab, and tender veal … It is a place of intimacy, grace, style, first-rate horses, first-rate jockeys, first-rate trainers, first-rate stewards.

For the first nine days, despite lovely sunlight and the close feel of the horses, I went into the graveyard. I hardly held on through the daily card and nine times in succession my triactor picks placed 1, 2, 4. This was perverse and punishing. It kept me awake at night because it is hard to sleep when the devil has his porch light on. Too many good horses kept sneaking in from nowhere … I couldn't get a rhythm. Logic faltered, concentration slipped away. Losers began to latch onto me under the maple trees.

You begin to smell it between your own sheets. It is the loss of a sense of yourself: after all, betting is, among other things, a confirmation of the self. To fail is to fail yourself. Still, I tried to start each afternoon with a freshness: I looked for a sign, an opening, a move. To surrender is to suck wind.

On the day of the Travers, the big stakes race of the meet, I found myself in disarray, caught between anger and dismay. I'd fallen into the slough of a bettor's despond, second-guessing myself, making my choice and then betting against myself. So, I decided to just back off and wait, wait and see if that still moment of perception would show up. I would let the rhythm find me since I couldn't find it.

The Travers promised to be an extraordinary race, with the three winners of the Triple Crown — Conquistador Cielo, Gato del Sol and Aloma's Ruler — running against one another. Runaway Groom, a Canadian-bred grey, was also entered, a horse I'd bet on once at Woodbine, and which had finished second in the Queen's Plate, and now I looked at it sentimentally but not seriously, until I saw that Jeffrey Fell was the jockey, an excellent rider who sits ramrod straight in the saddle, just the kind of rider to go into the Valley of the 600. The odds were 19 to 1 (Conquistador Cielo was then 2 to 5) but then I thought, those are not long enough odds for an unknown horse: someone had put money on the grey. For days I had been alone with the loneliness of the loser. Suddenly I felt a quickening and pressed close to the parade rail to look at the horses. I was astonished. Conquistador Cielo was wearing front bandages. I knew the horse had never worn bandages, and I thought, "No horse bandaged for the first time should be going off at 2 to 5." I hurried to the windows, noting the odds had gone down another point, put $40 to win on Runaway Groom and, suddenly seized by conviction, by the belief that I was right, wheeled him for the late double (that is, bet him with every horse in the field in the next race). When, a few minutes later, the Groom turned into that graveyard stretch, coming from

20 lengths off the pace, surging, his long neck straining, the crowd roared in disbelief as the Groom ran down Conquistador Cielo and Aloma's Ruler and won at the wire. I felt as if I'd come back from the dead, blessed by my own best judgement, and that grey, running from nowhere, appearing as if he'd come out of the dark morning mist at Sha Tin, had suddenly put out the devil's porch light. Suspicion and second-guessing, gloom and disarray, disappeared. Runaway Groom had come to me like a gift of grace, and when I left Saratoga ten days later, I had not only taken the healing waters but had both feet out of the grave. I had beaten the track. Down the killing stretch of the last days of the meet, clear judgement had clicked in, still moments of clarity had come to me. But as I left town on a bright morning, I saw two old men in their black coats, the coats billowing in the wind as they hurried away from me, birds of night, and somehow I knew that the strange fascination began in the dark of that cold, steel shed at Sha Tin was over. I had come back from the dead, I had been given a gift, but now the gift was gone. After Saratoga, there was nowhere to go.

It had been a summer of sunlight and horses, good talk and laughter, self-indulgence and hard work. Having won the triactor 71 times, I dedicated the book of translations, *Singing at the Whirlpool*, to the boys of my summer:

for
George Yemec,
Patrick Donohoe, Michael Magee,
Fred Dobbs,
Shoebox Victor, Statistician Steve,
Nelson the Bat,
Gardos,
King Clancy
and
the dream numbers
2 3 9

Editor's note: By the time Woodbine closed for the season, Mr. Callaghan had won the triactor 101 times. This is probably a North American record.

(First appeared in *Saturday Night*)

WIMBLEDON REVISITED

Jane O'Hara

The last time I was at Wimbledon, I was a player. It was 1968. I was 18 and it was Carnaby Street and Beatlemania and I had longer hair then, like a hippie. Except that I wasn't one.

I was a player. Not a great player, mind you, but that didn't really matter. I was playing at Wimbledon, with the best of the bunch — Ashe and Wade, Newcombe and Roche, Kodes and Goolagong, King and Court. That was what mattered. I entered the grounds in a player's car, a big, black Bentley that flew the Wimbledon colours from its hood ornament as it sailed through the wrought-iron gates and parted the crowds.

What struck me first was how overwhelmingly green everything was, from the buildings to the grass courts to the canvas backstops. It was not lush and muscular like a jungle, but ordered and English, like the repeated patterns of a brocade. There was a simple geometry to it. The lawns hadn't so much been cut as trimmed, the ivy seemed to creep rather than climb. It was a place that intimidated me with its perfect table manners.

Everything about Wimbledon seemed eccentric. There were three levels of locker rooms and we were assigned to them based on our ranking. The lower-ranks went to the basement, the top seeds took the penthouse. Wimbledon didn't have showers, it had big bathtubs, a plumbing feature, I suppose, that dated back to the days when women didn't sweat, they perspired. The masseur, on call throughout the fortnight, was a man who was blind. The woman who kept order in the locker room acted like her last job was running a field hospital during World War One.

I remember the Players' Tea Room with pork chops on Tuesday and I'll never forget the first time I saw Centre Court before the tournament began. It was silent as a cathedral and smaller than I had imagined considering the big things, I'd heard, that had happened there.

To be honest, although I played there, I never really felt I belonged. Canada had never really had a rich tradition of sending players to Wimbledon. The rest of the players looked upon us as an easy draw, almost a bye. And no wonder. The only grass we'd ever played on was in our backyards.

Grass is a surly surface. Playing on it is no walk in the park though the great players make it look easy when you watch them on TV.

The closest I can come to explaining how it feels to play on grass is this: imagine playing shortstop on marbles with the one-hoppers coming every four seconds. The footing is often lousy. The ball doesn't really bounce it skids, low, fast and unpredictably. It's why a serve-and-volley game works the best and, after being raised on slow, dependable clay courts, it was a game I never possessed. I'll never forget the first time I received serve from Margaret Court at Wimbledon. It was only in the warm-up, before she'd even started trying. Still, she smacked the ball so hard and it came off the grass so fast she almost knocked my racket out of my hand.

I spent most of my time at Wimbledon feeling scared and nervous. Scared that I would make a fool of myself at the most famous tennis tournament in the world. Scared, the first time I walked through the crowds to get to my court to play Linda Tuero, an American, who later married the man who made *The Exorcist*. I wasn't afraid to lose, I was afraid to set foot on the grass and begin my match. Because I knew the sooner it began, the sooner it would end. And I didn't want it to end.

Twenty-some years later, I am here again, this time as a reporter — an outsider, not an insider.

The other day, I wandered away from the men's semi-finals, the fire-bombing serve-and-volley matches, that were on Centre Court. I walked out to the calm green of the outer courts where the veterans, the people I competed against, were marooned, playing their version of Wimbledon.

There, in a corner of the stands on Court 3, I sat and watched as Goolagong, perfectly preserved, and her sister-Aussie Kerry Reid, played a gentle doubles against Americans Rosie Casals and Sharon Walsh.

And there was Billie Jean King, winner of so many Wimbledons, travelling down a walkway and nobody bothering to ask for her autograph.

On a distant court, I could see Stan Smith, still balding, start up his stiff-armed serve. He was playing against Britain's Roger Taylor, while his teenage boys looked on.

Playing too were Newcombe and Roche, slapping high-fives now to celebrate a point. While above it all Maria Bueno, thrice a champion here, watched from the players' balcony. Even she must have paused at the present play of these former giants, with their oh-so-slow serves and tame volleys, and forehands that quietly floated into the net.

I once beat Bueno. I lost to Goolagong and I used to practise with Billie Jean King.

As I sat in the stands, watching them all, I wondered if I should go up to them and say, "Hi. Remember me?"

But no, I was scared at Wimbledon again. They probably wouldn't remember me. But I remembered them and that I played at Wimbledon. Who could possibly forget?

(First appeared in the *Toronto Sun*)